BROKE

JOHN MUMFORD

BROKE

—— WHAT EVERY ——
AMERICAN BUSINESS
MUST DO *to* RESTORE OUR
FINANCIAL STABILITY

—— A N D ——

PROTECT OUR
FUTURE

WILEY

John Wiley & Sons, Inc.

Published by John Wiley & Sons, Inc., Hoboken, New Jersey.

Published simultaneously in Canada.

For general information on our other products and services or for technical support, please contact our Customer Care Department within the United States at (800) 762-2974, outside the United States at (317) 572-3993 or fax (317) 572-4002.

Wiley also publishes its books in a variety of electronic formats. Some content that appears in print may not be available in electronic books. For more information about Wiley products, visit our web site at www.wiley.com.

Library of Congress Cataloging-in-Publication Data:

Mumford, John, 1939-
    Broke : what every American business must do to restore our financial stability and protect our future / John Mumford.
        p. cm.
    ISBN 978-0-470-50461-1
    1.   Industrial management–United States. 2.   Financial crises–United
States. 3.   Leadership–United States. I. Title.
    HD70.U5M85 2009
    658–dc22   2009023575

Printed in the United States of America

10 9 8 7 6 5 4 3 2 1

To

Karen for her great patience and long-standing love
Our beautiful grandchildren:
Zachary, Caroline, Ellis, Emma, and Laine

and to

Your beautiful children and grandchildren
With the hope that they may all enjoy the same blessings
and abundance that we have enjoyed . . . until now

Honoring the memory of two outstanding young men:

Keith Warren Mumford (1968–2009)
Jesse John Payne Kay (1988–2007)

With special thanks to

Lindi Stoler for her invaluable suggestions and coaching
Sarah Tackett and Ron MacDuff for their timely help with edits
and production

and to

Dan Ambrosio of John Wiley & Sons, Inc., for his outstanding professional
guidance and leadership in this effort
Christine Moore, Ashley Allison, Kate Lindsay, and the superb team of
professionals of John Wiley & Sons, Inc., for their outstanding editing and
production work.

Contents

CONTENTS

Preface

When almost any one of us thinks about the United States of America, we envision one of the world's greatest civilizations. We picture a great empire. We think of democracy, freedom, and abundance. We think of taking care of others. We imagine a superpower and leadership. We think of the land of the free. We think of people who have it all.

However, because we busy Americans have full lives, many of us have not stopped very often to think about where this great country is in the course of history. We are too preoccupied with living our lives. We are busy soccer moms taking out kids to their practices. We are harried executives, rushing off to the next meeting. We are active at the gym, trying to stay fit. We are occupied on the golf course with our buddies for our weekly relaxation. We are busy at our next power lunch, or on our next business trip, or on our next cell phone call. Or we are busy just trying to make ends meet and to survive from one day to the next.

Most of us are busy doing everything we can to keep our own and our families' lives running well. So, although many of us may have an occasional talk or in-depth conversation with friends or family about the future of our nation, we do not typically focus too heavily on the future of the United States. This is especially true if our own lives are going along well. In other words, our nation's well-being is not what most of us are staying up worrying about at night.

If we *are* up worrying about something, it is probably an issue related to our own individual problems or our families. It is more likely that we worry about whether that next big business deal will go through; whether our health is okay; whether our marriage is in trouble; or whether our kids will win their next big game.

The average person doesn't stay up at night agonizing over national debt, the strength of the dollar, whether we are prepared for the next disaster, the state of our educational system, our failing health care system, an upcoming housing crisis, or where our country is headed and how it will impact us, our children, and their children. These issues are far too vast and complex for even the most motivated of us to study on a consistent basis.

Unfortunately, all of us would surely be shifting our worries if we knew where the United States of America is headed—and how it may affect each of us. *Broke: What Every American Business Must Do to Restore Our Financial Stability and Protect Our Future* is a startling, factual account of America's challenges in 17 different areas that should be of great concern to business leaders. Most of us care deeply about our nation and its future. That is why I wrote this book: to help each U.S. business achieve financial stability; to protect its future; and to show our citizens a way to meet head-on the problems that we, our children, and their children are facing. Business must lead the way in engaging both the problems and the solutions. We are at a crossroads, and business must lead the way to recovery.

Broke will describe the deep financial holes that we have created. It will also detail our three substantial deficits—financial, ethical, and leadership—on each issue. Most importantly, *Broke* will provide business leaders with a series of immediate steps that they can take to *restore theirs and our financial stability and protect our future!*

Only business has the capacity to lead our turnaround and transformation; and only business has so much at stake in keeping our nation's economic ship on an even keel. So business must point the way. Many Americans realize that our drift downward has occurred during the past 45 years. *Broke* says that the financial train wreck that is roaring toward us must be stopped now.

How did we get here? A trusted colleague of mine for more than 25 years said sadly that "We are fools [to have allowed these disasters to occur]." But how could we be so foolish?

One explanation lies in the nature of our daily battles—those that we see and those that rage in the mind and in the unseen. Prominent among them is the battle between good and evil that many ignore as foolishness. Another is our misunderstanding of the values and ethics of belief that drive behavior and that have haunted the United States since its founding. The first value set—the Judeo-Christian ethic—is the basis for the Constitution, the American system of common law, and most of the institutions that have been created in the United States during our 234 years of history.

Clearly delineating the forces of good and evil, this ethic holds that man is inherently evil; so he must confront this evil and look to God as the ultimate source of guidance, redemption, and ultimate accountability. These are the principles upon which this republic was established. Alexis de Toqueville describes the profound speed of development of an early America, because of its focus on community and associations dedicated to serving others in his 1832 epic study, *Democracy in America*. But that was then.

More recently, an opposing system of thought has taken hold of the American consciousness—secular humanism: a doctrine, philosophy, and way of life that rejects a supernatural God and stresses the dignity, worth, and capacity of the individual for self-realization through reason.[1] This system teaches that man, and not God, is the ultimate being. Further, it teaches that man is a captive of society—a society that has obligations to those who have grown out of the historic reality of one class exploiting individuals for the gain of others. Therefore, society is the source of man's problems, and these problems must be addressed and rectified by those in authority (presumably government at all levels) in the interest of righting past wrongs to individuals.

The source of hope for the secular humanist, therefore, is the revolutionary change of society. This new hope is the result of an enlightened and *progressive* new ethic, which will bring a new selfishness of all individuals who in turn strive for a new and enlightened *success* that they will enjoy until death—the end of everything.[2]

Business, however, cannot succeed if its members base their actions and efforts at exploiting one class for the benefit of others. The tragic outcomes of the economic meltdown of 2007 to 2009 are only the most recent evidence of this failed ethic and system of values. Business professionals must act on the basis of overcoming man's inherent weaknesses and serving his needs in line with his better instincts. This battle is a continuing one. If the United States is to overcome the leadership failures that brought about our current state during the past half century, business will be the institution that leads the way. In so doing, it must successfully confront all of these seen and unseen obstacles, as well as the obstacle of the "elite minority"[3] that sees the cures differently.

The late Bob Slosser—author, theologian, and educator who died in 2002—had a more subtle explanation for the changes in the United States during the last four decades. In his 1984 book, *Reagan Inside Out*, Slosser describes the fresh but pervasive influence of a new public force: "The Elite Minority." Recounting the events leading up to the 1979 General Election in Great Britain, which resulted in Prime Minister Margaret Thatcher's rise to office and the 1980 election of President Ronald Reagan in the United States soon thereafter, Slosser describes what he calls the "unusual impediment to the execution of the popular will" that had impacted electoral politics in both nations. Slosser boldly faults this "unusual impediment" for systematically thwarting the will of the majority in both British and U.S. electoral politics. He describes the reality in this way:

> Quite simply, there is the nation, which is the people, and there is the "political" nation, which runs things. Put another way, there is a

common majority and an elite minority. Strangely, in this marvelous democratic republic, the majority has not prevailed, at least for many years, certainly not in the last twenty years.[4]

What does this mean for us? In essence, it means that those in politics will listen more to the elite minority than they do to the majority. What did it mean to Thatcher and Reagan, who were elected "without the support—indeed, with the opposition of influential and articulate groups in the civil service, the academies, the media; and also against the wishes of 'progressive' businessmen, political writers, critics, trade union leaders, clergymen, entertainers, and professional humanitarians?[5] . . . Thus," Slosser concluded, "President Reagan and Mrs. Thatcher [were] merely in office, not in power."[6]

There is a third reason that the United States may have come to its current position of serving the priorities of its citizen-politicians. The nation's Founding Fathers saw public service as a part-time calling of motivated citizens. Citizen-public servants were in the legislature (or equivalent elected office) for only a small part of the year, and each of them managed a farm or business for the balance of the year. After a time, they left public service and another part-time public servant took their places. This practice has largely been abandoned in recent years, however. Since the mid-1960s, there has been a permanent class of politicians. At the federal level, for example, these full-time legislators have made permanent public service a career. Their reelection rates have exceeded 90 percent, because they set the rules for the opposition. Their health care and pension benefits exceed all but the highest levels of wealth or position. As a result, their priorities reflect their career aspirations: (1) being reelected by virtue of contributions of interested parties, (2) serving their partisan causes to remain in favor and appointed positions of power, and (3) serving the nation—in that order. You will likely agree that third on the list is a low priority.

Business cannot follow the path of pleasing only a few, well-heeled customers. It must serve every qualified customer that it can find. Business cannot survive if it serves only narrow partisan interests. It must address the larger markets of human need and opportunity. And lastly, business cannot survive if the nation and the institutions that set the rules and provide the healthy economic platform for its proper function vanish. Unfortunately, this, too, has occurred.

Where have these changes taken our businesses—those on Main Street who do not belong to the elite minority? *Broke* will explain.

Part I of *Broke* will take you on America's modern business and economic journey, starting in the mid-1960s and continuing to the present, and covering the good, the bad, and the ugly. It will examine key issues impacting the financial stability of businesses and the economic future of the United States, with emphasis on the attributes and actions of principled leaders, as contrasted with others who would give only the *appearance* of service, wherever they may be.

In Part II, *Broke* sets forth a complete action plan for business—to restore financial stability and to protect our future. Business stands to lose its economic platform unless principled business leaders take bold action: first, to strengthen their individual enterprises for the turbulent markets that now exist, and second, to step forward and lead the transformation of the nation from its current, weakened financial and physical state to a new economic and tangible reality. The time is right to shed what some would see as a culture of arrogance and reveal ourselves as a culture of realism. And it is right to move from what is all too often a deteriorated self-serving political culture in business to a culture of principle. The future is at stake.

Part II will also offer two first-step national solutions to rebalance our larger national interests and to begin restoring the financial foundations of government at the federal, state, county, and local levels, as well as the strength of our culture at home and abroad. Chapters 13 and 14 detail these first, vital steps to launch the United States' larger transformation. *Broke* explains how these two solutions will overcome and reverse past leadership failures in our finances.

Part III explains how the proposed solutions will enable the nation to overcome past leadership failures and launch transformation in our management of resources, international relationships, and global resources. It will conclude by taking the reader on a journey into the two possible Americas of the future—one in which we followed our current path (America Without a Turnaround); and one—America With a Turnaround and a Vision for the Future—wherein we will have launched the transformation called for in *Broke*. You will like the second story much more than the first.

Fasten your seat belt.

—John Mumford

Acknowledgments

The nearly 6,000 work-hour journey that resulted in *Broke* started late in 2004, when a outstanding and dedicated former federal civil servant, Fred Tillack, challenged me to develop a strategy to realign many of the business systems that are used to manage our nation's defense activities. The project was so exciting that it motivated me to look broadly at a number of issues that confronted the United States and its leaders in business as we began the 21st century. One year later I had catalogued 24 major issues facing the United States and had begun to see the common threads of values, leadership excellence, corporate responsibility, and, yes, the failures that ran through each of them.

In early 2006, Harvard Business School Associate Dean John Quelch invited me to be one of four panelists for a June 2006 Global Leadership Forum, sponsored by the Business School and held in Washington. The panel was to examine the commonalities and differences of public and private sector leadership. Dr. Quelch assembled a superb panel consisting of then Labor Secretary Elaine Chou; Mr. Craig Coy, who had just completed a very successful job with MASSPORT, and Mr. John C. Read, CEO of Outward Bound, Inc. The panel discussion and audience participation energized me so much that I put the writing project into overdrive, returning to Boston many times over the next several years to meet with Dr. Quelch and other endorsers.

In July 2006, Mrs. Roberta Hromas, CEO of a worldwide ministry organization, referred me to Ms. Lindi Stoler of STOLER MEDIA, a California-based public affairs and media management firm. Lindi patiently walked me through the myriad of lessons and techniques that turn ordinary writers into ones who earn readers—a three-plus year journey. Lindi has often provided guidance and support numerous times in the same week, and she never lost faith in the effort.

During those early days Jeff Ross and his daughter Megan, then a senior at the University of Virginia, offered a series of excellent recommendations on organization of the material and content so that the reader could better associate issues with their origins and collective impact.

As I reached out to potential endorsers, I was so fortunate to align with men and women of courage whose lifelong passion for truth and integrity had been a model for me—Steve Reinemund, former CEO of PEPSICO, whose call for business responsibility was so pivotal to this work; Fred Barnes, whose candid writing and speaking delight millions; Governor Tommy Thompson, whose life in public service is admired by millions; former Governor and Senator Zell Miller, whose life and courage in public service as a governor and later as a U.S. senator are legendary; Dr. John Quelch of Harvard, who has succeeded in demonstrating that educators can also manage complex public enterprises (Boston's MASSPORT); Dr. Larry Kotlikoff of Boston University, whose writing and sterling example of deep love of country helped to stir my passion for America's future; Dick Schubert, whose leadership in government, private industry, and in the non-profit sector always championed the American worker and inspired me; Vern Grose, whose life of integrity, writing, public service, and genius for risk management are the envy of the world and this long-term fan; Dr. Barbara Williams-Skinner, whose career and leadership in both public and non-profit enterprises has impacted and continues to influence thousands of the nation's future leaders; Dr. George B. Weathersby, whose career in public service, enterprise management, and writing has had a worldwide impact; and Stan Cottrell, who has won friends for the United States in 44 countries as an athlete and in numerous commercial enterprises as a manager and leader. I could not have been more fortunate.

During the many months of laboring over text, message, and content, I had the benefit of the steadfast encouragement, suggestions, and detailed comments on key passages from Dr. Vern Grose; Ralph Rosenthal, a professional of the highest caliber who read every line that I drafted; and Mrs. Jeanne Woodside, a friend whose love of country matches her love for books. They were invaluable, and I can never thank them enough.

During this long work period, two colleagues, Robert S. Strain, a Virginia businessman, and Dr. Vern Grose, CEO of Omega Systems Group, Inc., were instrumental in helping me to articulate the critical differences between principled leaders and principled politicians both of which make enormous contributions to our institutions. Moreover, they were able to guide me through the discussion of the elements of the political process and to show how leaders of high character and principle are able to accomplish so much, without compromising values and by looking only at the interests of those whom they serve. Of course, these wise counselors also enabled me to sharpen the distinction between these people of principle and the very different outcomes that result when self-serving leaders or politicians act only for the special interests that support them. Employees, citizens, and/or taxpayers all suffer when this occurs. I am most thankful for their superb advice and assistance.

Equally valued with the counsel of Vern and Bob was the enthusiastic and steadfast support of John E. Bishop, an experienced Maryland businessman; Van L. Lanier, Managing Director of Lanier Turnaround Consulting; international businessman Michael J. Feeley; New Jersey businessman Frederick P. Guttroff; and Outward Bound CEO John C. Read. None of these distinguished business leaders ever lost sight of our important goals in this effort, and they supported my efforts at every opportunity. No one could ask for better allies.

Charles B. Brown of North Carolina and Conrad R. Harper and Michael H. McDaniel of Virginia provided insight, wisdom, and encouragement at many important junctures in this journey as well. Their support has never subsided and continues to this day.

More recently, Mrs. Kay Coles James, CEO of the long-famous Gloucester Institute in Gloucester, Virginia, provided some important insights on African-American contributions to our modern history. Moreover, her experience as Chair of the Joint Financial Management Improvement Program for the federal government filled a long-missing section of the vision for standardization in financial reporting, accountability, and financial management for all federal programs.

Of course, I am deeply grateful for my wonderful friends from Atherton High School in Louisville, Kentucky, the U.S. Military Academy at West Point, and from Harvard Business School in Boston—and you know who you are—who were constantly ready to listen to a proposition, offer a suggestion, or add a word of encouragement at many stops on this long journey. Truly, "a man's riches consists of his friends."

And to Sarah Tackett, and the amazing team of professionals at John Wiley & Sons, Inc., whose skills in editing, coaching, questioning, producing, marketing, formatting, word processing, and indexing made good work look outstanding, I shall long be grateful.

Of course, to my Karen, who had to put up with an 8:00 A.M. to 9:00 P.M. work schedule for months on end, persevered as much or more than I did. She has been a constant reminder of the importance of leaving a better world for our grandchildren. I am forever in her debt.

Business Leadership in Twenty-First Century America

Down a Dark Road

There is no truth on earth that I fear to be known.

—Thomas Jefferson

The test of the morality of a society is what it does for its children.

—Dietrich Bonhoeffer

A Proud History—A Great Experiment

The United States of America will always be referred to in recorded history as one of the great experiments in democracy. This noble enterprise in statecraft will undoubtedly be appreciated because of the genius of its founders, the passion of its people for innovation and progress, and for its basic commitment to one set of values for much of the nation's history.

But democracies are fragile; they must be nurtured and protected. Like a good crop of wheat or tomatoes, they must be watched, guarded, and cared for each day if they are to survive and flourish. This book provides the future focus that is needed for this great adventure in freedom and democracy to continue.

How Long Do We Have?

Some years before (1770) when our original 13 states adopted their new constitution, Alexander Fraser Tytler, a Scottish-born British lawyer and writer, is reported to have said about the fall of the Athenian Republic some 2,000 years prior:

> A democracy is always temporary in nature; it simply cannot exist as a permanent form of government. A democracy will continue to exist up until the time that voters discover they can vote themselves generous gifts from the public treasury. From that moment on, the majority always votes for the candidates who promise the most benefits from the public treasury, with the result that every democracy will finally collapse due to loose fiscal policy, which is always followed by a dictatorship.[1]

Tytler very perceptively recognized the frailties of human nature in a democratic culture—falling prey to the temptations of deception, delusion, and denial in the form of promises made by public office seekers, who promise support and assistance to citizens who want or need it. This assistance is paid for with the taxes collected from others and thus comes at no real cost to the recipient. In the end, this practice brings an end to the democracy and to the government whose promises exceed its ability to pay.

Tytler saw this process as a repeating cycle in human history, as civilizations, emboldened by spiritual faith, emerged from bondage to achieve liberty, only to succumb to greed, complacency, and an ultimate return to bondage. The Tytler Cycle is shown in Figure 1.1.[2]

Since 1700, the U.S. pilgrimage matches this sequence. Unfortunately, the United States has now reached Stage 9 substantial dependence. And we've only been pushed there because of a stunning array of financial and leadership breakdowns that have occurred in recent years. The combination of failing to address the most significant national problems in the past four decades, spending well beyond our income, and borrowing in

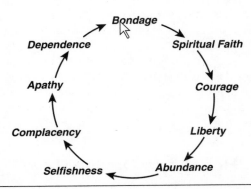

Figure 1.1 The Tytler Cycle
See *http:sanpetrepublic.com/?p=338.*

excess of our ability to repay has placed the United States in bondage to its financial obligations.

This book serves as a warning. As one reviews the many signs of our nation's movement (in the wrong direction), it is clear that for nearly half a century, we have placed too much trust in self-serving politicians instead of principled leaders in many of our institutions—business, organized religion, education, and government—and we are now headed for collapse. The nation's trajectory must be reversed as it enters the twenty-first century. And only business can lead this transformation—because it has the most at stake in a failure to do so.

Role of Institutions

Our four primary economic institutions—business, organized religion, education, and government—are at the center of this poorly directed movement. These institutions have abandoned many of the values[3] that served as the original basis for American government and culture in favor of satisfying more self-serving appetites, short-term goals, and compromised ideals. Much of this change has occurred in the past 40 years. Today's culture no longer aligns with the core principles that the nation followed for many decades prior.

Tracing these changes and their impact on the culture inevitably draws us to recognize the stature and quality of our leaders during the past half century—who they were, what roles and functions they have (or should have) performed, and what they and we are handing down to our children. However, this book will not single out individuals. It will assess the direction of our institutions during this period in the context of the attributes of principled leaders. Leaders reflect, and often determine, values in practice. These values are therefore the core elements of governance for institutions. Institutions guide and reflect the nation and its changing culture; and the nuclear family (husband, wife, and children) is at the center of the culture. The family binds and cuts across all four economic institutions; as such, the family is the centerpiece of the culture and the object of service and support from all four economic institutions. Unfortunately, the family may also be the most eroded of the nation's core institutions.

Each of the four economic institutions—business, organized religion, education, and government—has an unique agenda and core values that steer its behavior, define its role in the culture, and determine current cultural norms. Some institutions have put their interests above those of the nation. Others have stood by while the nation declined. And it is only principled business leaders who can reverse this decline and refocus our interests on the areas that matter.

Perhaps we are no longer a nation "of the people, by the people, and for the people," as stated in the preamble to the Constitution. You may indeed conclude that our four primary economic institutions have been hijacked by *self-serving* politicians, defined in the broadest sense, who individually and collectively are *not* serving the people and are instead serving themselves—their own special interests and political futures—at the expense of coming generations. This book is a call to the majority interest—not the special interests or to the elite minority.[4]

Leaders establish values; values set the direction of institutions; and institutions determine the course of nations. Any decline in the state or positive influence of our institutions is a failure of leadership—a deficit. The former comptroller general of the United States, David Walker, often stated that our country has "four major deficits—a fiscal deficit, a trade deficit, a balance of payments deficit, and a leadership deficit."[5] Forty years ago, such a statement would have drawn cries of outrage from across the nation—especially considering its source: a senior federal official. Ironically, however, the statement was not reported, except when it was originally broadcast on C-SPAN. Leadership failures now plague America: Seven million lost jobs, millions of foreclosed homes, and nearly $18 trillion in lost wealth bear stunning present-day witness to those failures.

Noted author and pastor Reverend Henry Blackaby was invited to Africa in 2006 to address a meeting of African heads of state. In November 2005, he previewed his planned remarks to a Virginia seminar audience of some 500 people, saying, "I can tell you right now what I plan to say to those leaders. Every problem in Africa is a problem created and/or allowed by you, the leaders of Africa or by your predecessors."[6]

Like our nation, businesses are all too often led by self-serving business politicians instead of principled leaders. The priorities of self-serving politicians are clear and limited—their self-interest and reselection or reelection, their partisan interests, and their wider community or country—in that order. This is true no matter where they serve—business, organized religion, education, or government. They are all the same. Institutions, however, do not thrive (or in many cases, survive) if the priority of the leader is his or her interests. This self-interest is what forces this type of leader to attempt to please everyone—for the sole purpose of securing his or her position. Unfortunately, seeking to please everyone is usually the path to pleasing no one. The bitter divisions among and between America's institutions are ample evidence of governance by special interests and not by principled leaders. Who will bear the cost of this twentieth century hijacking of the American dream for the twenty-first century? Our children. Is this the legacy that we wish to leave them? Are they not the future of

America? Have we put ourselves and our short-term interests ahead of our children's future?

A Shameful Legacy

Do we love ourselves more than we love our children? Pulitzer Prize–winning author of *From Beirut to Jerusalem*, Thomas Friedman, raises this question when he recounts a 1984 dialogue with a 54-year-old Lebanese Druse merchant, Nabih, and Nabih's 15-year-old son, Ramsi, in the village of Qabr Chmoun. The Druse had recently taken over the region from the Phalangists, who had responded with endless artillery barrages and machine gun attacks—some of which nearly destroyed Nabih's shop. As Nabih described the "savagery" of the attacking Phalangists, Friedman could see there were no remaining windows, and the interior ceiling of his shop had been reduced to a mess of hanging wires and steel rods.

The Phalangists had failed to retake the region. Nabih beamed with pride as he told how his son, Ramsi, had behaved in the fight. Ramsi echoed his father's pride as he told of leaving school to fight those who were killing his people. Friedman was puzzled at the story and its obviously deeper implications for the tiny country, and he recounted the event some weeks later to his friend—American University psychologist-counselor Richard Day—whose job was to counsel youth suffering from the trauma of internal civil war. Day responded with a question: "When will there be peace in Lebanon?" Answering himself, he went on to answer: "When the Lebanese start to love their children more than they hate each other."[7]

The same question applies to the current generation of Americans. Do we love ourselves more than we love our children? Our actions as a nation would suggest that we unfortunately do, because we are handing our children a nation that is economically, financially, morally, and socially bankrupt. The failures of our leaders have led to the state of our nation. Only principled business leaders can reverse this movement in the wrong direction. If leaders continue to default, politicians will continue to dominate our institutions and manage America's inevitable journey to mediocrity. Today's shortcomings will seem insignificant when that occurs. The suffering will be widespread. We are fast becoming victims of the four Ds of disaster: debt, deception, delusion, and denial.

In the absence of values, there is no standard by which the people can discern and refute the ever-present deception, delusion, and denial that become part of any culture. Our lives are saturated with them in all four of our economic institutions. Principled leaders don't allow entropy to take root and live; self-serving politicians do. Americans are like the frog in the pot of water coming to a boil—oblivious to the rising temperature of the water until it is too late.

The Warning

Sadly, the modern United States may not have the courage to prevent its own fall because:

- No one wants to hear bad news;
- The roots of our worsening situation are not fully understood;
- We are *broke*; our safety nets and financial systems are technically bankrupt;
- The best measure of our financial integrity—our currency—continues to decline in value;
- Our dual value systems continue to interfere with honest searches for cause; and
- Those in control may not care about the future of the nation as much as they care about short-term self-interest.

Collapse occurs in part because people in positions of entrenched power—the elite—in the four main institutions act to benefit themselves and the special interest groups who fund them. Those in authority pass on problems and growing excesses to future generations to resolve and pay the bills. They fail to reverse entropy.

Geographer Jared Diamond, who has studied the collapse of civilizations, was recently asked whether he thought the United States could survive. "I would give us a 51 percent chance," he responded. When asked what the critical factor would be in our survival, Diamond said that his studies indicate that "if the elites are not directly affected by the difficulties faced by others in a culture, its survival is unlikely."[8]

History Is Not on Our Side

Forty-nine empires have fallen of their own weight and arrogance.[9] Twenty-four civilizations have collapsed because they failed to see the long-run implications of their own actions or inactions. Moreover, only a few have succeeded in reversing the trends that ultimately caused their collapse. America has not reversed entropy.

So we must ask ourselves: Do we love ourselves more than we love our children?

Is There Hope?

This is a book of hope. It is a hope rooted in the reemergence of our long-standing, individual passion for reality, for progress, and for solutions and in our rejection of self-serving values. It will require a decade of sacrifice and action. But we must change course. There is still time to do the right thing, "to do the harder right rather than the easier wrong."[10] Taking the hard steps to forge a different future is still an option. We cannot say that we did not know, because history is rich with empirical examples of both collapse and survival. The choice is ours.

We cannot say that we did not have an opportunity to change our trajectory, first by establishing and maintaining a leadership culture built upon unifying values, and then on sacrifice and dedication to stopping the fall. Too many others have done this before us.

We cannot claim that the neoconservatives and liberals are at fault. Both share part of the responsibility. It is the 300 million of us who bear the ultimate responsibility, as we ignored debt, deception, delusion, and denial instead of paying attention to our future.

This surrender has left us *broke*. Some saw it coming in January 2006, as one of the nation's large annual investment conferences concluded in Orlando, Florida. One participant reported on the results. Summarizing the three-day meeting in two sentences, he reported "All of the managers tell me that it is time to get our money out of the United States. We are '*broke*.'"[11]

The Bottom Line

Our nation has now passed through four decades, three wars, several government-induced recessions, several energy crises, and more money than was spent by any entity in history—without truly resolving a single major issue on either the domestic or the international fronts. We have piled up more debt in the process than was ever created, and we have nothing to show for it. We are handing our children a country that is bankrupt morally, socially, spiritually, and financially, while we justify unconscionable waste that only serves the special interests of a select few. Are we ready to change this legacy?

CHAPTER
2

The Dilemma—Is America Off Course?

Dissent is the highest form of patriotism.

—Thomas Jefferson

A politician only looks to the next election. A statesman looks to the next generation.

—Thomas Jefferson

The Celebration

His name is Ross Gregory, and yesterday was his college graduation. He can't believe that the day is finally here—June 10, 2011. He had his twenty-first birthday just last week, then it was the walk across the stage to receive his diploma; today is a day to celebrate! He scans the backyard of his family's modest home and takes note of all the people who have joined him to celebrate his graduation and the new job he will start next week.

Dad is at the grill; Mom is busily arranging plates and food on the serving table. There must be 40 people who came to share the day with Ross and his family. Ross is an only son, which makes this type of occasion especially meaningful to his parents. They have done a wonderful job raising him. Both worked hard to support Ross, and their only recreational purchase over the many years of sacrifice is the new motor home that now sits in the driveway. Several days ago, they packed it for a long post-graduation trip they had planned months earlier. Now, it is all loaded and ready to go.

Ross's eyes continue to survey the scene before him. All four of his grandparents are here, and they are so proud of Ross as they reminisce with other parents and friends at the party. Ten of Ross's friends have also come to celebrate with him, and every neighbor on the block is there. Ribbons and banners are strung from tree to tree. Lights ring the yard so that the party can continue past dusk and into the evening. There is a table on which each of the guests has left a card, a small gift, or a souvenir for the occasion. Overall, this is a great day.

Later in the evening, after dinner has been served, it is time for Ross to open his presents. Ross and his parents sit at the old picnic table near the house, where the light shines out from the kitchen. The first present that he opens is from his parents. Surprisingly, it is the loan payment book for his college education. Ross is stunned to see the 10-year payment book with his name on each of the monthly stubs! He opens the second gift—a payment book for a home mortgage in his name. There are 20 years left on the loan. The third is the payment book for his new car, and the fourth is the payment book for his parents' new motor home. The process continues. There are health insurance payment books, prescription drug payment books, property tax coupons, life insurance coupons, burial insurance coupons, and others. Ross is dazed but grateful for all that his family has done for him. But, what is the meaning behind all of these payment books? His father and mother are only 57.

The party ends soon after the opening of these unconventional and unexpected gifts. A few friends linger and laugh with Ross about all of the good times in school and how their friendships have progressed. Most of them, like Ross, are single. Like Ross's family, most of his parents' friends had only one child, maybe two. It was just too expensive to have more.

As the last guest leaves, Ross's parents bring out a big envelope filled with the payment books he had just received. They hand it to him and say good night.

Early the next morning, Ross's parents depart on their cross-country trip and wish him well in his new job as they pull out of the driveway. He returns to the house and takes out all of those payment books that will be his for the next 20 years and adds up the obligations. When the total shows up on the machine, Ross realizes that he must somehow write checks for more than $85,000 per year for the next 20 years just to pay the current and anticipated debts that his parents have left for him. This amount must begin to be paid before he has even started his career or paid his own taxes. How can this be?

The Long, Hot Summer

As the summer wears on, Ross hears regularly from his parents. They are having the time of their lives. Ross, on the other hand, uses the summer to try to make some sense of the world around him. An avid reader, his stack of history and current events books grows by the day. His fervor for reading opens his eyes—and arouses his concern.

Ross's recent research into the prior collapses of cultures and civilizations has been particularly shocking; he is beginning to realize that many of the deficits that caused these ethnic disintegrations are now prevalent in the United States. The environmental losses, misuse of resources, overuse of land, overfishing of local waters, loss of forest land, unwise expenditures, and the like, are all failures of leadership in Ross's mind.

He realizes that similar problems exist in his own community. Ross knows that the local police force and firefighters have been protesting in City Hall because their pension fund has not been adequately funded. Their health care benefit plan has been cut as well, and other city employees are also complaining as they begin to find themselves in similar positions.

Ironically, property taxes have been raised every year for the past decade with no increase in services. Roads are going without repairs. Water quality suffers because of an aging water treatment plant. Bridges are closed because there is no money to repair or rebuild them. City council meetings have turned into hordes of angry people.

The county government is also in trouble. Wholesale retirements in the sheriff's, fire, and police departments—and even in the wastewater treatment department—have occurred. New replacements are very slow in coming because of a long-term wage freeze. Other citizens are openly bitter about the county's failure to successfully cope with the large numbers of illegal immigrants who have descended upon them, which has led to the taxing of emergency rooms for health care, the packing of already overcrowded primary and secondary schools, and the overtaxing of police and fire services. There are also new gangs, growing drug sales, and an increased rate of serious crimes.

It is the national picture that disturbs Ross the most, however. He is alarmed to learn that his country is risking bankruptcy as it balances huge security outlays, bloated domestic spending, massive unfunded obligations, and growing debt service costs, with dropping tax revenues. Then there was the subprime loan crisis and the takeover of two of the world's largest government-sponsored enterprises (GSEs) several years ago, while the insiders still collected millions in severance pay. That crisis followed an earlier one that caused the collapse of two of Wall Street's oldest securities and investment banking names. Soon thereafter, the federal government bailed out two of the three biggest automakers—one of them for the second time!

And it doesn't end there. Consumers, whose home values had earlier plummeted because of the subprime meltdown, had to turn to credit cards for living expenses. Their home equity lines had long since been drained. Their credit cards have hit their limits, and their stagnant pay levels won't allow them to keep up with interest payments. One major credit card company has collapsed; others have filed for bankruptcy protection.

This tenuous situation did not go unnoticed around the world. The first groups to begin selling U.S. Treasury securities and GSE bonds were Asian central banks. Several had been looking for such an excuse to dump their U.S. Treasury securities in favor of gold. As the dollar plummeted in value, the economic dominoes soon began to fall throughout Asia and Europe. Even more tragically, several developing nations in Asia and Africa, who survived on exports to the United States, saw their central banks collapse because of the value decline in their holdings of U.S. Treasuries.

After attempting to swallow this new information, Ross emerges confused and puzzled. His thoughts and questions regarding each issue follow.

America's Institutions

Ross now realizes that the public no longer trusts what it is being told by government, businesses, schools—and even organized religious institutions. Social service groups are overwhelmed, because churches and charities will not take on the burdens of the past. Since he is now a businessman, Ross decides to focus his research on how business should provide leadership to address these issues.

America's Economic Challenges

Ross quietly considers the staggering array of issues that has confronted him since graduation. His parents are now gone. His inherited debts and financial obligations are overwhelming. His community is failing. His friends are, like him, dismayed and confused.

Sadly, he is only now aware of a larger set of issues confronting the nation: a declining dollar, massive debts, a tsunami of risky derivatives, unforeseen disasters with no provisions for overcoming them, lurking inflation, declining infrastructure, millions of jobs lost to overseas employers, stagnant wages, rising unemployment, and a host of international challenges that rival any peacetime era in his country's history. The economic meltdown of 2007 to 2009, he learns, has stolen nearly half of the value of many families' savings and investments.

Even more disturbing, Ross realizes that the nation, like his community, is deeply divided and without a unifying set of values on a host of economic and social issues.

Lastly, employers—the engine of free enterprise—are struggling to meet their financial obligations, since bank credit dried up after the meltdown. New investments are being postponed. Plants are being closed. Employers and employees alike are deeply angry. They realize that America's challenges are the result of bad leadership over a long period. Now it's time to deal with each of those issues. Ross is still hopeful, as he considers the future.

The Dollar The dollar has lost 95 percent of its value since 1957, and half of its value since the late 1990s. Ross also discovers that the United States has had a positive balance of payments only a few times in the past 60 years, further weakening the dollar. This chronic balance of payments deficit must be repaid by the sale of U.S. Treasury bills, thereby giving IOUs to foreign central banks. He worries that the value of his future savings will be wiped out by the failing dollar, and wonders—What should business do?

Debt Federal, state, county, and local governments are all deeply in debt and are looking for ways to fund pension plans that are now underfunded. If this weren't bad enough, average citizens are hopelessly mired in personal and credit card debt. How did this happen? And what should business do to resolve the issue—not to mention the debts of the nation as a whole?

Derivatives The market for derivatives—hedges against certain types of financial risks—has grown worldwide at a high rate. By the end of 2009, the total derivatives outstanding had reached nearly $700 trillion—more than 10 times the size of the world economy, 70 times the size of the U.S. economy, and hundreds of times the total capitalization of the banks with derivatives on their books. Again, Ross wonders, what should business be doing?

Disaster More than half of the U.S. population now lives within 50 miles of the nation's coasts—and therefore is more vulnerable to natural disasters. Many cities are on earthquake faults, while others sit astride pipelines carrying oil and natural gas. We borrow, send out grants, and then borrow again to repair storm damage. How should business remedy this?

Inflation Inflation has reached 10 percent per year, excluding food and fuel, and it is silently cutting the spending value of savings accounts and pension funds. Inflation is only the friend of borrowers, and it is the enemy of lenders, so the nation *inflates* away its debt, while it borrows to pay current bills. How should business respond?

Liquidity   The money supply has grown so dramatically in the past five decades that the dollar is worth only a fraction of its 1957 value. People's savings are worth little because low interest rates allow for so much money creation. Federal Reserve money supply expansion is rampant, as low interest rates spur cheap bank borrowing and big lending margins. Is this causing foreign governments to replace the dollar as the world's reserve currency, Ross speculates? Should business demand policy changes?

Pensions   Ross knows that slightly more than half of all Americans even have a pension plan, and that fewer still are in fully funded pension plans. Many public pension plans are underfunded, and a significant number lost value in the 2007 to 2009 meltdown. Can business right this situation?

Security   The federal government spends more than its net tax receipts for security—the Department of Defense, Department of Homeland Security, Department of Veterans Affairs, and, rightly, interest on the national debt. Should business make us pay off our large debts? Ross is pretty sure that we can't be secure if we are *broke*.

Restoring Our Economic Future   Ross ponders this urgent set of facts and indicators of the financial condition of his country. He is alarmed and dismayed, and his dismay turns to irritation and anger as the reality sinks in that so many of the nation's financial resources have been spent without regard for the needs and opinions of the majority of Americans. Business should lead the call for change, he decides.

America's Domestic Challenges

Then there is the challenge of other domestic issues: demographic imbalances, drugs and other addictions, education underachievement in many cities and states, continued energy overuse, nagging environmental problems, overstressed middle-class families, persistent health deficits, plummeting home values, an aging infrastructure, inequities and inefficiencies in the legal system, and the failure to manage one of the nation's most valuable resources—water.

Does business have a role in overcoming these deficits? Can it ignore them—perhaps at its peril? How much more delay can the nation tolerate, while politicians listen only to special interests? Should business take the lead in putting forward solutions? Ross begins to feel a sense of exhilaration as he considers the sheer magnitude of the challenges that lie ahead. What an opportunity this is!

Demographic and Population Trends   The United States is aging. Ross remembers how in 2007, 77 million baby boomers began to retire and sell their retirement assets and securities. The markets had several bad years, made all the worse by the meltdown. The times were turbulent. What was even more alarming, Ross recalls, was how 60 percent of all federal, state, county, and local employees began to retire starting in 2010. Many job losses followed.

At that time, U.S. birthrates were below replacement levels (2.1 children/1,000 women per year), while the illegal population was growing at a much faster rate. Ross now ponders the relationship between children lost to abortion (1.4 million per year since the 1960s) and the illegal immigrant workers who replace them in numbers. He also sees jobs going overseas because of high corporate tax rates. The unpleasant conclusion to the matter is that members of his generation will be caring for their children and parents at the same time.

Drugs and Addictions   Ross finds it surprising to learn that marijuana has taken over as the biggest cash crop in the United States. Why do Americans fall victim to this scourge in such large numbers? The long-declared war on illegal drugs appears to have long since been lost. Ross can't find a single illegal drug that doesn't result in physiological or neurological damage to the user. Sadly, he also learns that the health care, rehabilitation, and other economic costs of alcohol and drug abuse had already reached nearly $250 billion in the year in which he was born (1990). These costs are probably $1.0 trillion now, he concludes. Should business assert more leadership in this arena? he wonders.

Education   According to the 2006 results of the Program for International Scholastic Assessment (PISA), a testing program for 15-year-old students in OECD nations, U.S. students are fifteenth in reading and science and twenty-sixth in mathematics, as compared with 30 other OECD members (Norway, Germany, and others).[1] Ross's frustration begins to mount. Will U.S. businesses really want or need uneducated workers? Is it any surprise that business is turning to better-educated international workers for many of its new hires?

Energy   The United States uses nearly 70 percent more energy per capita than any OECD nation but two—Iceland and Canada, both of which have colder climates and much smaller populations. Ross recalls the skyrocketing gasoline costs in 2008, and he's aware of the nation's dismal record of having paid subsidies to oil companies and corn farmers, while taxing imports of ethanol from Brazil—an energy-independent state with no fossil fuel imports. Renewable energy efforts faltered when the electric grid didn't reach the areas where renewable energy was produced, and the electric cars introduced in 2011 helped only slightly. Ross grows angry as he considers the mounting challenges facing business.

Environment   Though the United States has pioneered many facets of environmental law, it has not come close to meeting its environmental objectives. Ross was in grade school when the United States rejected the Kyoto Treaty on air emissions. He remembers when chlorine was outlawed, and chlorine interests sabotaged many water plants. Wastewater plants also suffered when the breakdown in overage water systems reached levels that threatened public health. Superfund and brownfield sites remained a draw for legal fees, while few were restored and reused. Air quality problems now plague 450 cities. Many civilizations, he notes, failed solely because of their arrogance in environmental matters.

Families   Ross is beginning to realize that families seem to have suffered the most during this same 50-year period. His reading indicates that births out of wedlock have become the majority in many post-2009 communities. He learns about the continued pressure from stagnant wage levels and non-stop growth in property and income taxes, increased job turnover and job losses, export of high-skill manufacturing jobs to lower wage areas, and the rise of Asian manufacturing prominence. Even two-wage families are in trouble. Ross begins to wonder whether *he* should ever marry and have children.

Health Care   Nearly half of all Americans have a serious health issue facing them. Many avoid visiting the doctor because they know their treatment will be costly. Even the Internet and efforts at growing transparency in health care treatment regimens and costs have only served to slow the health care cost increases. He is astonished to find that lifestyle management (diet, exercise, rest, etc.) and prevention (regular checkups, screenings, dental care) have not affected insurance rates. Epidemics of obesity, diabetes, and kidney disease have crippled a growing share of the workforce and added to the long-term health bill. How should business respond?

Housing   Ross reads about the housing rush of the late 1990s and early years of the twenty-first century. Past rules of borrowing had been set aside, and mortgages were used to fund living costs. Then there was the sub-prime meltdown, when it all broke loose. Homeowners' property values plummeted. Ross' own parents' home fell victim to this overborrowing disaster. In 2009, home foreclosures reached nearly 4 million units. How does this economic catastrophe affect business customers, markets, and future growth?

Infrastructure Ross can't help but note the deteriorated state of the nation's infrastructure—roads, bridges, electric lines, dams, schools, public buildings, and other public use facilities—as a great concern as well. He is surprised to note that 25 percent of the nearly 600,000 bridges nation-wide are outdated and that 270 levees are in urgent need of repair. The electric power grid is so outdated that renewable energy production is no longer feasible. No new power plants can be added. Modernizing the nation's infrastructure could be a major source of new jobs—*if* there were capital to fund it. How can business lead an infrastructure turnaround?

Law and Order Ross is dismayed to learn that the United States has more people in prison than any other country in the world. Of course, he realizes that most nations do not report accurately on their prison populations, so these statistics are not the best comparisons. What he *does* learn is that the court system is overflowing with criminal cases that it can't address, civil cases that clog its dockets, and a growing calendar of unmanageable civil litigations. Ross concludes that only a massive culture change can cure this broken institution. Can business help?

Water Ross learns about another hidden risk: potential future shortages of clean water. The nation has overstretched its water supply, and agriculture is a big waster of water. (One cow, for example, needs 150,000 gallons of water during its lifetime, and the United States has 100 million cattle!) The water table under San Francisco has had major problems with saltwater encroachment, and the one under Phoenix has been drawn down below 500′ of depth—when it had been at 25′ less than 50 years prior. Ross concludes that water will replace oil as the cause of twenty-first century wars. What should business do?

Restoring the Homeland

Ross quickly concludes that the financial and leadership models of the last half-century no longer work in today's global economy. The nation is *broke*. Moreover, the money spent since the mid-1960s far exceeded that collected in taxes. The rest was new debt. And there is no new leadership model to help the nation establish new approaches and boundaries. But the present-day problems don't stop at home.

America's International Challenges

America has been the dominant force in the international world for nearly half a century following the close of World War II. Tragically, the world has emerged from this period with as many failed states, wasted expenditures, poverty-stricken states, health crises, education shortcomings, polluted waterways, missing forests, and corrupt leaders as it began with. Has our approach failed? Have our priorities been misplaced, or have our international contributions been misdirected? Does business have better solutions? What a great challenge for genuine business leaders in this new century!

Foreign Affairs   It is clear to Ross that the old international relations model may be just as ineffective as the domestic systems the United States is still using. Non-state terrorists with political ambitions may be succeeding in destroying the U.S. economy, while the new Asia asserts its political and economic will. The United States can't compete, because it is *broke*. How can principled business leaders help remedy this situation?

American Empire   Several past failed civilizations have fallen prey to ambitions of empire. While the United States has no territorial ambitions in the world, it now has military representatives in more than 130 countries. Ross concludes that trillions in public funds have already been invested in military alliances, troop garrisons, weapons systems, and military aid programs in countless other nations, and he believes that this empire mentality needs to be tempered. Can business help to rationalize our ambitions?

Avoiding Further Technology Losses   Ross learns of previous unsuccessful programs to protect U.S. technology. Asian countries, he discovers, had secured nearly $5.0 trillion in new technologies developed by the United States. The bureaucratic wrangling between universities and commercial companies eager to sell their technologies, and the Departments of Defense, State, and Commerce who never managed technology controls have been futile. Ross wonders what business can do to change this.

Terrorism   Terror has been a central strategy of extremists since the early 1970s, but it wasn't taken seriously by more than a few until 2001, when the World Trade Center buildings were felled. Despite the massive expenditure of resources, numerous terrorist networks remain, most of which are funded by oil-rich states. Large areas have been commandeered by extremist groups. Drug gangs operate similarly, as they seize whole cities. It is clear that the terror groups seek to destroy the U.S. economy. Can business change this perilous trend?

Developing World There is extreme poverty in certain areas of the world, where the depressed state and tragic living conditions have existed for decades. The absence of clean water, education, health, infrastructure, and community development in these regions persists. Is there a more efficient way for the countries of means to assist those in need? Ross wonders. Is this something that business can facilitate in any way?

International Environment The United States should act as a leader in restoring the environment. Unfortunately, it hasn't yet done so. Ross concludes that the reason for this might be the fact that large business interests have opposed cleanup, while environmental advocates have opposed modernization. International environmental cleanup is also in gridlock. Can business offer alternative and effective strategies?

Restoring the Nation's International Standing

As Ross took in all of the news and information he studied over the summer, what disappointed him most was that no one had intercepted and reversed these bad steps. Self-serving politicians seemed to control everything; perhaps short-term greed got the best of them. The United States seemed to have three glaring, substantial deficits—financial, ethical, and leadership—on each issue. He was even more disappointed to realize that business, organized religion, education, and government have all contributed to the problems. It isn't a partisan political issue, it is a U.S. issue. So what should business do?

Ross laments that self-serving politicians haven't told the truth and that they tend to worry about their own jobs first. *Then* they worry about their political party, and only after addressing these concerns do politicians concern themselves with the state of the nation.

Detrick Bonhoeffer, a German Jewish theologian who perished in a Nazi prison camp in the closing days of World War II, states, "The test of the morality of a society is what it does for its children." How could the United States have failed this test so miserably? And what can the nation possibly do to reverse this series of detrimental decisions?

Taking Responsibility for the Future

Generations of Americans have spent their lives trusting political leaders to do the right thing. Unfortunately, these *leaders* may have been deceived, been deluded, or denied the truth about the future. Most significantly, they failed to stop the nation's decline.

Can business turn this situation around? Are there principles business leaders can follow to restore confidence in the nation and in its economic future? Why business? But then, why *not*?

Business can establish a new ethic, a new value system, and a new leadership model—one that positions the nation for transformation. Business, Ross concludes, can act to *restore our financial stability and protect our future*!

- The political responses to current U.S. financial crises are headed in the wrong direction. Government does not—and never has—*created* jobs. That is the role of *business*!

- Business in the latter half of the twentieth century allowed the United States to gradually move from a *business-based* market system toward a *government-based* economy. Therefore, business must reverse this trend toward creeping socialism and restore the market to the American people.

- Historically, business innovation has solved most of the world's economic and technical challenges. Other institutions may support a renewed United States, but business must take the lead and assume the largest share of that responsibility.

- Business has a golden opportunity to lead the nation back to prosperity by modeling the fundamental, time-tested values of principled leaders.

CHAPTER

3

Applying Timeless Principles to Business Leadership

The only safe ship in a storm is leadership.

—Faye Wattleton

A leader takes people where they want to go. A great leader takes people where they don't necessarily want to go, but where they ought to be.

—Rosalynn Carter

A Long Look Back

Ross Gregory and his father are celebrating five years since Ross completed his schooling. It is now June 2016, and they have decided to take a trip to Idaho for two weeks of fly-fishing. Much has changed since Ross's graduation, and the two talk endlessly each day. But their conversation inevitably returns to Ross's post-college studies, and his extensive reading about the changes in the United States.

Nowadays, there are fewer of many things—automobiles, suburban houses, manufacturers, banks, colleges, densely populated cities, seniors, schools, and international commitments. Similarly, there are more bicycles, children, families, home jobs, small farms, and small communities. Ross and his father both agree that these changes have led people to become healthier and happier.

The nation has experienced a number of major transformations during the years since Ross's graduation. Gone are the massive budgets, overextended military forces, balance of payment deficits, fiscal crises, environmental disasters, and complex economic systems—all the trappings of superpower status. New superpowers now occupy the world stage, and new issues have emerged for them to address. The United States is about the business of healing from its heavy dose of twentieth century economic overindulgence. Although there is much less of everything, there is a new spirit of unity and anticipation of the future.

Ross and his dad sit quietly, reminiscing about those challenging years. Although they can't quite put their fingers on the catalysts that brought about the enormous changes of the period, they both agree they are much better off. It must have been the new business and government leaders. What was their nature, their character, their approach to leadership? How did they make decisions? What were their models? Ross's father suggested several historic examples that have saved nations in the past.

A *Great* Leader—Joseph

Those thought to be leaders are most often politicians of one sort or another, whether they serve in business, organized religion, education, or government. Though two great leadership examples—Joseph and Nehemiah—come from long ago in recorded history, their stories are still compelling and applicable today.

Joseph made his mark in history by saving ancient Egypt from starvation. He was awakened in a dream as a boy and made aware of his long-term call to be a steward of resources—and a great leader. In fact, Joseph was so sure of this calling that he boasted to his brothers with typical boyhood exuberance, and his overconfidence angered them. The final straw came when Joseph's father gave him a beautiful coat to reflect his pride in his youngest son.

The brothers wanted to put a stop to Joseph's constant talk of his ambition and future. Though they didn't fully understand his calling, they did know that his self-confidence and enthusiasm irritated them greatly. So they plotted to put an end to his boasting—and even to Joseph himself. The means they chose was to kill a lamb, spread the blood on Joseph's new coat, and throw him into an abandoned well to be left for dead. His brothers returned home to report to their father that Joseph was dead, and they provided his bloodied coat as evidence. Their father was incredibly distraught; Joseph was his favorite son.

Meanwhile, Joseph's cries for help from the well soon attracted the attention of the masters of a passing caravan. They pulled Joseph out and decided to sell him at the slave market in Egypt, where they were headed. A slave trader for the House of Pharaoh purchased Joseph—an event after which his life was never to be the same.

But Joseph's personal qualities allowed him to turn a less-than-ideal situation into an opportunity. Because he was handsome, energetic, thoughtful, and likeable, his good work resulted in his assignment to the house of Potiphar—a wealthy officer in Pharaoh's service. Soon, Joseph was appointed master of the household.

Potiphar's wife, a woman of great beauty and cunning, was attracted to the handsome Joseph—and attempted to seduce him. He fled, but not before she had torn away a portion of his work coat. She later accused Joseph of trying to lure her into intimacy; using the coat as evidence, she convinced her husband that Joseph was the wrongdoer. Potiphar immediately—and understandably, in light of the evidence—took his wife's side and had Joseph cast into prison—Joseph's home for the next 14 years.

But even in prison, Joseph was a model citizen. He was appointed lead prisoner soon after his arrival. The guards trusted him the most of all of the captives, and the prison's master extended special privileges to Joseph because of his good behavior.

When two of Joseph's fellow prisoners had disturbing dreams about their futures, they immediately asked him for his interpretation. He obliged and explained that one of them was headed for greatness in the kingdom of Egypt, and the other was headed for death. He asked the one who was destined for greatness to remember him and to help to secure his release when he was free. Unfortunately, the former prisoner forgot Joseph when he was released. Joseph continued to languish in prison—an innocent man.

Joseph's ability to interpret dreams soon came to Pharaoh's attention. When Pharaoh had a bad dream, he sent for Joseph to give an explanation. Again, Joseph obliged, and again, the news was not good. Joseph informed Pharaoh that Egypt was headed for seven years of famine following seven years of plenty. Distraught, Pharaoh asked that Joseph help him figure out what to do—and Joseph responded with a solution. Pharaoh was so impressed with Joseph's interpretation and advice that he immediately ordered Joseph to be released from prison and appointed him as the equivalent of the prime minister of Egypt to implement his plan.

Joseph swung into action. First, he imposed rigorous taxes on the grain harvests. A one-fifth portion of the harvest was set aside in government-controlled storage buildings for use during the upcoming famine. Then he enforced strict controls on the currency and fiscal management to ensure that Egypt's money was not devalued—in order to save the people of Egypt.

Famine came, and Joseph's plan worked. He enforced his rules meticulously. When some of the people needed grain, he made sure that they paid a fair price to Pharaoh for it. Joseph's plan guaranteed that the nation survived. Even those who could not pay traded their land to Pharaoh for food.

When the famine hit Joseph's homeland of Israel, his brothers learned that Egypt had a surplus of grain that could be purchased; and so they journeyed to Egypt to buy it. They did not realize their brother—whom they had given up for dead many years earlier—was now the prime minister of Egypt. Joseph, meanwhile, learned of their coming visit, and he summoned them to visit his palace without revealing who he was.

When Joseph's brothers arrived, he decided to test their character after the many years of his absence. He had one of Pharaoh's silver cups planted in one of the bags of grain that were being taken back to Israel. Then Joseph dispatched soldiers to find the silver cup and to charge his brothers with theft of palace property. Although they pleaded their innocence, Joseph had them leave his youngest brother as a hostage and directed that they return with their father. He wanted to see his aged father once again before he died. When his brothers returned with their father, Joseph revealed his identity, and the family had a tearful reunion.

Joseph had suffered patiently for many years. When he was appointed to leadership, he was diligent and highly successful. He wisely used the resources entrusted to him, and he did not use the resources of future generations. Joseph performed powerfully to fulfill a vision to save Egypt.

Lesson for Principled Business Leaders. Joseph heard the call to leadership, and he responded to it by controlling with diligence. Because of his elevated mission, he heard the warning of hard times in advance through the interpretation of Pharaoh's dream. He then fulfilled a leader's roles and functions to prepare Egypt for these difficulties. He also demanded that the people act with integrity in fiscal and monetary matters in an effort to maintain the value of their currency. His example personifies an incredibly important lesson: never compromise principles.

Lesson for Principled Business Leaders. The United States needs men and women with bold visions and unshakable values to change the reality around them. Does the United States have a Joseph—a person driven by principle and not by passion alone? Does your business have a Joseph?

Another *Great* Leader—Nehemiah

Like Joseph, Nehemiah responded to a call to leadership with boldness and decisiveness in a time of urgent national need. Nehemiah was among the thousands of Israel's hostages in Babylon (near modern-day Baghdad). Taking hostages was common in the culture of that period, as it is now, and Nehemiah's native city of Jerusalem had fallen into ruins. The walls of the city had collapsed or been destroyed, and the infrastructure was in ruins. Nehemiah was heartbroken over the plight of his homeland.

Nehemiah's anguish continued for many days of prayer and fasting. He emerged from his time of reflection and prayer and concluded that he alone had been called to restore Jerusalem to prominence and to change the course of its people. Nehemiah then did what few would do: He went to the king who held him as prisoner and asked for the resources to rebuild the walls of Jerusalem.

To Nehemiah's great surprise, the king consented to give him the materials to restore the city's barriers. He was also granted permission to lead the effort—despite his status as a captive and former hostage. The king released Nehemiah so that he could fulfill this important calling.

The work that Nehemiah faced was difficult. The people were arrogant and lazy after many years of languishing without leadership. The detractors were persistent, and the critics were plentiful. But Nehemiah had a single focus, high standards, a relentless commitment to accountability, and a passion for hands-on supervision. He was successful in rebuilding the walls of Jerusalem in 52 days—a remarkable leadership accomplishment!

Lesson for Principled Business Leaders. Nehemiah did not stop with this achievement. He mobilized the people to turn in a new direction. He called them away from their declining values and apathy, and urged them to righteousness and good character in the public square and in the family. He relentlessly challenged them to change their ways. U.S. businesses have many Nehemiahs today—all of whom realize that execution is everything.

Lesson for Principled Business Leaders. Nehemiah thought strategically. He was systematic in the way that he focused upon defined outcomes. He also had a clear strategy to achieve the desired goals.

Lesson for Principled Business Leaders. Joseph and Nehemiah had unique leadership styles and unique ways of demonstrating similar leadership attributes. Both men confronted daunting obstacles and persevered in achieving their goals and their unique calls to action.

Lesson for Principled Business Leaders. Joseph and Nehemiah had similar leadership attributes including:

- A great vision
- Strong values

- A sound strategy to achieve the desired outcomes, and consistent, strategic thinking
- Effective, well-supervised organizations
- Knowledge of the *full cost* and of the resources needed to succeed
- Clear priorities to guide allocation of all resources
- Standards for the effective use of resources and for systematically managing risks
- High-quality support systems to assist their people in their work
- Full accountability for execution with high standards
- Flawless implementation with precision, passion, courage, measurement, and modifications to instructions as needed to ensure fulfillment of the vision
- Continuous effort to intercept entropy and to catch and resolve possible future problems before they became serious issues
- Standards of action and leadership for the long-term in all that they did
- Highest possible example and use of best practices
- Organizations designed and staffed for long-term success
- Plans and provision for emergencies and unforeseen obstacles
- Continuous training of new leaders to meet future needs
- Full engagement of volunteers and other helpers, when possible
- Development of the next generation of leaders to meet future needs to overcome deficits
- Absence of hypocrisy because their words matched their deeds
- Truth in all matters and absence of deception, delusion, and denial[1]

How did each leader demonstrate these attributes? Table 3.1 explains.

Each of these attributes builds upon the prior one; each is therefore a systematic step forward. Each step requires boldness and clarity, and requires objectivity in focusing on the *what* (defined outcome) before focusing on the *who* (of individual responsibility) and accountability for its realization.[2]

There are many significant similarities to recognize between leadership and management. One anonymous author distinguished them by saying that, "Leadership deals with people, and management deals with things." Both are important; but again, we must address the *what* before we address the *who*.[3]

Table 3.1 Searching for Motive—The Attributes and Actions of Principled Leaders

Attribute	Definition of Attribute in Principled Leaders	Actions of Principled Leaders
Vision	Principled leaders always have a great vision.	Principled leaders develop and communicate a simple, measurable vision for the future with defined outcomes to describe that scenario.
Values	Principled leaders always have strong values, principled character, and unquestioned integrity.	Principled leaders demand principled action, based upon sound doctrine and not merely on whims. Their integrity is strong and unwavering.
Strategy	Principled leaders always think strategically—and they always have a sound strategy.	Principled leaders lead with courage and passion based upon a strategy that defines expected outcomes precisely.
Structure (organization)	Principled leaders always build and staff good organizations.	Principled leaders build their organizations to use each person's gifts, abilities, and motivations for best results.
Resources	Principled leaders always know what resources are needed to succeed.	Principled leaders set priorities for all tasks and for the use of all resources.
Priorities	Principled leaders always set clear priorities.	Principled leaders put first things first. They make sure that the "main thing is the main thing."[4] They allocate resources to match their priorities.
Risk	Principled leaders always manage resources and risks systematically.	Principled leaders systematically assess risk and act to mitigate the greatest risks.
Support	Principled leaders always push their subordinates toward success with staunch support.	Principled leaders manage support systems to achieve the desired outcomes and to fulfill the highest priorities.

(continued)

Table 3.1 (*continued*)

Attribute	Definition of Attribute in Principled Leaders	Actions of Principled Leaders
Accountability	Principled leaders always hold people accountable.	Principled leaders ensure that: Everyone is held accountable, everyone is involved, and everyone has a role to fulfill and a task to complete.
Execution/ performance	Principled leaders always measure performance and manage execution.	Principled leaders ensure that performance and execution are managed and changed as needed in order to fulfill the vision.
Intercept entropy (decline)	Principled leaders always look for indications of future failure and act to limit the adverse impact. They intercept entropy (normal decline).	Principled leaders pursue and act upon early warning signs of future problems. They confront these problems and reverse them before they become serious.
Long-term strength	Principled leaders always lead with the future in mind.	The higher the level of the principled leader, the further in the future he or she looks forward and leads. A principled leader has a generational view and instills strong values and high character in subordinates.
Example	Principled leaders always set the highest example.	Principled leaders walk their talk, and they insist that other leaders do as well.
Legacy	Principled leaders always build legacies with those who will follow in mind.	Principled leaders want to leave their successors an easier job and will take the necessary steps to do so.
Emergency preparedness	Principled leaders always provide for emergencies.	Principled leaders allocate resources for unforeseen crises, and they ensure that plans are made to confront emergencies and to minimize their adverse impacts.
Future leaders	Principled leaders always raise up and train new leaders to meet future needs.	Principled leaders seek to equip at least three new leaders for every future leadership job.

(*continued*)

Table 3.1 (*continued*)

Attribute	Definition of Attribute in Principled Leaders	Actions of Principled Leaders
Volunteers	Principled leaders always engage volunteers and other helpers when possible.	Principled leaders ensure that qualified volunteers are used to their potential and equipped for the work to be done.
Leadership deficits	Principled leaders build the next generation.	Principled leaders seek to prepare the next generation to overcome expected challenges and existing deficits.
Hypocrisy	Principled leaders always eliminate differences between words and deeds.	Principled leaders adhere to the highest standards in walking their talk.
Truth	Principled leaders deal only in truth.	Principled leaders do not allow deception, delusion, or denial in any form.

The Importance of Measurement

Measurement is the basis of gauging performance against the defined outcome. It is also the basis of knowing whether the defined outcome has been realized.

"Measures shape behavior, and behavior creates culture."[5]

Leadership Models

George Washington, Benjamin Franklin, Thomas Jefferson, Abraham Lincoln, Harry Truman, and Dwight Eisenhower are just a few who exhibited these attributes in government. More recent leaders in business and science, like George Washington Carver (agriculture), Olive Beech and William Boeing (aviation), Harold T. Geneen and William T. McGowan (telecommunications), Michael Dell and William Gates (computers), F. Trammell Crow and James W. Rouse (real estate), Walter E. Disney and Michael R. Bloomberg (entertainment and media), Warren E. Buffett and Richard H. Jenrette (finance), William Darden and Thomas Monaghan (food and restaurants), Eli Lilly and Jonas Salk (medicine), Paul O'Neill (metals), Kenneth T. Wessner and Fred Smith (services), and William Brosnan and Edward V. Rickenbacker (transportation), have displayed these attributes.

Likewise, leaders in education, like Thomas Jefferson, John Harvard, Albert Einstein, and Margaret Mead, had these attributes. This is also true of the great leaders in religion over the centuries: William Wilberforce, C. S. Lewis, William Tyndale, Pope John Paul II, and William Hybels, to name a few.

The American Revolution would have surely been lost had it not been for one remarkable leader—George Washington. Washington was by no means a military genius; in fact, he was barely qualified to fulfill the roles thrust upon him. Politicians abandoned him in countless ways over the five years during which he led the Revolutionary forces. They moved the Congress from Philadelphia to the present-day site of Washington, DC, as the war came south from New York to New Jersey. They consistently failed to provide enough resources to Washington's army. Self-serving politicians made Washington's work all the more difficult.

But Washington remained steadfast in his leadership. Without regard for the conditions—lack of military acumen of his army, battlefield wins or losses, fair and foul weather, hardship of a night-crossing of the Delaware, the few times he could celebrate victory and the many instances of suffering in defeat—he was in full command. He was even present when he was needed to break up a fight between two soldiers.[6] And although they lost countless battles along the way, he became a historical icon by leading the Revolutionary Army to ultimate victory.

Lesson for Principled Business Leaders. Great leaders do not stop until the goal has been achieved—no matter what the circumstance.

Lesson for Principled Business Leaders. Principled business leaders objectively assess their personal leadership attributes.

Table 3.2 will enable you as a business leader to assess your leadership motivations and attributes. In order to do so, select the point score based on whether column (c), (d), or (e) most closely matches your leadership approach and level of accomplishment. Place the numerical score (1, 3, or 5) in column (f). Total your score for all 20 attributes in the block on page 39. A score below 50 suggests that your strong leadership attributes are still in formation.

Stretch Goal for My Enterprise. What attributes are missing in your leadership score—and in your organization as a whole? What are your priorities to build these or other qualities into your organization? How will you measure success? Are there other attributes that you might add to this list and demonstrate in your enterprise? Does your enterprise mirror these or other attributes in its overall performance?

Questions to Ponder. Have you ever known a leader who possessed all of these traits? How did he or she demonstrate them? How did his or her leadership attributes affect others in the organization? What was the organization able to accomplish that was truly remarkable under the leadership of this person? What was the single most influential attribute that enabled him or her to lead the organization to this level of achievement? How many of the attributes do you have at present? How many would you *like* to have?

Table 3.2 Evaluating Your Leadership Attributes

Leadership Attribute (a)	Definition (b)	Low (1) Standard (c)	Medium (3) Standard (d)	High (5) Standard (e)	My Leadership Score (1–5) (f)
1. Casts the vision and builds support for the vision throughout the organization culture.	Widely accepted view of where the organization is headed and how to know when the goal is attained.	Vision is widely accepted and matched by defined outcome(s) in 0–50% of all activities.	Vision has wide acceptance, clear milestones, and defined outcomes in 50–89% of all activities.	Vision has wide acceptance; clear milestones; and defined, fulfilled outcomes in 90–100% of all activities.	[ ] Score
2. Has strong values and principled character. Sets sound doctrine and consistent core values.	Equitable rules/ values that all will follow to benefit future generations.	No rules but my rules for my time and let those after me solve this and their problems.	Rules for the establishment of improved environment and benefit of all now and in the future.	Rules to apply/benefit all now and in the future applied equitably.	[ ] Score
3. Develops and implements sound strategy.	The leader thinks strategically. Realistic, achievable approach to achieving full success.	Strategy is documented, but unrealistic or unachievable.	Realistic, well documented, widely accepted and achievable in available time.	Realistic, achievable within set time and with available resources.	[ ] Score

4. Establishes and manages effective organizational structure.	Organization is in place; structure fully supports performance at lowest cost and lowest overhead; right people are in the right positions.	Organizational structure matches strategy; performance meets expectations in 0–50% of all missions; right people are in right positions.	Organization is optimal; performance meets expectations in 50–89% of all missions; overhead is limited to 10%; right people are in the right positions.	Organization is optimal; performance exceeds expectations; overhead is limited in 90–100% of all missions to 10%; right people in right positions.	[ ] Score
5. Assesses all resource requirements and counts the full cost of success.	People, funds, and equipment allocated to the task in right priority for structure; resources used do not exceed those available.	Some of required resources known and available from current staff and income to fulfill (under 50%) the vision requirements.	All required resources known and available from current staff and income to partially fulfill (50–90%) vision.	All required resources are available and applied from current staff and income and utilized in proper priority to completely (90–100%) fulfill vision.	[ ] Score

(continued)

33

Table 3.2 (*continued*)

Leadership Attribute (a)	Definition (b)	Low (1) Standard (c)	Medium (3) Standard (d)	High (5) Standard (e)	My Leadership Score (1–5) (f)
6. Sets clear priorities and allocates resources by priority.	Fair priorities established, followed, and measured in all aspects of effort.	Priorities are arbitrary or everything is a priority; resources allocated by priority to top 50% of all required tasks and missions.	Sound priorities are set, announced, measured, followed, and reported; resources are allocated to fulfill 50–90% of all required tasks and missions.	Sound priorities are set, announced, measured, followed, reported, and adhered to with right resources; resources are allocated to fulfill 90–100% of all required tasks and missions.	[ ] Score
7. Manages resources and all risks systematically. Establishes and implements related budgets and control systems	Systems in place to allocate and manage all resources and risks systematically.	Control systems allocate and oversee the use of resources and management of risks within established priorities and schedules.	Control systems ensure that resource use is within priority, budget, and schedule, and risks are managed systematically for 50–90% of all tasks and missions.	Control systems ensure limited use of resources by priority and schedule, and all risks are managed systematically for 100% of all tasks and missions; overhead is consistently <10%.	[ ] Score

34

				[ ] Score
8. Ensures maximum effectiveness by establishing and implementing sound support systems.	Support systems (ADP), supplies, materials, etc., are in place and managed effectively.	Support is accurate, timely, and effective for up to 50% of all tasks and missions.	Support exceeds expectations in effectiveness for 50–89% of all tasks and missions.	Support exceeds expectations; cost is consistently lower than expected and within priorities for 90–100% of all tasks and missions.
				[ ] Score
9. Assigns specific tasks and establishes accountability and performance standards for every person.	Specific persons are responsible for achieving defined outcomes at specific times.	Some persons are accountable (0–50%) for each task and mission; some (0–50%) of all tasks and missions are measured and reported.	Most persons are accountable (50–89%) for each task and mission; some (50–89%) of all tasks and missions are measured and reported.	All persons are accountable (90–100%) for each task and mission; some (90–100%) of all tasks and missions are measured and reported.
				[ ] Score
10. Executes with passion and courage. Measures and evaluates performance by task and makes needed changes to ensure that vision is fulfilled.	Standards of acceptable performance equitably applied to all tasks. Success is measured systematically.	Standards exist; most (>50%) tasks are measured and applied equitably.	Standards exist; most (51–80%) tasks are measured and applied equitably.	Standards exist; all (81–100%) tasks are measured and applied with uniformly good results versus vision.

(continued)

Table 3.2 (*continued*)

Leadership Attribute (a)	Definition (b)	Low (1) Standard (c)	Medium (3) Standard (d)	High (5) Standard (e)	My Leadership Score (1–5) (f)
11. Intercepts entropy (decline).	Principled leaders always look for indications of future failure and act to limit the adverse impact. They intercept entropy (normal decline).	Routine and systematic efforts to find flaws, absence of best practices, and poor performance exist in more than 50% of all products and services.	Routine and systematic efforts to find flaws, absence of best practices, and poor performance exist in 11–49% of all products and services.	Routine and systematic efforts to find flaws, absence of best practices, and poor performance exist in 90% or less than 10% of all products and services.	[ ] Score
12. Exhibits long-term strength.	Principled leaders always lead with the future in mind.	Business plans, leadership development, and budgets are set for three years.	Business plans, leadership development, and budgets are set for five years.	Business plans, leadership development, and budgets are set for ten years.	[ ] Score
13. Leads by example.	Principled leaders always set the highest example.	Employees seek to serve in half of all work units.	Employees seek to serve in at least 50% and up to 80% of all work units.	Employees seek to serve in at least 80% and up to 100% of all work units.	[ ] Score
14. Leaves behind a legacy.	Principled leaders always build legacies with those who will follow in mind.	Supervisors and leaders are respected and have strong legacies in 50% of all work units.	Supervisors and leaders are respected and have strong legacies in 50–80% of all work units.	Supervisors and leaders are respected and have strong legacies in in >80% of all work units.	[ ] Score

15. Demonstrates emergency preparedness.	Principled leaders always provide for emergencies.	Business continuity is ensured in 50% of all work units in emergencies.	Business continuity is ensured in 50–80% of all work units in emergencies.	Business continuity is ensured in >80% of all work units in emergencies.	[ ] Score
16. Develops future leaders.	Principled leaders always raise up and train new leaders to meet future needs.	Supervisors and leaders have three qualified successors in 50% of all work units.	Supervisors and leaders have three qualified successors in 50–80% of all work units.	Supervisors and leaders have three qualified successors in >80% of all work units.	[ ] Score
17. Recruits and engages volunteers.	Principled leaders always engage volunteers and other helpers, when possible.	Volunteers are valued and are active in up to 50% of all work units.	Volunteers are valued and are active in up to 80% of all work units.	Volunteers are valued and are active in up to 100% of all work units.	[ ] Score
18. Deals with deficits.	Principled leaders build the next generation.	Every worker has three qualified successors in up to 50% of all work units.	Every worker has three qualified successors in up to 80% of all work units.	Every worker has three qualified successors in up to 100% of all work units.	[ ] Score

(continued)

Table 3.2 *(continued)*

Leadership Attribute (a)	Definition (b)	Low (1) Standard (c)	Medium (3) Standard (d)	High (5) Standard (e)	My Leadership Score (1–5) (f)
19. Opposes and eliminates hypocrisy.	Principled leaders always eliminate differences between words and deeds.	Fewer than 20% of all work units have experienced leadership or best practices violations.	Fewer than 10% of all work units have experienced leadership or best practices violations.	Fewer than 5% of all work units have experienced leadership or best practices violations.	[ ] Score
20. Embodies and exemplifies truth.	Principled leaders deal only in truth.	Fewer than 20% of all work units have experienced false reports or inaccurate information in five years.	Fewer than 10% of all work units have experienced false reports or inaccurate information in five years.	Fewer than 5% of all work units have experienced false reports or inaccurate information in five years.	[ ] Score
MY LEADERSHIP SCORE					[ ] Total Score

The following questions will help you develop an action plan, based on your leadership score and personal/organizational goals.

Action Steps

1. What is your leadership score? (Add the numerical ratings in the column at the right to get your score. A score of 100 is perfect. If you exceed 50, you are on a promising leadership path.)
2. What will it take to get you above a score of 50? What steps will you take in priority order? What is the expected outcome for each step?
3. What steps are you prepared to do to reach this level of leadership? What work sacrifices or lifestyle changes are required?

Key Measures of Success

Missing Attribute	Target Date to Adopt	Weakest Function(s)	Corrective Action Steps	Resources Needed
1.				
2.				
3.				
4.				
5.				

Suggested Reading

Bennis, Warren, and David A. Heenan. *Co-Leaders: The Power of Great Partnerships*. New York: John Wiley & Sons, 1999, 312 pp.

Ellis, Joseph J. *His Excellency: George Washington*. New York: Alfred A. Knopf, 2004, 312 pp.

Feiner, Michael. *The Feiner Points of Leadership*. New York: Warner Business Books, 2006, 265 pp.

Iacocca, Lee. *Where Have All the Leaders Gone?* With Catherine Whitney. New York: Simon & Schuster, 2007, 274 pp.

Landorf, Joyce. *Joseph*. Old Tappan, NJ: Fleming H. Revell Company, 1979, 319 pp.

MacArthur, John F., Jr. *Nehemiah: Experiencing the Good Hand of God*. Nashville: W Publishing Group, 2001, 122 pp.

McCullough, David. *1776*. New York: Simon & Schuster, 2005, 386 pp.

Sanborn, Mark. *The Fred Factor*. Colorado Springs: WaterBrook Press, 2004, 110 pp.

4

Business Leadership and the Political Process

The roots of violence—
Wealth without working,
Pleasure without conscience,
Knowledge without character,
Commerce without morality
Science without humanity,
Worship without sacrifice,
Politicians without principles.

—Mahatma Ghandhi

Solving the Puzzle

It is Ross and his father's last night of their two-week-long fishing trip on the Salmon River in Idaho. The two men have just completed their final supper at the cabin; they return home tomorrow.

Ross has been thinking about the conversations he's had with his father over the past week about the nation's current situation—and he has been puzzled all day. How did so many failures occur in the United States in the first place? Although the outcomes were positive, and the social and economic pain of getting through the process are now behind them—Ross still wonders how leaders of principle could have allowed things to fall apart as they did. How was it that no one stopped the precipitous collapse of the

41

dollar on the heels of a half-century of massive federal budget deficits, the nagging international balance of payments shortfalls, the countless enterprises failures in the economic meltdown, and the hundreds of city and county bankruptcies? Of course, the biggest issue is the impact on businesses and jobs—often innocent victims of leadership failures at other levels. His questions continued all evening, and eventually, his father began to question him in return.

"Do you know the definition of 'self-serving'? Do you know the meaning of this term when it is attached to politicians in any institution? Are all politicians self-serving, or are there politicians who are also principled leaders? What distinguishes a self-serving politician from a principled leader? Can you give me examples of both?"

Ross was beginning to understand. The lights were coming on, slowly. There is a difference between the two, he realized. His father went on.

"What is the nature of the political process? Does the political process have to work in every organization or institution? Where does the political process end and the leadership process begin?"

By the end of the night, Ross was exhausted. But his eyes lit up; he was starting to see why the nation had gotten itself into such trouble. For the last half-century, *U.S. institutions had been led more by politicians than they had by principled leaders.* That was it! Ross had discovered the pivotal issue that led him to ask the important questions: Where does politics end, and principled leadership start? How had the political process tolerated financial decline; cultural divisions; government gridlock; pervasive mistrust of businesses, government, schools, and religion—all as the United States entered the twenty-first century?

These certainly wouldn't be easy questions to answer—of that much Ross was sure. But he was too tired to wrestle with them. Upon coming to this realization, Ross and his father blew out the kerosene lamp. It had been a long day.

Leadership and the Political Process

One must view all aspects of the political process with a wider lens, as Ross has done—whether it applies to business, religion, education, or government—based upon long accepted norms both for the political process and for politicians as a group. It's also important to adopt the proposition that the political process—whether in business, religion, education, or government—is a potentially vast reservoir of current and future leaders for our twenty-first century institutions. Historically, this massive stockpile of political talent has been—and will continue to be—the obvious place to start our search for principled leaders with understanding of these times of turbulent and profound change.

We should seek to select leadership candidates who are people of great integrity, capability, capacity, gifts, and talent—those whom any citizen would readily support or serve in a variety of institutions to strengthen the nation. They should be persons of vision who inspire, motivate, guide, and challenge citizens to accomplish magnificent deeds—regardless of the difficulty or sacrifice needed and without compromising the principles listed in Chapter 3. This wellspring of potential leadership talent is the primary hope for the future of the United States.

Third—given the United States' current difficult circumstances—one must weigh where the nation stands with regard to that fundamental trajectory so remarkably established by our founding fathers. If the United States is indeed missing that intended orbit, the reader must understand why this may have occurred and what responsibility the political process—or more accurately, self-serving politicians—may bear for this errant direction.

Fourth, of all of our institutions—business, organized religion, education, and government—isn't business the one that is the most capable of taking on the challenge of leading a U.S. turnaround? Shouldn't business be able to guide the nation to a sustainable twenty-first century?

Finally, and most importantly, one must question whether the United States has the wherewithal to produce the principled leaders needed at this time in our history. Should they not be available, no amount of chatter, frustration, anger, fear, or dialogue will alter the nation's failing trajectory. If there are no principled leaders, solutions in any form or for any issue are mere conversation. This is no time for mere conversation.

If, however, principled business leaders *do* emerge among us, they must first ensure that their individual enterprises are in top shape and positioned for long-term sustainability in any economic environment. Then they can address the two most important U.S. deficits—national financial bankruptcy and the absence of a widely shared personal commitment to national community—as a first priority. Solutions to these two massive shortfalls can reverse the nation's downward trajectory and reorder it into an upward destination of future greatness. The solutions to these overriding needs will be proposed with honesty, integrity, candor, and realism—but wholly dependent on the availability of principled leaders to carry them forward.

There is also the reminder introduced in Chapter 1. The daunting reality is that history is not on the side of the United States. There are few instances of cultures and civilizations that have successfully turned around once they were in decline, or once citizens had become dependent upon the government to survive. And, in fact, the United States may have already passed that point. One must first have a clear understanding of the political process that has brought us here.

Perhaps the best way to begin is by asking ourselves some very basic questions: What is politics? What is the political process? And what—or who—are politicians? What separates a great politician from a great leader? Consider the great achievements during our nation's history, accomplished in all sectors by selfless politicians who were also great leaders. How permanent are the recent changes in our nation? What makes any reversal temporary or permanent? What is the lasting legacy of politicians who have a different value system and who seek to benefit only special interests rather than the larger body of citizens whom they serve? One must begin with a broad definition of politics, politicians, and the political process, as they apply to all of the institutions—business, religion, education, and government—the source of potential future leaders.

We can assess the attributes of any politicians using the criteria in Chapter 3, and we can also gauge the actions of politicians against those of great leaders. To what extent have politicians in the past guided groups, institutions, or nations without gaining the trust of the members? At what point does serving others transform to becoming *self*-serving? While it is certainly possible to have great political leaders, recent failures suggest that this is not the case in many current institutions and enterprises.

It will probably not surprise you to realize that although selfless politicians have a natural path toward leadership positions, history reveals that few such politicians rise to become great leaders as well. It is tragic that only a small percentage of the politicians in any of our institutions are currently viewed as great leaders. In terms of our own nation's leadership, President John F. Kennedy was the last president to challenge Americans to serve their country instead of asking what the nation could do for them. Few if any national figures since that time have posed this challenge, and the United States appears to have backed away from President Kennedy's call. How could the host of subtle changes shown in Chapter 2 have occurred in just 40-plus years since Kennedy made this appeal? How have we gone from a nation where principled leaders call citizens to service to one where politicians are promising gifts from the public treasury to those who vote for them? Are we on a dead-end street? It's time to answer these questions.

Business, organized religion, education, and government all seem to have fallen victim to these subtle changes as they have compromised their values, standards, and commitment to the public. The United States has entered an era of the *winner take all* economy, and the winners may have indeed taken it all—leaving middle-class families, shareholders, citizens, investors, voters, pensioners, and seniors holding an empty bag. We may have been *Madoffed* by a lot of thieves.

We must, however, consider whether there are other reasons for such changes or decline—the rise of the first among equals, persons of extra privilege, special interests, or the *elite minority* mentioned in the preface. Have we allowed ourselves to be the victims of false, misleading, inaccurate, biased, or deceptive information and advertising, or is it just plain old greed? Have we trusted the media, an elite minority, or the *institutional aristocrats* who may have slowly engineered these changes to pull it off? Have politics trumped principle? I hope not, but the current state of our country is certainly a cause for concern.

Is the absence of leadership a political party problem? Many in the current public debate attribute our failures to one or the other political party when, in actuality, neither is to blame. Both political parties—as well as many of our universities, the media, and special interest groups—have used the past 50 years to give them all what one anonymous author might now call a "firm grip on an empty bag."

If we measure by accounting standards, the United States may be technically bankrupt. Happily, the Federal Reserve creates money, so outright bankruptcy is not a reality, at least not right now. Of greater concern is the absence of unifying values, as the nation shamelessly spends future generations' resources without blinking and presses toward what may become a multifaceted collapse—all in record time.

There are members of the business community who know that there has been immoral behavior for at least two decades and who know that business has been a "bad boy"[1] for longer than it should have been. These leaders of business may be in the minority now, but this can change at any time. These principled leaders with substance, courage, and the guided passion to turn the United States around can become the majority. They can be ready to move forward, as soon as they have a plan they can trust. And that time is *now*. Our deeds of tomorrow can, at last, match our words.

Unfortunately, the lack of progress on the major issues outlined in Chapters 5 through 23 have a high potential to harm the nation, which would suggest the contrary. Sadly, none of these issues have been satisfactorily addressed. Can what has been hailed as the greatest nation on earth not resolve any central fiscal, social, or economic problem? Perhaps it is those who benefit from our failures and inaction who have the most influence. They gain more if the problems remain unresolved. But the problems *can* be worked out, and the United States can return to its former strength and fortitude with greater influence than ever—if the principled men and women who lead our businesses act immediately!

This is not a partisan political story. The many references and short essays included in this book are broadly representative of the full political spectrum. Some writers are liberal, some are conservative, some are independent; virtually all are recognized in their fields. Every effort has been made to provide both liberal and conservative viewpoints on each issue, and yet it remains a chronicle of leadership failure.

Regardless of the causes, the reader is likely to conclude that we—citizens, employees, members, and other participants—may bear the ultimate responsibility for any deficits that we have allowed to come into being, that is, unless principled business leaders come forward and launch the transformation. The full plan of action is here, but leadership fails if standards of excellence are compromised, principles are set aside in favor of passions, self is put ahead of others, and accountability is compromised or eliminated. Any one of these factors can clear the way for a new, even more harmful political leadership process to appear.

As we've discussed previously—and as Ross has discovered through his research and conversations with his father—the United States has undergone profound change. Were all of these changes the product of self-serving special interests? How did so many phonies come into power in our institutions, and how did our nation ignore its misdirection? How did key U.S. institutions fall under the direction of self-serving politicians? How could the vast reservoir of potential leaders—honorable, principled people—first be so selfless and later become so corrupt? A brief comparison of the attributes and actions of self-serving politicians may be helpful (see Table 4.1).

You may now have a better understanding of how self-serving U.S. politicians may have unwittingly brought about a sea change for the worse on a number of vital national issues—all of which have led to business failures, decline of the dollar, accumulation of debt, damage from derivatives, demographic imbalances, uncontrolled addictions, declining education performance, failing health levels, clean water shortages, failed energy policies, lagging environmental cleanup, declining international relations, technology losses, terrorism, and a slew of other problems. These losses have occurred over the past 40-plus years because principled leaders have failed to take charge or refused to act in the long-term interests of the nation.

Table 4.2 contrasts the actions of self-serving politicians with those of principled leaders on three of these issues.

Lesson for Principled Business Leaders. Four decades of marginal accountability and sporadic leadership are penalizing employees, families, and middle-class taxpayers who must now contend with quickly rising prices; flat or low wage gains; growing job losses; destabilized investment markets; growing home foreclosures; and countless other devastating forces. All of these outcomes are the unintended consequences of short-term, politically motivated actions, leadership failures, or the abandonment of sound values in the modern United States.

Lesson for Principled Business Leaders. You can now decide for yourself who you believe to be a principled leader versus a self-serving politician—in terms of your own experience. It's up to you to judge whether the public servants and private leaders whom you know—the mayors,

Table 4.1 Searching for Motive—The Attributes and Actions of Self-Serving Politicians

Subject	Attributes of Self-Serving Politicians	Actions of Self-Serving Politicians
Vision	Politicians have a short time for action with no clear goals or desired outcomes except their personal gain and extended control.	Politicians offer vague and general visions to which neither they, nor their allies, can be held accountable. There are few, if any, defined outcomes.
Values	Politicians are interested in expediency; they have few strong values and malleable character traits.	Politicians follow the passions of the moment and cater to the loudest complainers to realize short-term gain at the lowest cost. They have few guiding principles.
Strategy	Politicians have no strategy—except to be elected to power.	Politicians heed to the most demanding constituents and seek personal job security without a related institutional strategy or accountability.
Structure (organization)	Politicians use people to achieve personal goals instead of attempting to build effective organizations.	Politicians build organizations to reward the most vocal constituents and assign work based upon the demands of process and not on priorities. They bypass accountability.
Resources	Politicians love money and the control of people and other resources. They use people to achieve personal gain.	Politicians seek resources only for allies, and they use public resources as a means to extend personal control.
Priorities	Politicians set no priorities except those needed for short-term gain.	Politicians attend only to short-term crises and set no long-term priorities or accountability levels.
Risk	Politicians seek to control resources and react only to loss.	Politicians ignore priorities and do not systematically define, manage, or mitigate risk. Only friends and allies receive resources.

(continued)

Table 4.1 (*continued*)

Subject	Attributes of Self-Serving Politicians	Actions of Self-Serving Politicians
Support	Politicians seek to be first and seldom empower subordinates. Control is their primary standard.	Politicians do not manage support systems to ensure the highest potential for success. They provide support to friends and allies.
Accountability	Politicians avoid accountability—personal or organizational.	None are accountable because only a few are carrying loads—and all disperse blame for failure.
Execution/performance	Politicians do not measure or manage performance; they focus only on the process.	Politicians provide jobs to those whom they favor and ignore performance unless a crisis demands otherwise.
Intercept entropy (decline)	Politicians ignore indications of future failure and do no act to limit adverse impact. They ignore entropy (normal decline).	Politicians heed only immediate crises and ignore any warning signs of impending future problems or failure. They only act when forced to do so.
Long-term strength	Politicians lead only for the short term and self-interest.	Politicians act only for short-term gain. They are motivated more by self-interest than by wider or long-term realities. They only seek to avoid crises on their watch. They ignore warning signs.
Example	Politicians only follow the example of the moment.	Politicians speak only to those in hearing. Actions and words seldom match.
Legacy	Politicians build coalitions only for the short term.	Politicians only want to succeed themselves. Their interests are in short-term gain. They ignore the future.
Emergency preparedness	Politicians do not provide for emergencies.	Politicians use all resources for immediate reward. They ignore risk and pending emergencies.

(*continued*)

Table 4.1   *(continued)*

Subject	Attributes of Self-Serving Politicians	Actions of Self-Serving Politicians
Future leaders	Politicians do not raise and train new leaders to meet future needs. They live for now.	Politicians use information and power to control others. They ignore future leadership needs.
Volunteers	Politicians engage volunteers only to meet personal, self-serving goals.	Politicians use volunteers for personal benefit and only for as long as is needed to realize the politician's short-term gain.
Deficits	Politicians build only for the present generation.	Politicians ignore current and potential future deficits. They focus on short-term crises and ignore the long-term interests of the institution.
Hypocrisy	Politicians tolerate and exemplify hypocrisy.	Politicians have no sense of the match of words and deeds. They work and talk only for the moment.
Truth	Politicians have no standard of truth.	Politicians craft their words to suit the immediate need and audience. Problems and hard issues are set to the side and ignored so that their self-interest is served.

county commissioners, assembly people, judges, heads of corporations, employers for whom they work, company presidents, members of congress, or current political candidates for office—have been principled leaders or self-serving politicians.

Stretch Goal for My Business. Are the core values and leadership principles of operation of my business codified, shared widely, and adhered to in my enterprise? Do I have a responsibility to ensure that this is done?

Questions to Ponder. To what extent does *politics* influence my *business*—and vice versa?

- How can *business* exist and operate free from *politics*?
- What role should *business* play in *politics*?
- Which is a priority to myself and to my organization—*politics* or *business*?

Table 4.2 Comparing Self-Serving and Principled Action on Public Issues

Example	Actions of Self-Serving Politicians	Actions of Principled Leaders
Debt	Use massive debt at all levels to advance short-term political agendas—regardless of the impact on future generations.	Abhor excessive debt and insist on its timely retirement and actuarially sound reserves and pensions.
Energy	Allow special interests to control the energy supply, subsidies, and distribution.	Insist on economic realism, prudence, and principled conservation.
Terrorism	Misapply the resources needed to conquer terrorism on special interest projects and phony political priorities. Fail to match urgency of risk and remedial action to mitigate risk.	Systemically reduce and eliminate terror risks consistent with their severity. Apply suitable countermeasures. Spend within available resources and reserve funds for emergencies based upon a systematic risk analysis.

Action Steps

Principled Business Leaders Must:

1. Ask the top supervisors in your organization to outline the core values of the business. Do they match your own?

2. Ask your employees to confidentially share their feelings about the decision-making process in your enterprise. Where do principles leave off and politics start? Is there a common perception of this dividing line? Is the dividing line where it should be?

3. Review the steps being taken to move decisions, promotions, and incentives toward principles, firm criteria, and standards, and away from internal politics?

Key Measures of Success

No.	Qualitative Standard	Quantitative Standard	Success Cases/ Total (%)
1.	Decision-making criteria	Involvement of affected-staff Post decision feedback Accountability for results	
2.	Promotions based upon merit	Job output measures Productivity measures	
3.	Incentive standards	Individual output measures Group output measures Organization output measures	
4.	Market share/position	Market share (%) Product position/share ($)	
5.	Long-term (five-year) potential	Current market position versus prior; Current product position versus prior	

Suggested Reading

de Tocqueville, Alexis. *Democracy in America*. Boston: Tichnor and Fields, 1862. Current edition published by Barnes and Noble, 2003, 808 pp.
Slosser, Bob. *Reagan Inside Out*. Waco, TX: Word Books, 1984, 203 pp.

Principled Leadership and Financial Stability

The Vital Role of Business Leaders—Getting Your Enterprise in Top Shape

In crisis lies opportunity.

—Chinese proverb

A Scary Future

R oss Gregory and his friends arrive for a final evening of discussion for 2016. The group has been meeting monthly for nearly five years, and December 2016 seems to have come quickly. After a quiet dinner, the group decided to spend the balance of the evening discussing the lessons of their five years together.

As the discussion wore on, the tone of the group changed from light-hearted laughter and joking to somber storytelling and hushed voices. Bonnie Hughes told of conversations with many of her customers at the bank where she works part-time. Many continue to struggle with credit problems but are still borrowing to support their lifestyles. Bonnie was especially sensitive to this problem because she works in the consumer loan workout department, which oversees loans in default.

Mark Baker told about his part-time work with the Social Security Administration and of the dire straits of the many consumers who had no savings and were recently outraged when their monthly payments were decreased to provide for interest payments on the national debt. Tad McGraw told about his part-time work with the state social services directorate, where he had been given the unfortunate task of telling unemployed and undocumented workers that no funds remained in the unemployment security accounts to help them with job training and interim unemployment benefits. Tens of thousands of these workers—and larger numbers of unemployed citizen workers—all have the same problem. Tad's office had been filled with shouting people from the moment the doors opened at 8:00 A.M., and when the doors closed at 5:00 P.M., it often took help from the local police to remove the people still waiting after closing hours.

Tim Cullen, who had interviewed for a job at the State Department, learned of a recent riot at an airport in East Asia. Tim was visibly moved as he shared the story that his interviewer had told him of screaming women and children who blamed the United States for the collapse of their central bank the year before and used this as an excuse to attack the U.S. consul. His shirt was torn off; his luggage was taken, opened, and scattered across the square and into the nearby market. Only the local police had saved him from being cut with broken glass bottles and struck on the head with bricks and paving stones. "Should I look for another job?" he asked the group.

Charlie Eichelberger related a story about his family's filing for bankruptcy when their entire savings was devalued by half as a result of the recent, precipitous fall of the dollar. His mother died shortly thereafter because of health complications and the termination of the local medical assistance program for indigent families. Bill Woolfalk's parents had also filed for bankruptcy, and they were now living with him—an ironic turn of events. Joe Kellerman told the story of an uncle in the northeast who had finally turned to illegal drugs following the collapse of his lifelong employer, Atlantic Power and Light, when their delinquent customer base grew so large that the company ran out of cash. It was a tragic situation.

The stories continued until well past midnight. While the many situations of hardship saddened some and angered others, Ross encouraged everyone to think about all that they had heard and wait until another evening to discuss answers. The goodbyes were muted as each of his former classmates left for home. They had to put together some real answers; 2016 had been a hard year. Ross felt a knot begin to form in his stomach.

The Issue. New U.S. graduates and job seekers will be increasingly confronted by a staggering array of conditions that had not existed when they entered high school or college. Business leaders may be able to help in resolving some of the issues.

The Vital Role of Future Business Leaders

Business is the one institution that has operated successfully in the face of a 40-plus year decline in leadership values. Setting a bad example all too often, business leadership failures mirrored political leadership failures to produce a new class of victims—innocent middle-class taxpayers. As 2010 begins, U.S. businesses may be at a crossroad, facing many more years of adjustment. Enterprises that took massive risks, for which they could not pay during the prior decade, got us here. Principled business leaders must get us out of this mess.

Excess business risk is not to be confused with the ordinary risks that informed entrepreneurs take in the launch of a new product, the development of a technology, or the offer of new services in underdeveloped markets. These risks went *well* beyond prudence, and many of them also moved conflict of interest to a new high. While entrepreneurial gambles are an ordinary element of the capitalist system's risks and rewards, payment for these failures from excess risk has been passed to innocent taxpayers. In their wake is $18 trillion in lost wealth, $14 trillion in direct government payments and guarantees, and an economy that must carry stunning new levels of public debt. It is one thing for entrepreneurs to risk their capital; it is quite another for misguided policies to threaten the viability of the free market system.

Unfortunately, the landscape of business history during the past four decades is now littered with tragic leadership failures that have hurt many innocent, well-meaning, and well-behaved citizens. In many cases, these victims are the ones who have worked hard, paid their bills on time, raised their children well, and attempted to save enough to look forward to some good years as seniors. In far too many instances, they have instead lost their jobs, savings, investments, retirement savings, and college savings for their children—through no fault of their own. Table 5.1 contrasts the severity of the current recession with those of the past 65 years. As you can see, the trough that began in 2007 has already set (or nearly set) records in gross domestic product (GDP) losses, unemployment, and duration from peak to trough.

Looking for Causes   The taproots of today's crises are found in many of the same causes of the 1930s Great Depression era—debt, overconsumption, overinvestment, decline in trade (today, this is an imbalance in trade and not a decline), malfeasance by industrialists and bankers, and delusion or incompetence by government officials—all of which ultimately led to a collapse of consumer confidence. To this list of causes, we have now added excess liquidity; subprime mortgages; over-leverage; flat middle-class wages for nearly two decades; inflation that outstrips those flat wages; the intermittent but persistent decline in the value of the dollar; rampant and

Table 5.1 The Worst Downturn Since the Great Depression Recessions Following World War II

| Peak | Trough | Duration in Months | | Peak-to-Trough % Change | | Jobless Rate | | |
		Recession Peak to Trough	Expansion Trough to Peak	Real GDP	Non-Farm Employment	Low	High	Change
Dec. 2007	**Dec. 2009**	**24**	**73**	**-3.9**	**-5.1**	**4.4**	**9.8**	**5.4**
March 2001	Nov. 2001	8	120	-0.4	-2.0	3.8	6.3	2.5
July 1990	March 1991	8	92	-1.3	-1.5	5.0	7.8	2.8
July 1981	Nov. 1982	16	12	-2.9	-3.1	7.2	10.8	3.6
Jan. 1980	July 1980	6	58	-2.2	-1.3	5.6	7.8	2.2
Nov. 1973	March 1975	16	36	-3.1	-2.7	4.6	9.0	4.4
Dec. 1969	Nov. 1970	11	106	-1.0	-1.4	3.4	6.1	2.7
April 1960	Feb. 1961	10	24	-1.3	-2.3	4.8	7.1	2.3
Aug. 1957	April 1958	8	39	-3.8	-4.4	3.7	7.5	3.8
July 1953	May 1954	10	45	-2.7	-3.3	2.5	6.1	3.6
Nov. 1948	Oct. 1949	11	37	-1.7	-5.1	3.4	7.9	4.5
Average for past recessions		10	57	-2.0	-2.7	4.4	7.6	3.2

Sources: NBER, BEA, FRB, BLS, Moody's Economy.com.

unregulated derivatives; excessive public spending; underfunded pensions; and countless other issues. Where were the genuine leaders when all of this was taking place? Where did those in control bring us? The full list of leadership failures since the 1960s, many of which occurred in just the past five years, is truly stunning. (See Appendix A for a complete description of a half-century of U.S. government/entrepreneurial/business leadership failures.)

The economy's partial collapse in the 1970s occurred when foreign competition and technology took away certain elements of the United States' commercial advantage, cut into its manufacturing dominance, and caused many companies to either divest poor performing businesses or outsource work to gain needed efficiencies. Made worse by the oil embargo, imposed by OPEC nations angry at U.S. policy toward Israel, this downturn slowed the U.S. economy to a walk for more than 20 months. It was only the steadfast courage of then-Federal Reserve Chairman Paul Volcker in the early 1980s—and the pain of three years of oppressive interest rates (in the high teens) and the accompanying monetary contraction—that edged the economy back from that precipice and prepared the way for future expansion. It took a courageous leader to administer the hard medicine of limiting the money supply to restore order.

The resulting economic reverses, job losses, and business failures produced a spate of new business regulations, which strengthened worker benefits and protections, lowered rampant inflation, and reversed the downward spiral of unemployment. The energy shortages and bank failures of the 1970s finally yielded to this hard medicine to open the way for expansion in the mid-1980s. No other economic problems were resolved, but a new set of bank problems emerged—the savings and loan (S&L) collapse of 1989 to 1991. In this instance, special interest pressure to deregulate the savings and loan industry gave rise to thousands of new banks, loans, and commercial development, much of which collapsed because of the

> ... high and volatile interest rates during the late 1970s and early 1980s, which exposed thrifts to interest-rate risk (caused by a mismatch in duration and by interest-rate sensitivity of assets and liabilities); phaseout and eventual elimination in the early 1980s of the Federal Reserve's Regulation Q, which caused increasing costs of thrift liabilities relative to many fixed-rate assets and adversely affected industry profitability and capital; adverse regional economic conditions; state and federal deregulation of depository institutions, which allowed thrifts to enter new but riskier loan markets; the deregulation of the thrift industry without an accompanying increase in examination resources (for some years, examiner resources actually declined); reduced regulatory capital requirements, which allowed thrifts to use alternative accounting

procedures to increase reported capital levels; excessive chartering of new thrifts during the 1980s; the withdrawal in 1986 of federal tax laws (enacted in 1981) that benefited commercial real-estate investments; the development during the 1980s of the brokered deposit market; and delays in funding the thrift insurance fund during the 1980s and the RTC during the 1990s, which led to regulators' failure to close many insolvent institutions in a timely manner.

As a consequence of all these factors, during the 1980s the thrift industry realized unprecedented losses on loans and investments. The result, as noted, was the failure of hundreds of thrift institutions and the insolvency by year-end 1986 of the FSLIC, the federal insurer for the thrift industry. As of year-end 1986, 441 thrifts with $113 billion in assets were book insolvent, and another 533 thrifts, with $453 billion in assets, had tangible capital of no more than 2 percent of total assets. These 974 thrifts held 47 percent of industry assets. In response, Congress created the Financing Corporation (FICO) in 1987 to provide funding to the FSLIC by issuing long-term bonds. By the time FIRREA was passed two years later, FICO had contributed $8.2 billion in financing to the FSLIC, an amount insufficient to deal with the industry's massive problems.[1]

The savings and loan collapse marked the first time that public money had been used to effect the rescue of an entire industry. When the final analysis was completed by the FDIC in 1999, the total private sector losses were put at $29.1 billion, the public sector losses were set at $123.8 billion; and the total was $152.9 billion.[2] Table 5.2 on the following page details the annual failures and asset losses to investors.

The 1980s also brought deregulation of airlines, public utilities, energy, and banking, among others, followed by tax cuts, investment incentives, and a concerted effort to build U.S. businesses. Incomes soared, wages began to rise dramatically, and the age of technology that was to dominate the next decade began. Black Monday—October 19, 1987—was the first casualty as the trusting investors saw their market investments drop by 23 percent. Innocent Americans, who had placed their confidence and hard-earned money in the stock market, lost billions.

The 1990s brought the savings and loan crisis that came on the heels of Black Monday. One thousand and forty-three of the deregulated savings and loan associations collapsed, and U.S. taxpayers had to shell out $152.9 billion through the Federal Savings and Loan Indemnity Corporation (FISLIC) to repay depositors and then recover and resell the failed industry's assets. Investors lost another $36 billion.[3] The first casualty of 1970s bank deregulation and the 1981 law allowing the sale of mortgages by savings

Table 5.2 Thrift Failures, 1986–1995 ($ Millions)

	FSLIC		RTC	
Year	Number	Assets	Number	Assets
1986	54	16,264		
1987	48	11,270		
1988	185	96,760		
1989	9	725	318	134,520
1990			213	129,662
1991			144	78,899
1992			59	44,197
1993			9	6,148
1994			2	137
1995			2	435
Total	**296**	**125,019**	**747**	**393,998**

Source: Curry and Shibut, "The Cost of the Savings and Loan Crisis: Truth and Consequences," FDIC Banking Review, 1999.

and loan banks was soon followed by another—the real estate collapse of 1990 to 1992.

These bundled mortgages of the 1980s became the forerunners of the collateralized debt obligations (CDOs) of the late 1990s, which were bought by Wall Street at a deep discount and resold as government-backed bonds to Fannie Mae, Freddie Mac, Ginnie Mae, and others to build a new foundation for the next financial collapse—savings and loan failures. The largest of these—Home State Savings and Loan of Cincinnati (1985), Lincoln Savings and Loan, and Silverado Savings and Loan—cost the taxpayers and innocent investors in the billions.

The *dot.bomb* and real estate collapses of the 1990s and 2007 to 2008 were eerily similar to those that had preceded them. In these instances, many of the banks bailed out in 2008 were the biggest contributors to both political campaigns in the November 2008 election, as bailout (TARP) monies proved to be a handsome repayment for their political contributions. Specifically, many of the initial nine banks that received $250 billion in new federal capital in October 2008 were top contributors to the presidential campaign, while another 402 banks received $38.1 billion from the U.S. Treasury for preferred stock purchases. Two of these, Morgan Stanley and Goldman Sachs, were approved by the Federal Reserve to become banks on a warm September 2008 weekend so that they could join the parade to the TARP window!

Modern American business leaders have been on a torturous walk, bouncing back and forth through a virtual lifetime of cyclical leadership failures that have caused massive economic disruptions across broad economic sectors. Sadly, these failures have had a devastating impact upon innocent consumers, investors, employees, retired persons, and other supervisors in one enterprise after another. The impacts have often had an effect far beyond the United States' borders and are often all the more intense—as many innocent, low-income citizens in Asia and other areas of the world suffered job losses and dislocations due to leadership failures in U.S. businesses.

It is a tragic irony that the top business-politicians in control of these failed enterprises have often benefited the most from their collapse. They still received their "golden parachute" severance packages, despite the businesses failures or emergency taxpayer aid needed to restore them to solvency. Americans are angry, and rightfully so. Continued job losses and business collapses have stoked the raging fires of their outrage. Perhaps it is time for new leadership culture in U.S. business. What do we have to learn from this tortuous journey that has penalized the millions of current and future taxpayers without their consent?

Lesson for Principled Business Leaders. Business leaders must manage enterprise finances on a pristine, conservative, cash-focused, and prudent basis in order to compensate for the highly volatile, politically motivated management of monetary and fiscal policy that in turn gives rise to regular economic collapse due to:

- Systematic and pervasive conflicts of interest by regulators, managers, and global financial engineers;
- Failures in financial market leadership by officers and managers at the global enterprise level;
- Failures in government supervision, product regulation, and operations oversight, made possible by overlapping conflicts of interest, lack of disclosure and transparency, and self-serving greed at all levels;
- Ineffective oversight and supervision by many business boards of directors, the Congress, and industry leaders, many of whom also had conflicts of interest;
- Unchecked greed by corporate executive officers who were more interested in extracting value than in building value;

- Massive influence by special interests through substantial donations and breathtaking control of the legislative process;
- Wide swings, overlaps, duplication, and lack of measurement in regulation, deregulation, and oversight;
- Vague and burdensome accounting rules, which permitted billions in off-balance sheet manipulation, along with on-balance sheet accounting games aimed at *puffing* or managing earnings for the maximum benefit of insiders;
- Fraudulent mortgage and subprime loan documents that were baked into 40 percent of all subprime loan transactions;
- Deceptive manipulation of accounting reports and investor communications meant to benefit insiders' bonus ambitions and public stock prices in both public and government-sponsored enterprises (Fannie and Freddie et al.);
- Failure to regulate and manage new markets in high-risk securities, subprime loans, and derivatives, based upon technicalities and oversight gaps;
- Massively complex corporate tax policies and regulations that benefit special interests and give unfair advantage to select businesses while driving jobs offshore;
- Ponderous tax, reporting, and regulatory burdens for small business, which heighten the risk of failures, job export, and job cuts;
- Routine government practices to hire oversight regulators from the regulated industries (thereby causing slack oversight of sophisticated organizations) to keep the exit path of departing staff open to lucrative industry jobs; and to put inexperienced, junior professionals in roles for which they are ill-equipped and ineffective—
- . . . all of which combine to systematically undermine the free-market system and the wider world order for the benefit of scarce few insiders and at the expense of millions of innocent, hard-working, tax-paying middle-class citizens, their children, and their grandchildren.

Lesson for Principled Business Leaders. The history of U.S. economic leadership failures suggests that economic downturns will continue to occur every two to four years. Therefore, your enterprise must be prepared to operate effectively in spite of the leadership failures at any other level.

Lesson for Principled Business Leaders. Business leaders must:

- Take a long-term view, build coalitions and teams, and share rewards of success with employees;

- Sell their boards of directors on also taking a long-term view of the business, its innovation needs, and its product development needs, instead of focusing on short-term goals that threaten long-term survival of the enterprise;
- Build the leadership team in depth, and create a leadership culture; and
- Set the example of responsible, principled leadership for the United States to follow, and demand that government follow that example in order to realize a turnaround in the nation's perilous financial situation.

Lesson for Principled Business Leaders. Business leaders must actively seek to self-regulate at the local and national level to ensure principled customer relations and industry practices. They can do this by:

1. Joining a local industry association in order to take the first steps toward self-regulation in their industry.
2. Assisting with national industry self-regulation, where it is feasible.
3. Routinely employing best practices in their enterprises so that they can offer the benefit of their good experience to national and local industry associations.

Lesson for Principled Business Leaders. Business leaders must first ensure that their enterprises are operating effectively in a period of declining markets and turbulent economic activity so that they will perform well in any environment regardless of their size—sole proprietorship to small- or mid-cap public company.

Questions to Ponder. How does my business perform compared to other companies in the same industry? Does my business routinely use best practices in all of its operations? Does our performance and share of market improve over time? How good are we? Are we in top shape?

Action Steps

Stretch Goal for My Enterprise. Can my enterprise score 50 or higher in its readiness for the present and for the coming economic future? Is my enterprise in top shape?

Standards for measuring your enterprise readiness are displayed in Table 5.3. Award 1, 5, or 10 points based upon the best description of your enterprise condition from columns (c), (d), and (e). Your score should be entered in column (f) and totaled at the bottom of the table.

Table 5.3 Measuring My Enterprise Readiness

Action Item (a)	Desired Outcome (b)	Low Score (1) (c)	Medium Score (5) (d)	High Score (10) (e)	My Score (f)
1. Business/economic environment	Full assessment of current economic environment and its impact on our enterprise.	We have a full understanding of every relevant factor affecting our short-term (one-year) market and customer base.	We have a full understanding of every relevant factor affecting our mid-term (one- to three-year) market and customer base.	We have a full understanding of every relevant factor affecting our long-term (three- to five-year) market and customer base.	[ ] Score
2. Market evaluation—long-term (one year), customer by customer	Complete assessment of my customer base and its durability for the coming fiscal year.	We know at least 20% of our customers by name; we know their planned purchases by month for the coming year and have verified their financial condition/ability to pay on time.	We know at least 21–59% of our customers by name; we know their planned purchases by month for the coming year and have verified their financial condition/ability to pay on time.	We know at least 60% of our customers by name; we know their planned purchases by month for the coming year and have verified their financial condition/ability to pay on time.	[ ] Score
3. Market evaluation—long-term (five years)	Complete assessment of my product/customer base and its durability for the next five years with both our current and our planned product/services.	We have a full buildup of likely product/service sales to a minimum of 20% of our customers by name for the next five years.	We have a full buildup of likely product/service sales to a minimum of 21–59% of our customers by name for the next five years.	We have a full buildup of likely product/service sales to a minimum of 60% of our customers by name for the next five years.	[ ] Score

(continued)

Table 5.3 *(continued)*

Action Item (a)	Desired Outcome (b)	Low Score (1) (c)	Medium Score (5) (d)	High Score (10) (e)	My Score (f)
4. Product/service evaluation	Full assessment of every product and service with contingencies for supplier interruptions, financing failure, or unforeseen market failures.	We have examined every product or service in our portfolio, and we have contingencies to overcome any supplier or financing loss for the coming year. We know what to eliminate in the event of a 20% sales drop.	We have examined every product or service in our portfolio, and we have contingencies to overcome any supplier or financing loss for the coming year. We know what to eliminate in the event of a 40% sales drop.	We have examined every product or service in our portfolio, and we have contingencies to overcome any supplier or financing loss for the coming year. We know what to eliminate in the event of a 60% sales drop.	[ ] Score
5. Cash flow	Up-to-date, real-time cash flow plan and management for current operations.	We have a realistic cash flow plan for the next year at current sales volume with collection schedules, purchasing controls, and no unplanned purchases.	We have a realistic cash flow plan for the next two years at current sales volume with collection schedules, purchasing controls, and no unplanned purchases.	We have a realistic cash flow plan for the next five years at current sales volume with collection schedules, purchasing controls, and no unplanned purchases.	[ ] Score
6. Cost analysis	Up-to-date cost buildup for every product or service.	We know the cost profile of our top 10 products/services.	We know the cost profile of at least half of our products/services.	We know the cost profile of all of our products/services.	[ ] Score
7. Break-even plan	Capability to break even at 50% of current sales for five years.	We have limited variable costs, so we can break even at 80% of current sales volume.	We have limited variable costs, so we can break even at 60% of current sales volume.	We have limited variable costs, so we can break even at 40% of current sales volume.	[ ] Score

	CONTINGENCY PLAN	Low Items ( )	Mid-Range Items ( )	High-Range Items ( )	
8. Workforce/management compensation contingency plan	Full plan for workforce and management staffing and compensation for all contingencies.	We have a full plan to limit work time and management compensation while preserving our normal margins at 60–80% of our current volume.	We have a full plan to limit work time and management compensation while preserving our normal margins at 30–60% of our current volume.	We have a full plan to limit work time and management compensation while preserving our normal margins at 30% of our current volume.	[ ] Score
9. Liquidity/financing	Full capacity to secure credit and maintain liquidity to fulfill five-year business plan.	We have available cash flow, invested reserves, and approved credit arrangements to fund our enterprise for the next full year.	We have available cash flow, invested reserves, and approved credit arrangements to fund our enterprise for the next three years.	We have available cash flow, invested reserves, and approved credit arrangements to fund our enterprise for the next five years.	[ ] Score
10. Raw materials/parts/supplies	Full capability to secure raw materials/parts/needed supplies from solvent primary and backup vendors to fulfill five-year business plan.	We have ensured a reliable supply of raw materials/parts/supplies from all primary vendors for 50% of our products. We have solvent backup vendors for products that realize up to 40% of our gross revenues for the coming business year.	We have ensured a reliable supply of raw materials/parts/supplies from all primary vendors for 50% of our products. We have solvent backup vendors for products that realize up to 60% of our gross revenues for the coming three business years.	We have ensured a reliable supply of raw materials/parts/supplies from all primary vendors for 50% of our products. We have solvent backup vendors for products that realize up to 80% of our gross revenues for the coming five business years.	[ ] Score
MY SCORE	CONTINGENCY PLAN	Low Items ( )	Mid-Range Items ( )	High-Range Items ( )	

Key Measures of Success

Measurement Number/Date	Point Total	Weakest Function(s)	Corrective Action Steps	Date to Complete
1. __/__/__				
2. __/__/__				
3. __/__/__				
4. __/__/__				
5. __/__/__				

Suggested Reading

Kawasaki, Guy. *The Art of the Start—The Time-Tested, Battle Hardened Guide for Anyone Starting Anything*. New York: The Penguin Group, 226 pp.

Labovitz, George, and Victor Rosansky. *The Power of Alignment*. New York: John Wiley & Sons, Inc., 1997, 242 pp.

Peterson, Peter G. *Running on Empty*. New York: Farrar, Straus and Giroux, 2004, 239 pp.

Schiller, Robert J. *The New Financial Order*. Princeton, NJ: Princeton University Press, 2003, 366 pp.

CHAPTER 6

Overcoming the Declining Dollar

Some men worship rank, some worship heroes, some worship power, some worship God, and over these ideals they dispute and cannot unite—but they all worship money.

—Mark Twain

In the past we have sacrificed the economy to preserve the currency. This time we have sacrificed the currency to save the economy.

—David M. Darst

Realignment

A good friend of Ross Gregory's named Art Kay—who graduated three years after Ross—is now in his third year at a new job. Fortunately, Art's company lets him do some of his IT work at home; otherwise, the cost of gas to get to work every day would be a crushing financial burden for a relatively new employee like Art. Yesterday he filled his gas tank, and it cost $300. Gas has just risen to $15 per gallon.

Since Ross has been living on the financial edge since graduation, he continues to be deeply concerned with his staggering debt and living expenses. He accurately senses that the economy, prices, and the value of the dollar continue to deteriorate as they have for the past five years.

Ross glances at an old news clipping at Art's house, a business article about the 2006 OPEC conference in Caracas, Venezuela, seven years earlier. The article tells the story of the Venezuelan president's call to the OPEC members to begin pricing oil in gold, in euros, or in a currency other than the dollar. The OPEC members, the article reports, had courteously acknowledged the Venezuelan proposal, but no decision was made on the matter at that meeting. Four years passed. Then came 2010.

That was the year that the Middle East peace process collapsed. Ironically, the demise of the peace process also helped to bring on the decline of the U.S. dollar. More and more OPEC nations joined Venezuela to push for denominating oil sales with the euro. They gave in to the local pressure of Venezuela, Iran, Russia, and several other exporting states to replace the dollar as the world's reserve currency. Oil exporters cited the staggering level of U.S. debt obligations and the precipitous rise in interest rates that had followed several dollar devaluations.

China then joined the debate as well. Having quietly made a number of policy changes following the 2008 Olympic Games in Beijing, the country's views were well respected. They first pressed the United States for guarantees on their past and future purchases of U.S. Treasury bills. Japan's Central Bank followed suit in its own defense, and Europe was close behind. Then came the meltdown—a worldwide event that halted trade, caused industry shutdowns, precipitated millions of job losses, forced numerous dislocations, brought on a general wage collapse, and produced a host of crushing economic reversals. From this, two strange ironies emerged.

First, it became clear to all that U.S. consumption until 2008 had been underwritten by the savings of millions of Asians, and the world was angry, as repayment was either delayed or done in devalued dollars. Second, the dollar, once the safe haven for most of the available international liquidity, began to decline in value at a faster pace after 2010. So the demands for a new reserve currency, combined with the staggering levels of new federal debt created after the meltdown, began to drive up the interest rates paid by the U.S. Treasury to refinance their existing and new debt. Third, the 2007 to 2009 meltdown, which had destroyed a large share of the domestic and international wealth accumulated over the prior three decades, continued to drag down economies around the world for the next seven years. The pace of decline increased annually. Consumers worldwide suffered. The U.S. economic situation became desperate, and the dollar continued to sink in value.

Ignited by the U.S. subprime mortgage meltdown in 2007, the rolling collapse saw the demise of some of the largest names in banking, finance, and investment in the two years that followed. First, oil prices dropped by 75 percent as demand slackened. OPEC was angry, and Russia was even angrier. OPEC first cut production, and then made the long-threatened pricing change away from dollars to euros in 2011. The many OPEC members who had been badly hurt by the earlier market collapse were unanimous in their decision.

The United States responded by hurriedly implementing a massive infusion of debt-financed spending for domestic energy, infrastructure, and social programs aimed at stimulating the U.S. economy. Unfortunately, the investment requirements were so large and the available money was so little of the amount needed that the new stimulus was a fruitless exercise. Additionally, big oil companies slowed their exploration and development efforts when pricing changed to gold. Oil prices rose to $300 per barrel. Gold went to $1,800 per ounce and then to $2,800 per ounce in another year. The energy-starved U.S. economy continued to slow to a walk.

Ross knows that 2014 is going to be a tough year, and he wonders if there is a lower-paying hourly job that he can get within cycling distance from his home. As he ponders the situation, he begins to piece together the causes of the nation's decline. First, he concludes that the United States has two value systems—the humanist value system and the Judeo-Christian value system. The diverging value systems caused the nation to pay for two differing governance strategies—a security one and a social one, both of which took as much money as the annual net (after entitlements) tax revenues.

Second, the long-forgotten 1971 closing of the gold window for exchanges of dollars for gold broke loose the dollar from its moorings. Gold prices skyrocketed from the mandated $35 per ounce, while the dollar began its headlong fall—a decline that has not slowed since.

Listening to Art tell of his experiences, it became clear to Ross that the humanist system had put all wisdom in the hands of people who followed only one set of rules—their own. Meanwhile, the Judeo-Christian ethic was largely abandoned as debt piled up and the dollar continued its decline. The taxes of the next three generations were spent before the first of them was born.

Ross also realizes that politicians had bought-off both sides of the political spectrum for more than four decades—always with more debt. Excess spending, unbridled liquidity (the creation of fiat money in massive amounts by the Federal Reserve Board), and the abandonment of the gold standard all contributed to this irresponsible financial mess. So as a result—the value of the dollar continuously fell for much of this time, while the nation attempted to pay for the programs of the two sharply differing value systems. The dollar, no longer *as good as gold*, collapsed, along with millions of savings accounts, pension funds, and foundation trust accounts. Is it time for business to lead the turnaround? Ross and Art agree; the answer is *yes*.

The Issue. The safety of the *dollar* is critical to *business* strategy, employee benefits, employee pensions, and business survival in many sectors. Business leaders know the lunacy of borrowing one's way to prosperity. This simply won't work. Business must instead lead the call for prudent financial policies—first in their enterprises, and then in the nation. The winner-take-all economy of the past 50 years is history. The "winners" took it all. Business must support the need for a strong dollar as the world's reserve currency, just as it has supported sound consumer savings, investments, and pensions for five generations. If business does not act to improve its financial stability and preserve our economic future, it will be the victim; because without the dollar, business has no solid economic platform on which it can function.

The dollar is now the world's reserve currency. It is also the basis for the sale of oil in most of the international markets. Since the dollar is the world's reserve currency, the United States has the advantage of holding zero interest rate loans in every major economy, as well as purchasing oil without having to finance the purchase. Scores of small states have turned to dollars to stabilize their economies. Unfortunately, the dollar has declined in value for many of the past 40 years, notwithstanding the Department of the Treasury's stated "strong dollar" policy and other official "strong dollar" pronouncements of the U.S. government. A strong dollar is in the best interests of the United States. But it is a long-faded reality. Al-Qaeda must be delighted. They win without firing another shot.

So who wins? The current financial community wins. Who loses? Our children and their children to follow are the losers from such an irresponsible practice. One Texas congressman eloquently described this history on February 15, 2006. He spoke of the link between the strength of the dollar and the strength of the United States and of our long-standing habit of using military force to demand continued worldwide use of the dollar for exchange—regardless of its deteriorating value—by saying:

> This is why countries that challenge the system—like Iraq, Iran, and Venezuela—become targets of our plans for regime change. Ironically, dollar superiority depends on our strong military, and our strong military depends on the dollar. As long as foreign recipients take our dollars for real goods and are willing to finance our extravagant consumption and militarism, the status quo will continue regardless of how huge our foreign debt and current account deficit become.

> But real threats come from our political adversaries who are incapable of confronting us militarily, yet are not bashful about confronting us economically. That's why we see the new challenge from Iran being taken so seriously. The urgent arguments about Iran posing a military threat to the security of the United States are no more plausible than

the false charges levied against Iraq. Yet there is no effort to resist this march to confrontation by those who grandstand for political reasons against the Iraq war.

It seems that the people and Congress are easily persuaded by the jingoism of the preemptive war promoters. It's only after the cost in human life and dollars are tallied up that the people object to unwise militarism. . ... Concern for pricing oil only in dollars helps explain our willingness to drop everything and teach Saddam Hussein a lesson for his defiance in demanding euros for oil.

And once again there's this urgent call for sanctions and threats of force against Iran at the precise time Iran is opening a new oil exchange with all transactions in euros. Using force to compel people to accept money without real value can only work in the short run. It ultimately leads to economic dislocation, both domestic and international, and always ends with a price to be paid.

The economic law that honest exchange demands only things of real value as currency cannot be repealed. The chaos that one day will ensue from our 35-year experiment with worldwide fiat money will require a return to money of real value. We will know that day is approaching when oil-producing countries demand gold, or its equivalent, for their oil rather than dollars or euros. The sooner the better.[1]

Against this backdrop of a century of forceful stewardship—and the reality that the United States no longer controls the oil market—we must also consider the relevance of recent world events to the nation's insatiable energy needs and consumer costs. (See Chapter 15.) For example, OPEC again heard the call to move away from the dollar in Caracas when President Hugo Chavez of Venezuela offered an impassioned plea to have OPEC price oil in euros or even in a new South American currency.[2] Additionally, OPEC watchers had long since begun their speculation on the future of energy costs and the fortunes of the dollar. For example, Iran has priced its oil in euros for some years and began work to establish an oil bourse in 2006. Saddam Hussein had also priced Iraqi oil in euros since 2000. Venezuela transferred a large portion of its foreign reserves out of U.S. Treasuries and into euros last year. OPEC will at some point agree with such a plan, if the dollar continues to fall, because—as Florida analyst Martin Weiss claims—

. . . a declining U.S. dollar hurts Arab oil sheiks who do tons of business, vacationing, and shopping in other currencies. Given the dollar's fall, their revenues are worth less every day. And that's not just when they're shopping in Europe. It's almost everywhere—Japan, China, even Latin

America. As of February 2006, OPEC held a whopping $84.9 billion in U.S. Treasuries. And that excludes OPEC's holdings through British banks. In short, now, the value of their holdings are plunging with the dollar. That's going to make them more receptive to dumping the U.S. currency for pricing their oil.

And Venezuela doesn't care if the U.S. gets hurt or not. Chavez is convinced that he can replace U.S. demand for oil by selling to China's booming economy. He's also aiming to shift strategic alliances and establish a power block that's outside of the dollar's realm.

But Venezuela has another set of problems.

Rigzone, a publication that follows the industry, says as many as 10,000 Venezuelan oil wells are now mostly useless. Venezuela can't even meet its current OPEC quota—it's allotted 3.2 million barrels a day but can only manage 2.5 million barrels per day! In fact, state-owned oil company Petroleos de Venezuela SA (PDVSA) is buying 100,000 barrels of oil per day from Russia to avoid defaulting on deliveries to clients.[3]

And there is another implication of the weakening dollar—the subprime mortgage meltdown of 2007 to 2009 and the potential collapse of the credit card financing market.

The Layoff Factor

This fear is based on the realization that—with the waves of layoffs sweeping through various economic sectors—the lowered available income is placing trillions in credit card and other consumer debt in immediate jeopardy. Several banks are setting up special task forces while others are increasing the size of operations in place to deal with this crisis—including attempting to negotiate write-offs and restructuring agreements on these unsecured loans to prevent defaults.

But as economist Lothar Kemp explained before the economic meltdown began:

> The problem is further compounded by the bundling of consumer loans into derivatives-based securities, which in turn have been used to prop up already weakened positions of effectively bankrupt banks, including mega-banks such as Citibank. If there are too many write-offs, and if there continues the already accelerating trend toward

defaults on this debt, Greenspan would be faced with the prospect of a quick-term banking collapse, and the need for bailouts that would make the Argentine crisis pale by comparison.

Greenspan and the Federal Reserve are thus encouraging an effort to pump, potentially, trillions into the banking system by encouraging people to take higher-valued mortgages in order to transfer the vast majority of the money back into the banks, as the old mortgages are paid off and the "cash out" is used to pay off credit card debt. The key thing here is a gimmick: In doing this, the unsecured credit card debt is converted into a "secure" real estate loan.

When will the credit pyramid come down? According to the Jerome Levy Economics Institute in the United States, the "implosion" has already started. The Levy Institute belongs among those institutions that themselves offer no solution to the crisis-other than perhaps a little bit of dollar devaluation coupled with a little bit of protectionism-but nonetheless present some useful analysis. In an 18-page investigation entitled "As the Implosion Begins . . .," the institute notes that its warnings have been circulating for years, that the expansion of the U.S. economy would sooner or later end up in disaster, "because it relied upon a continuing growth of private spending in excess of disposable income, and thus created an enormous growth of debt."

Many things are converging now, states the Levy Institute: Increasing numbers of households are no longer able to keep up debt payments. The bad loans in the banking system are growing, so that even (the then) Federal Reserve Board Chairman Greenspan had to acknowledge the "deteriorating" health of the U.S. banking system. The net inflow of foreign capital into the United States cannot be maintained. In sum, "all the ingredients are now present, including rising unemployment and reduced or stagnant asset prices, which normally characterize the inception of a self-reinforcing credit implosion."[4]

That was then. Look at it now. The major victim, beyond the people who are suffering, is the U.S. dollar.

The U.S. Dollar—A Painful Ride Down

Dennis Gartman, who publishes the respected *The Gartman Letter*, summarizes the fall of the dollar, as follows:

> With the benefit of retrospect, it does certainly appear that a huge top for the dollar has taken place. . . . Strength in the dollar is to be sold, not weakness to be bought.[5]

Sempra Metals, the firm that provided Figure 6.1, also notes that:

> The U.S. dollar has now lost more than a third of its value (−35 percent) against a basket of major currencies since February 2002. The decline is accelerating. The U.S. dollar has shed—12.5 percent of its value in the last year,—3.5 percent in the last month, and—1.5 percent in the last week alone.

When the dollar's purchasing power is examined in absolute terms, the picture is no better. Consider that it takes $21.57 today to purchase the same goods and services that cost $1.00 in 1913. In 1920, it cost $2.02; it then declined in 1925 and through the 1930s, illustrating the effect of the Great Depression when prices slumped. Prices did not pass $2.00 again until 1950. The U.S. Department of Labor, Bureau of Labor Statistics reports the average Consumer Price Index (CPI) index each year in measuring changes in the prices of all goods and services purchased by urban households. This process has been accelerating since 1965, however, as Table 6.6.1 illustrates.

In his 1796 farewell address, Washington admonished the nation to avoid "not ungenerously throwing upon posterity the burden which we ourselves ought to bear."[6] Americans today would be wise to heed Washington's timeless wisdom.

The warnings are not new. Clyde Prestowitz, president of the Economic Strategy Institute and author of the book *Three Billion New Capitalists*, delivered a blunt word of warning on September 6, 2005.

> There's an economic storm cloud brewing on the horizon; one that will sink millions of middle-class Americans into poverty and the economy into financial chaos. And the flailing U.S. dollar is to blame. Unfortunately, few Americans are aware of the train wreck ahead.
>
> ... for millions of Americans, the bulk of their investments, their life savings and their assets are tied up with the dollar—like an iron chain to a two-ton anchor. And right now, the U.S. dollar is the most widely held financial asset in the world. But it is also the most dangerously overvalued asset in the world. And one of the worst performing.
>
> It doesn't take any great stretch of the imagination to see what could happen if one of these central bank managers decides to dump dollars. We had a situation recently when a mid-level official at the Central Bank of Korea used the word *diversification*. It was a throwaway remark at some obscure lunch, but there was instantaneous overreaction. The U.S. stock market fell by 100 points in 15 minutes because the implication was that South Korea might be shifting out of U.S. dollars.

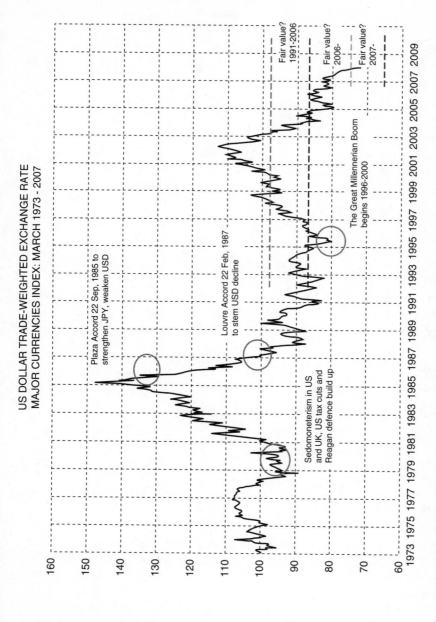

Figure 6.1 U.S. Dollar Trade-Weighted Exchange Rate

Source: Daily Kos blog, November 2007. Article written by London Yank. Chart furnished by Sempra Metals.

Table 6.1   Lost Purchasing Power of the U.S. Dollar (1913–Present)

Year	Amount It Took to Equal $1 in 1913
1913	$1.00
1920	$2.02
1925	$1.77
1930	$1.69
1935	$1.38
1940	$1.41
1945	$1.82
1950	$2.43
1955	$2.71
1960	$2.99
1965	$3.18
1970	$3.92
1975	$5.43
1980	$8.32
1985	$10.87
1990	$13.20
1995	$15.39
2000	$17.39
2001	$17.89
2002	$18.17
2003	$18.59
2004	$19.08
2005	$19.73
2006	$20.18
2007	$20.94
2008	$21.57

Source: Bureau of Labor Statistics, http://stats.bls.gov/.

Whether one agrees with Prestowitz or not, he isn't alone. Billionaire financiers Warren Buffet and George Soros have taken steps to hedge their currency positions against the possibility of a cataclysmic plunge in the greenback.

Then there's Paul Volcker, head of the Federal Reserve before Alan Greenspan, who has said publicly there is a 75 percent chance of a dollar crash in the next five years. "The lack of an alternative to the dollar is the only reason it hasn't taken a big fall already."[7]

Paul Volcker also sounded similar warnings on April 15 and July 21, 2005 as reported in *Liberty Dollar*: "Among other things, Volcker warns of a possibly dramatic shift in the relationship between U.S. consumerism and foreign investment—and the dire consequences that would have on Americans."

Some focal points of Volcker's speech:

- Volcker sees "disturbing trends: huge imbalances, disequilibria, risks . . ." in the U.S. economy.
- He claims these are the most dangerous economic conditions he has ever seen—and, he notes, he has seen "quite a lot."
- Though businesses are rebuilding their financial reserves, the federal deficit has offset these savings in only a few years.
- Home ownership has become a vehicle for borrowing rather than a means of financial security.
- U.S. citizens consume and invest about 6 percent more than we produce.
- The U.S. economy is held together by a foreign capital influx of over $2 billion each day.
- Foreign competition has kept interest rates relatively low, despite vanishing savings and rapid growth.
- In Volcker's words: "The difficulty is that this seemingly comfortable pattern can't go on indefinitely. I don't know of any country that has managed to consume and invest 6 percent more than it produces for long. The United States is absorbing about 80 percent of the net flow of international capital. And at some point, both central banks and private institutions will have their fill of dollars."
- Volcker says that to solve the economic crisis, "China and other continental Asian economies should permit and encourage a substantial exchange rate appreciation against the dollar. Japan and Europe should work promptly and aggressively toward domestic stimulus and deal more effectively and speedily with structural obstacles to growth. And the United States, by some combination of measures, should forcibly increase its rate of internal saving, thereby reducing its import demand."
- Volcker doesn't "know whether change will come with a bang or a whimper, whether sooner or later. But as things stand, it is more likely than not that it will be financial crises rather than policy foresight that will force the change."[8]

In another speech, Volcker claimed that he doesn't see how the United States can keep borrowing and consuming while letting foreign countries do all the producing. "It's a recipe for American economic disaster," he insisted. "If I were a biologist I'd call this a perfect example of symbiosis," he said during a February speech at Stanford University. "Contented American consumers matched against delighted foreign producers. Happy borrowers matched against willing lenders. The difficulty is, the seemingly comfortable pattern can't go on indefinitely."

Experts (Volcker and others) seem to agree that the current situation can't last. But will there be a smooth and manageable rebalancing of the global economy—created by a slow drop in the dollar combined with a spike in foreign demand? Or will the U.S. currency suddenly collapse, with skyrocketing interest rates that lead us into a global recession? Volcker believes a crisis is unavoidable, and he claims that investors will lose their confidence "at some point," creating serious dilemma for "both exchange markets and interest rates."

That was then; it has now happened.

The report in *Liberty Dollar* continued:

> As the United States faces the threats of a potential housing bubble, a massive trade deficit and the lowest level of American savings in history, the jury is out on the Federal Reserve's actions over the past five years. The *Wall Street Journal* reports that while the Fed acknowledges that its response to the 2000 Dot-Com crisis is partly to blame for current economic conditions, it claims it had no other viable course of action.
>
> To alleviate this problem, at some point, U.S. consumers will have to curb spending and concentrate on saving—plus the economy will be forced to forego foreign investment.
>
> Some economists warn that the Fed has simply replaced the Dot-Com bubble with a housing bubble that is ready to burst, draining consumer spending, driving foreign investors away from U.S. markets, and nurturing numerous other conditions that could lead to a serious recession.
>
> The former Fed chairman thinks we need to make sure foreign investors hold their confidence in the United States because they're the ones doing all the investing. They need to know "those trillions of dollars they are piling up are going to be protected against inflation."[9]

Again, that was then. It has now happened. It is strange, indeed, that Mr. Volcker—who is now Chairman of the Administration's Economic Recovery Advisory Council—has, so far, been silent in the midst of the current crisis and has offered no strategy to restore the dollar or the turnaround of the U.S. economy. Business leaders must have a strategy that addresses these conditions, nonetheless.

Lesson for Principled Business Leaders. The United States is in a "balance sheet" meltdown, not the typical, temporary consumption downtrend or sector failure. The balance sheet of the nation is in tatters, so the balance sheets of business must be strengthened to guard against irrational policy actions or credit losses.

Lessons for Principled Business Leaders. There are no actions that are currently addressing the fundamental weaknesses in the U.S. economy—debt, inflation, and erosion of the purchasing power of the dollar, among others. Businesses must therefore take protective actions to guard against these continuing losses in dollar purchasing power by:

1. Looking for alternative, less expensive suppliers, subcontractors, and vendors;

2. Eliminating every cost that does not drive your business to limit dollar exposure;

3. Building dollar-loss financial reserves; for example, gold funds, inflation protected securities (U.S. Treasury "TIP" instruments), and others; and

4. Including inflation protection into vendor sourcing and sales contracts.

Stretch Goal for My Business. Do I have adequate cash reserves, liquid business investments, and currency contingency plans that will enable me to survive a rapid (15 percent or more) loss in the value of the dollar in my enterprise each year?

Questions to Ponder. What is the impact of a declining dollar on *my* business? What impact will this have on my credit management, product sourcing, sales financing, and bank relationships? Do I have exports that may be aided by a devaluing dollar? Is the export sector one to exploit?

Action Steps

Principled Business Leaders Must:

1. Have non-dollar financial reserves to compensate for volatile financial and worldwide markets.

2. Include contingencies for dollar devaluation and/or its continuing decline in purchasing power.

3. Diversify investments into risk-averse currencies and other instruments.

4. Move every possible enterprise cost from fixed to variable to provide wider management options and avert financial risk.

5. Build real-time flexibility into work and product schedules in order to precisely manage cash and financial reserves.

6. Formulate steps to preserve asset value in the business and counter lost dollar purchasing power.

7. Take every possible action to strengthen their personal and business balance sheets for mid- and long-term financial security.

Key Measures of Success

Measurement Date	Topic	Level	Corrective Action Steps	Date to Complete
1. __/__/_____	Break even			
2. __/__/_____	Product margin(s)			
3. __/__/_____	Services margin(s)			
4. __/__/_____	Pricing move(s)			
5. __/__/_____	Profitability (%)			

Suggested Reading

Arnold, Daniel A. *The Great Bust Ahead*. Vorago-US, 2005, 64 pp.

Duncan, Richard. *The Dollar Crisis: Causes, Consequences, Cures*. Singapore: John Wiley & Sons (Asia) Pte Ltd., 2005, 269 pp.

Karmin, Craig. *Biography of the Dollar: How the Mighty Buck Conquered the World and Why It's Under Siege*. New York: Crown Publishing Group, Random House, Inc., 2008, 263 pp.

Kosares, Michael J. *The ABCs of Gold Investing—How to Protect and Build Your Wealth With Gold*. Omaha, NE: Addicus Books, 2005, 175 pp.

Leeb, Stephen, PhD. *The Coming Economic Collapse.* New York: Warner Business Books, 2006, 211 pp.

Lewis, Nathan. *Gold: The Once and Future Money.* Hoboken, NJ: John Wiley & Sons, Inc., 2007, 447 pp.

Rubino, John, and James Turk. *The Collapse of the Dollar and How to Profit From It.* New York: A Currency Book Published by Doubleday, 2004, 252 pp.

Schiller, Robert J. *The New Financial Order.* Princeton: Princeton University Press, 2003.

Wiggin, Addison. *The Demise of the Dollar and Why It's Great for Your Investments.* New York: John Wiley & Sons, Inc., 2005, 218 pp.

CHAPTER 7

Managing Business Debt (So It Doesn't Manage You!)

No generation has a right to contract debts greater than can be paid off during the course of its own existence.

—George Washington to James Madison, 1789

It is incumbent on every generation to pay its own debts as it goes. A principle which if acted upon would save one-half the wars of the world.

—Thomas Jefferson

Managing His Career

Ross will never forget that 2011 graduation party at home. Now 24, Ross is almost three years into a new job and struggling under a mountain of school, home, and personal debt . . .

And there is no time for a social life. The college loan payment book still has four years to run. He has made some progress on the house mortgage, but there are still 17 years left on the loan. Happily the car loan is paid off, but the note on his parents' new motor home has 17 more years on it. Then there are the normal bills—health insurance, prescription drug payment books, property tax coupons, life insurance coupons, burial insurance coupons, and more. He nods off to sleep just thinking about it all. What a mess!

Issue Summary. Through the eyes of Ross, you are witnessing your children's probable future. If the United States indeed wishes to rebuild its financial system, business cannot allow this debt tsunami to engulf it as it has the federal government. In order to address this massive debt load, every American expected to be on the U.S. taxpayer rolls in 2012 with a positive Adjusted Gross Income—all 79,404,282 of them (see Appendix B)—has an additional yearly individual debt payment bill of $81,718 due the first of every January thereafter (before they begin earning their living and paying income taxes on those earnings!). This payment is needed just to cover the nation's federal, state, and local debts; the annual interest bill; and the unfunded liabilities of the federal, state, and local governments.

Of course, Medicare, Social Security, and unfunded retirement benefits are included in this total liability. Since we have either spent or obligated ourselves to spend these amounts, the anticipated Social Security shortfall, past borrowings from the Social Security Trust Fund, the massive Medicare expense deficit that looms ahead, and the debt that virtually every state must pay to rebuild their now-depleted retiree health and pension plans—the time has come to act. Although such an approach as this has virtually no chance of being implemented, this extra yearly payment would have to continue for as long as 20 years (through 2031) to restore the financial health of the United States!

The central issue in the nation's financial jeopardy is rooted in the growing U.S. practice of attempting to borrow its way to prosperity—an approach that has few (if any) successful, historic precedents in nations that survived! Such an approach may have worked when the United States was the world's biggest manufacturer. But it won't work in a nation that is principally (75 percent) a service economy and already the world's biggest debtor! In light of this national weakness business leaders must translate the current economic realities to a practical action plan that can be implemented within the context of today's turbulent capital markets.

The nation is simply not able to afford this self-serving ethic of spending money that we don't have. The total amount of our current financial obligations is astonishing—$57.6 trillion in *total public* debt and $108.9 trillion in *public* unfunded liabilities.

Could the United States be technically bankrupt? This question is based on the traditional measures of its financial strength—assets, liabilities, interest coverage, fiscal management, solvency, and ability to repay debt. And the answer is yes! This may also true in many of the 84,000 units of state, county, and local government.

Business' Responsibility for Our Future

America is *broke*. It can't borrow its way to recovery. Only business can take the lead in demanding that U.S. debt be repaid; and business must also manage and cut its own debts *and* its long-term financial risks to prepare for the future in a turbulent, declining world economy. Business can demonstrate how retirement of unnecessary debt and managing innovation can bring both new jobs and higher productivity to twenty-first century America.

At the end of 2009, the total debt of the nation reached $57.6 trillion. The federal, state, and local portion of this debt is $14.3 trillion—nearly the equivalent of one year's economic output. Consumers owe $13.0 trillion. Businesses owe $11.1 trillion. And other domestic and foreign sectors owe $19.1 trillion.

But current debt is just the tip of the iceberg. Federal, state, and local government unfunded liabilities—payments that are required by existing law for which there is no reserve or current funds—have reached a staggering $108.9 trillion. This amount is growing by the day, as federal, state, and local government pension and health care plans continue to hemorrhage with new obligations, as is shown in Table 7.1.

This debt has a number of components. The Department of the Treasury and a series of related studies listed in Appendix B report that, as of September 2009, our debt had the components displayed in Table 7.1.[1]

Table 7.1   America's Debt and Unfunded Liabilities—2009

	Debt ($ Trillions)	Unfunded Liabilities ($ Trillions)
Consumer debt	13.8	
Business debt	11.1	
Federal debt and unfunded liabilities	12.1	5.0
Social Security		15.8
Medicare/Medicaid/prescription drugs		85.9
State debt and unfunded liabilities	2.2	2.2
Domestic financial sector debt	17.2	
Foreign borrowers debt	1.8	
Totals	57.6	108.9
Public debt only	14.3	108.9

There is a consistency in behavior between what the federal government and the last three generations of citizens have done: spent money well beyond their means to pay. Ironically, some businesses have done the same thing. Simultaneously, the federal government laments the excess spending and poor savings patterns of Americans. And yet, it does the exact same thing in practice. Business cannot follow this approach to managing its assets. In fact, business must set a *new* standard and call for a revamped financial management ethic. These irresponsible financial management habits have been in place for more than four decades—ever since the federal government decided to fight the war in Vietnam and to expand domestic programs without adding taxes in the name of short-term political gain. It was a failed demonstration that *guns and butter* finance policies are feasible. The dollar has never been the same, and the nation has not been out of serious debt since! Business must lead the way to replace this arrogance with a new financial ethic rooted in sound principles.

Even our government-sponsored enterprises (GSEs) followed this failed strategy and then rewarded the executives who brought them down with bonuses—just like what transpired on Wall Street. Federal National Mortgage Association (FNMA/"Fannie Mae") and the Federal Home Loan Mortgage Corporation (FHLMC/"Freddie Mac")—both chartered by the Congress to promote responsible home ownership—were both turned into printing presses for risky loans. Home and commercial mortgages, which in the days of the local bank were once written by the same local banker who would supervise and collect them, were bought and bundled by these lenders to be sold worldwide as mortgage-backed securities. The nation's securitized debt was then sold to domestic and foreign investors.

And that's not all. Congress has since spent the taxes of the next three generations of taxpayers. From 2007 to 2009, $18 trillion in U.S. wealth and $50 trillion in wealth worldwide was destroyed, and $14 trillion in public support was provided to the same people who had caused the meltdown—at the expense of innocent and now angry taxpayer-victims. Wall Street will never be the same. It will take three generations for Wall Street to recover its reputation and standing in the world financial system. Principled business leaders must not follow this failed course.

If all of this were not enough, the federal government is also in the direct loan business. It lends through the Export-Import Bank, the Small Business Administration, the College Housing Fund, the Rural Development Telephone Bank, and the Farm Credit Administration. Do we need to reserve for all of these obligations? Banks reserve for loan losses, so good practice and prudence would both require healthy reserves. Moreover, since we have no reserves for disasters other than modest insurance premiums that are paid to the Federal Flood Insurance fund and several others—including Terrorism Risk Insurance—the possibility of terrorist attacks and future natural disasters could easily cost more than any risk-rated loss reserves that might be set aside by prudent leaders.

As the saying goes—we are "up to our eyeballs in debt!"

In light of this massive burden of both secured and unfunded contingent liability debt, one can naturally ask: Do we love our children enough to *not* pass on this enormous risk and obligation to them? So far, the actions of the past three generations of politicians have said that today is more important than tomorrow—and they have piled on the debt. Leaders would never say or do this. For the sake of our future, it may be necessary for business to take the lead in calling for a plan to retire our public debts and reserve for emergencies and unfunded liabilities.

Lesson for Principled Business Leaders. Leaders already know the United States has too much debt. These obligations are tolerated without complaint because no one is asking taxpayers to repay it. The situation is now so extreme that business leaders must decide whether they have the commitment, courage, and capacity to preserve the nation. If the answer is yes, they must face the realities as they are and insist that those in authority do the same. Many of these same businesses have too much debt that must also be retired.

Lesson for Principled Business Leaders. Retiring the many layers of U.S. public debt will be the toughest leadership task of the twenty-first century. Business leaders must ensure the nation's debt does not further endanger the value of the dollar or the world economy. If they are to succeed, business leaders must set an example of fiscal restraint unmatched at any time since the Revolutionary War. Great leaders will rise to such challenges.

Lesson for Principled Business Leaders. Business leaders also need to take several courses of action to manage debt. First, they must act to limit spending to real cash income, less an amount needed to retire debt within a stipulated number of years. Second, they must restructure fixed costs so that debt retirement is achievable at lower revenue rates—should this occur. Third, it is prudent in times of economic uncertainty to lower debt service expenses to 20 percent of EBITDA (earnings before interest, taxes, depreciation, and amortization.)

Stretch Goal for My Enterprise. Is my enterprise able to systematically retire all existing business debt within five years, even if our sales volume drops by 50 percent? Do we wish to do so?

Questions to Ponder. What is the impact of a massive public debt on your business? What impact will it have on your credit management, product sourcing, sales financing, currency values, and bank relationships? Are there contingency plans for any alternative raw materials and parts sourcing in the event that the sales drop by 30 percent or more? Are such plans needed?

Action Steps

Principled Business Leaders Must Realize That:

1. Borrowing is *seldom* a reliable path to business prosperity unless it is being used for solely for prudent expansion, modernization, or asset purchases and not to pay for current operations. Cash planning and management is the key to business survival—not excessive debt.

2. Debt coverage ratios must be kept high (20 percent of EBITDA) for any future borrowings in volatile business and financial markets.

3. Personal services businesses cannot be leveraged with debt and still preserve their financial strength, stability, and future potential.

4. Business owners can manage cash best in difficult times by paying all employees, taxes, and vendors before they pay themselves.

5. Business owners must manage tax obligations by paying any taxes that are due *before* they pay themselves.

Key Measures of Success

Measurement Date	Debt Level	Retirement Progress	Debt Service as % of EBITDA	Responsible Person
1. __/__/____				
2. __/__/____				
3. __/__/____				
4. __/__/____				
5. __/__/____				

Suggested Reading

Bonner, William. *Empire of Debt: The Rise of an Epic Financial Crisis*. With Addison Wiggin. Hoboken, NJ: John Wiley & Sons, 2006, 356 pp.
_____. *Financial Reckoning Day: Surviving the Soft Depression of the 21st Century*. Hoboken, NJ: John Wiley & Sons, 2003, 306 pp.

CHAPTER 8

Avoiding Derivatives and Financial Tsunamis

We view them as time bombs both for the parties that deal in them and the economic system . . . In our view . . . derivatives are financial weapons of mass destruction, carrying dangers that, while now latent, are potentially lethal.

—Warren Buffett

The Big Party

It is years later, but Ross Gregory still remembers his first day of work at his post-college job as a dizzying blur of going from office to office, meeting new people, sitting for short orientations, and filling out form after form. Everyone had been very courteous, and the process had been efficient. Recently, Ross met up for lunch with Doug, his good friend from the high school class some years ahead of Ross. Doug has been working at the local office of a large, international bank for six years now.

As soon as they sat down, Doug told Ross about his job in derivatives valuation. Doug had asked to be assigned to this department when it was formed in 2007 so that he could use his accounting degree to its best advantage in a very popular insurance investment arena—derivatives. Before lunch arrived, Doug had told Ross how the international derivates investment system had become very popular in the 1990s. Doug also related the 1998 story about two Nobel laureates who had started a hedge fund to trade derivatives. When the markets turned against them, the Federal Reserve rescued them from financial oblivion at a cost of more than $3 billion. It had been a close call.

Since then, the regulations pertaining to valuing and managing derivatives had been under continuing discussion, while oversight regulations had been largely ignored. As a result, issues of transparency, pricing, trading, risk limits, timely clearing, and many others remain unresolved. Additionally, the derivatives market has become the so-called Wild West of the financial world. Banks and financial houses alike had all been in the market for some time with their guns blazing, taking large risks on the hope of continuing rises in housing, interest rates, and the GDP until the meltdown of 2007 to 2009. It was all very unsettling to Doug, who was monitoring the financial exposure. Doug explained how these ironies and the resulting meltdown gave birth to a valuation manual of 1,500 pages. He quietly said that he had overheard other, more senior accountants' comments in those early days that the real problems of managing derivatives had never been fully resolved. Many of the derivative instruments were not signed, others were untraceable to the real buyer, and still others had been kept off the official balance sheets of the trustee banks because the valuation work was weeks, if not months, in arrears. The back office operations were really a nightmare, he reported.

Moreover, many international banks had derivatives balances that were several times larger than their total assets and hundreds of times larger than their invested capital. So any collapse in the derivatives market could also cause the failure of the bank. It was a truly frightening situation.

As they finished their meal, Doug told Ross of the sad days after the collapse of the credit default swaps (CDS) market in his second year on the job. The bank and derivatives department had both been decimated, and the bank was still repaying money that had been provided to it in 2008 to pay the CDS counterparties to the federal government. It was truly ugly. Doug survived only because he worked 12 hours a day for nearly two years through the work-out period. He was like a combat veteran, who had survived countless bloody battles, while many others had not survived at all.

Issue Summary. In the search for growing returns on investment, certain fund managers have used an advanced form of futures investing to: (1) increase their use of leverage and (2) achieve vastly higher returns, while limiting to some extent their downside risks on direct investments. Not all bankers were fools, however. British Banker Sir Julian Hodge instructed his officers, "In no circumstances enter the derivatives trading market without first agreeing it in writing with me ... at some time in the future it could bring the world's financial system to its knees."[1]

Unfortunately, one person's reward is another person's risk; in this case, the economic base of the United States is and has been at risk for the benefit of a few riverboat gamblers on Wall Street and in the nation's largest banks. As we proved in 2008, the entire world can be threatened by the bad judgment of relatively few insiders. The 2008 $806 billion and the 2009 $736 billion bailouts of Wall Street and the series of bailout steps that continued into 2009 were not just a product of subprime debt; they were also a function of credit default swaps (one form of derivatives) gone bad at AIG, the largest U.S. banks, and many investment houses. The worldwide balance of derivatives had reached $683,725 trillion in mid-2008[2]—or 10 times the size of the world economy. Credit default swaps were about $60 trillion of this balance. Who gets rewarded? Investors, insurers, and banks. Who takes the risk? Central banks. Who pays the cost of the losses? The taxpayers. As we will learn, the crises are *far* from over.

Derivatives remain largely unregulated and continue to constitute one of the most significant risks to both the United States and to the world economy in an age of massive public debt, adverse demographics, failed accountability, poor reporting, and regulatory blindness by politicians.

Lesson for Principled Business Leaders. The derivatives risks to the world economy are more significant than public debt. Derivatives, which are an obscure financial instrument used by sophisticated managers to limit or remove their own financial risk while transferring that risk to the public, were at the heart of one near-meltdown in 1998, and they were the cause of many bank and insurance failures and near-failures in 2008. Derivatives are intended to counter financial risk in many forms—interest rates, commodity prices, credit default swaps (the current AIG villain), and futures prices, to name only a few. Instead, they have been used to transfer risk from financial firms to an unwitting public.

Although derivatives were at the center of the financial meltdown of 2008, the balance of derivatives worldwide has continued to grow, albeit at a slightly lower annual rate through June 2008. At the end of 2006, there were $300 trillion in derivatives worldwide, $100 trillion of which were held by U.S. banks. The outstanding derivatives balance worldwide was nearly $684 trillion in June 2008, and U.S. banks held $145 trillion in derivatives at that time. The bank risk from derivatives was nearly 20 times the banking industry's capital! Several of the continuing bank and business failures since 2008 were due in whole or in part to derivatives.

Citizen and taxpayer welfare took a backseat to the bailout of the large banks that had been at the center of the problem. The cost of loans, grants, and guarantees has reached $14 trillion. Six years of tax revenues have been risked on the bank and Wall Street bailout, and on making good the bad bets of the financial engineers. The public is angry—very angry. The derivatives meltdown is yet another leadership failure.

The Challenge—Gambling? Hedging Risk? Courting Disaster? What Are Derivatives?

As one expert writes:

> Derivatives are financial instruments that have no intrinsic value, but derive their value from something else. They hedge the risk of owning things that are subject to unexpected price fluctuations, e.g. foreign currencies, bushels of wheat, stocks and government bonds. There are two main types: futures, or contracts for future delivery at a specified price, and options that give one party the opportunity to buy from or sell to the other side at a prearranged price.[3]

Jerry Markham of the Futures Industry Association amplifies the definition as follows:

> Examples of derivatives include futures, forwards, options, and swaps, and these can be combined with each other or traditional securities and loans in order to create hybrid instruments. Derivatives play an important and useful role in hedging and managing risk, but they also pose several dangers to the stability of financial markets and thereby the overall economy.
>
> As a testament to their usefulness, derivatives have played a role in commerce and finance for thousands of years. The first known instance of derivatives trading dates to 2000 B.C. when merchants, on what is now called Bahrain Island in the Arab Gulf, made consignment transactions for goods to be sold in India.[4]

Aristotle discussed a case of market manipulation through the use of derivatives of olive oil press capacity in Chapter 9 of his *Politics* some 2,500 years ago.[5]

Legal expert Edward J. Swan, writing in 1993, illustrates the long history of derivatives trading which was thought to have occurred in Mesopotamia.[6]

Swan explains further that derivatives trading in an exchange environment and with trading rules can be traced back to Venice in the twelfth century.[7] The Japanese traded futures, like contracts on warehouse receipts or rice, in the 1700s. In the United States, forward and futures contracts have been formally traded on the Chicago Board of Trade since 1849.

Randall Dodd, formerly of the Derivatives Study Center, further illuminated the murky history of deeds and misdeeds in derivatives along with a series of recommended solutions to the derivatives risk problems at a Financial Policy Forum on November 15, 2001:

> Derivatives are useful for hedging the risks normally associated with commerce and finance. Farmers can use derivatives the hedge the risk that the price of their crops fall before they are harvested and brought to market. Banks and thrifts can use derivatives to reduce the risk that the short-term interest rates they pay to their depositors will rise against the fixed interest rate they earn on their loans and other assets. Pension funds and insurance companies can use derivatives to hedge against large drops in the value of their portfolios.
>
> As an indication of the dangers they pose, it is worthwhile recalling a shortened list of recent disasters. Long-Term Capital Management collapsed with $1.4 trillion in derivatives on their books. Sumitomo Bank in Japan used derivatives [in] their manipulation of the global copper market for ten years prior to 1996. Barings bank, one of the oldest in Europe, was quickly brought to bankruptcy by over a billion dollars in losses from derivatives trading. Both the Mexican financial crisis in 1994 and the East Asian financial crisis of 1997 were exacerbated by the use of derivatives to take large positions involving the exchange rate.
>
> The first danger posed by derivatives comes from the leverage they provide to both hedgers and speculators. Derivatives transactions allow investors to take a large price position in the market while committing only a small amount of capital—thus the use of their capital is leveraged.
>
> Leverage makes it cheaper for hedgers to hedge, but it also makes speculation cheaper. Instead of buying $1 million of Treasury bonds or $1 million of stock, an investor can buy futures contracts on $1 million of the bonds or stocks with only a few thousand dollars of capital committed as margin. The returns from holding the stocks or bonds will be the same as holding the futures on the stocks or bonds. This allows an investor to earn a much higher rate of return on their capital by taking on a much larger amount of risk.
>
> Taking on these greater risks raises the likelihood that the investor makes or loses large amounts of money. If they suffer large losses, then they are threatened with bankruptcy. If they go bankrupt, then the people, banks and other institutions that invested in them or lent money to them will face possible losses and in turn face bankruptcy themselves. This spreading of the losses and failures is known as systemic risk, and it is an economy wide problem that is made worse by leverage and leveraging instruments such as derivatives.

Another danger involves transparency. Some derivatives are traded on formal futures and options exchanges, which are closely regulated. Other derivatives are traded over-the-counter (OTC) in markets that are almost entirely unregulated. In the OTC markets there is very little information provided by either the private market participants or collected by government regulators. The prices and other trading information in these markets are not made freely available to the public like is the case with futures and options exchanges. Instead that information is hoarded by each of the market participants.

As a result of this lack of information in the OTC market, it substantially reduces the ability of the government and other market participants to anticipate and possibly preempt building market pressures, major market failures, or manipulation efforts.

Yet another danger involves the use of derivatives to evade, avoid, dodge or out-flank financial market regulations designed to improve economic stability. In the cases of this decade's financial crises in Mexico and East Asia, the financial institutions in those countries used derivatives called total rate of return swaps to outflank financial regulations limiting those institutions exposure to foreign exchange risk. Derivatives can also be used to evade tax laws and manipulate accounting rules my restructuring the flow of payments so that earning are reported in one period instead of another.

Foreign exchange derivatives can also be used to improve the ability of speculators to mount an attack on a developing country's exchange rate system. In 1997, speculators employed both foreign exchange derivatives and equity-linked derivatives on Hong Kong's stock market in order to launch their attack on Hong Kong's fixed exchange rate regime. Thus when the Hong Kong monetary authority tried to defend its currency by raising interest rates, the speculators profited when the higher interest rates pushed down the price of stocks.

In sum, the enormous derivatives markets are both useful and dangerous. Current method(s) of regulating these markets is not adequate to assure that the markets are safe and sound and that disruptions from these markets do not spill over into the broader economy.

There are two very important economic functions or purposes for derivatives markets are: risk shifting and price discovery. Risk shifting is also referred to as risk management and more traditionally as hedging and speculating. Risk shifting can improve the efficiency of the economy by facilitating the transfer of risk from those less willing or able to bear it to those more willing or able to handle it. Derivatives also improve risk management because of their ability to decompose or disentangle the various sources of risk involved. . . .

The presence of derivatives markets, and more recently their extraordinary growth, raises some important concerns about the vulnerability of the financial sector and the overall economy. As the poet once said, "How do I threaten thee? Let me count the ways."

1. Increases leverages and lowers expense of risk taking
   - Risk taking is an externality and thus is a market imperfection that is not solved by the market alone.
   - Derivatives make risk shifting, and hence risk taking, cheaper and more efficient.
   - Derivatives are sometimes used to outflank prudential regulations and taxation.

2. Destructive and unproductive activities
   - Destructively used to commit fraud on the market
   - Destructively used to manipulate markets and distort price discovery
   - Unproductively used to outflank prudential regulations
   - Lower capital requirement
   - Lower collateral and margin requirement
   - Avoid restrictions on assets and liabilities
   - Unproductively used to manipulate accounting rules
   - Unproductively used to avoid or evade taxation
   - Credit risk
   - Liquidity risk
   - Systemic risk

The following exposition will address each of the points enumerated above. Each of these concerns is linked to one or more concepts of market failure or market imperfections. These are the externality of risk taking, the externality of the information content of prices, the absence of destructive competition and systemic risk.

Expansion of Risk Taking. There is an external diseconomy from the activity of risk taking. It is an inherent property of risk taking in financial markets that it can have a deleterious impact not only on those entities that are not party to the transactions and even those that do not participate in the market.

This is akin to negative external diseconomies such as pollution and congestion.

Markets can discipline internal risk management and the risk-reward relationship for ownership of internalized risk taking activities. Financial markets price securities and other transactions based on their risk-reward characteristics. Financial markets also produce incentives for risk management through the use of collateral, margin and capital.

Markets cannot address and solve the collateral damage of bankruptcy and lesser events such as failure to perform on transactions obligations. This affects not only the immediate counterparties, who are supposed to internalize the credit risk of their counterparties, but also other non-counterparties in the market and others who are not in the market.

In financial markets, risk taking has an externality because bankruptcy affects more than the failing firm. Part of the impact on other firms is anticipated by their holding capital in reserve against just such problems. However, reserve capital is costly and competition between market participants drives them to avoid holding any excess capital. Therefore bankruptcy losses in excess of what they anticipate will adversely impact those firms and in turn the other firms and individuals that do business with them. This is most clearly a problem for "too big to fail" firms. If they are driven to bankruptcy or are unable to perform their usual market functions, then it will have an adverse affect on the overall economy unless the government must steps in to restore market order.

Linkages between the various investors and financial institutions are inherent in financial markets. My risk becomes your risk becomes his and her risk. The ability of market-based competition is limited to discipline market participants against taking on more risk or too much risk. Sometimes competition punishes above normal risk taking as more and more investors decline to do business with the exceptionally risky investor. Other times competition drives down the standard for prudent investing as the competition for capital and customers pushes investors to seek higher returns by moving into riskier investments. Although competitive markets work sometimes, it is the times that they fail which justify the role of the government to provide minimal prudential regulatory standards.

Externality of risk and bankruptcy extends not just to other individual investors but also to the economy as a whole when it strikes key financial institutions such as banks that are critical to clearing payments, dealing in or clearing U.S. Treasury securities, underwriting and dealing in other bonds or interest rate derivatives. The problem is that the cost to the individual for their risk taking is less than the social cost.

Derivatives, especially OTC derivatives, make it worse by reducing transparency.

The externalities inherent in the risk-taking activities in financial markets makes it economically necessary for the government to play a role in setting prudential standards. Competitive markets alone will not do this. This role of the government, though, is not justified by some paternalistic motive to protect fools from themselves. Rather it justified by need to *protect the rest of us from the fools*.

One of the most glaring illustrations of this notion is the failure of LTCM [Long-Term Capital Management].

Had the failure of LTCM triggered the seizing up of markets, substantial damage could have been inflicted on many market participants, including some not directly involved with the firm, and could have potentially impaired the economies of many nations, including our own. [Alan Greenspan before the House Banking Committee in October 1998]

Current U.S. regulations are in fact designed to address this externality.

- Capital requirements for financial institutions which are calculated based on internalization of counterparty exposure, but which also serve as buffer to other outside disturbances
- Restrictions on banks' balance sheets
- Segregated accounts
- Speculation limits on futures and options exchanges [CFTC just filed charges against a futures trader who exceeded position limit.]
- Margin requirements on stock transactions and futures and options positions
- Exchange trading halts and circuit breakers
- Appropriate person limit to certain types of transactions
- Regulatory oversight and supervision
- Know-thy-customer provisions in securities laws[8]

[Derivatives Regulation.] Potential regulations for financial markets in advanced capitalist countries [must include]:

1. Reporting requirements: In order to improve transparency and market surveillance, market participants report transactions information including price, volume, open positions, large trader positions, contract basics. Market price, volume and open interest information should be broadcast to the broad market like current stock prices.

2. Modernize capital requirements: capital requirements should apply to market risk (e.g. foreign exchange and interest rate exposure) and potential future risk as well as credit risk; and capital requirements (and restrictions on asset holdings) should to apply to consolidated balance sheet and off-balance sheet positions.

3. Establish requirements or standards for collateral and margin requirements—these are already in practice futures and options exchanges and the law for U.S. stock purchases.

4. Enforcement: It can be enhanced by requiring reporting of transaction as condition for legal enforceability, and requiring maintenance of audit trail.

5. Require OTC derivatives dealers to act as market-makers by maintaining bid-ask quotes throughout trading day. This obligation compares with the privileges of being dealers, and is similar to requirements in U.S. Treasury securities markets.

6. Know thy customer: Extend these rules to all financial institutions conducting lending, underwriting, repurchase agreements and securities lending transactions, and all derivatives transactions with entities in developing countries.

7. Modernize accounting rules to account for credit and market value of derivatives exposure, and to properly account for embedded derivatives.

8. Standstill provisions and other measures included in debt instruments in order to facilitate debt rescheduling and reorganization.[9]

Derivatives risk affects all of those levels of government and their pension plans where governments own them. How do derivatives make financial markets and businesses of all types vulnerable? How did they bring a near collapse to the U.S. economy from 2008 to 2009? The Director of the Derivatives Study Center in Washington provided a clear indication of the substantial risk nearly a decade ago:

> The first and most obvious concern is the way in which derivatives markets can [bring about an] expansion of risk-taking activity. By enhancing

the efficiency of transactions and capital, derivatives can increase both hedging and speculation.

Secondly, derivatives markets can also encourage destructive and unproductive activities such as fraud, manipulation, outflanking prudential financial market regulations, manipulating accounting rules and evading taxation.

The third concern involves the creation of new credit risk as derivatives contracts are traded in order to shift various types of market risk. The new credit risk, especially in over-the-counter markets (OTC), is *not* [emphasis added] subject to collateral or margin standards or requirements and is not treated in the most economically efficient way for purposes of capital requirements.

The fourth concern is the liquidity risk, especially in the interest rate swaps market, which can be suddenly arrested due to creditworthiness problems with one or more major market participant. The last concern is systemic risk, which arises from the non-transparent nature of most OTC derivative markets and the strong linkages between derivatives and the underlying asset and commodity markets. The paper will conclude with a proposal for prudential regulatory measures that will address these public interest concerns.[10]

Lesson for Principled Business Leaders. Notwithstanding the benign views of the financial press, derivatives have already directly or indirectly cost the nation three years' tax revenues, because they have:

1. Taken unfair advantage of inconsistent disclosure and valuation rules for derivatives;
2. Aided numerous off-balance sheet tricks and inconsistent derivatives accounting;
3. Punished the worldwide financial community as a result of numerous instances of fraud, self-dealing, and bank failure;
4. Injured unsuspecting U.S. employees, investors, and others through the misuse of derivatives by now-collapsed Enron and its massive corporate fraud; and
5. Victimized millions of taxpayers and investors who in 2008 had to bail out the public and private commercial enterprises who didn't properly manage their derivatives businesses.

Lesson for Principled Business Leaders. The public and worldwide risks posed by unregulated or poorly regulated derivatives are so great that the public should not be forced to pay the costs of these past leadership failures. Most businesses should therefore avoid derivatives.

Lesson for Principled Business Leaders.   Business leaders must realize that:

1. Derivatives pose high risks for banks and businesses in volatile worldwide financial markets.
2. Derivatives threaten the capital of many international banks and central banks.
3. They must reserve capital as a contingency against derivatives risks.

Stretch Goal for My Enterprise. Do we or any of our primary banks have any high-risk credit default swaps or other derivatives that cannot be replaced within one year with less risky insurance, credit arrangements, or risk hedges?

Questions to Ponder. Do you know what your banks hold in derivatives balances? Are you comfortable that their level of risk will not increase your level of risk on credit, factoring, or future lending because of derivatives? Do you have an alternative bank credit facility? Is your business maintaining the highest level of transparency and accountability? Is your bank doing the same? Have you asked them? Do you have a second and backup bank with standby credit, if needed?

Action Steps

My business will avoid derivatives and preserve asset values by:

No.	Action Step	Expected Outcome	Date to Achieve Outcome
1.	Developing and implementing a sound, systematic financial risk assessment/mitigation plan.	Priority list of risks; priority list of mitigation actions; priority list of mitigation expenses	
2.	Developing and implementing an improved cash management plan to compensate for risk.	Improved operating margins	
3.	Reviewing my financial controls for greater financial market risk in coming years.	Improved reporting and controls	

(continued)

Action Steps (*continued*)

No.	Action Step	Expected Outcome	Date to Achieve Outcome
4.	Examining my bank's policies on derivatives.	Avoid bank credit changes or withdrawals because of bank capital issues	
5.	Developing alternative credit sources, if needed.	Options for future credit in the event of needs	

Key Measures of Success

Measurement Date	Cash Total	Weakest Function(s)	Corrective Action Steps	Date to Complete
1. __/__/__	$			
2. __/__/__	$			
3. __/__/__	$			
4. __/__/__	$			
5. __/__/__	$			

Suggested Reading

Bonner, William. *Financial Reckoning Day: Surviving the Soft Depression of the 21st Century*. With Addison Wiggin. Hoboken, NJ: John Wiley & Sons, 2003, 306 pp.

Dent, Harry S., Jr. *The Great Depression Ahead—How to Prosper in the Crash Following the Greatest Boom in History*. New York: Free Press, Simon & Schuster, 2009, 400 pp.

Kunstler, James Howard. *The Long Emergency: Surviving the Converging Catastrophes of the Twenty-First Century*. New York: Atlantic Monthly Press, 2005, 320 pp.

Leeb, Stephen, PhD. *The Coming Economic Collapse*. New York: Warner Business Books, 2006, 224 pp.

CHAPTER 9

Preparing for Inevitable Disasters

A prudent man sees danger and takes refuge, but the simple keep going and suffer for it.

—Proverbs 22:3

The Warning

Ross Gregory's high school classmate, Van Marks, has become a student of the environment in line with his degree in meteorology. Van is home for the summer before he returns for his final year of graduate studies at one of the top Western universities in the subject. The faculty at his school is so respected, in fact, that its senior professors have faculty and student research projects ringing the globe.

Van tells Ross about his recent work—a systematic analysis of the most significant weather phenomena to affect the United States in the past century. He is ecstatic about this assignment. Ten of his classmates had also submitted thesis proposals on the topic, but Van had been chosen. He is working 14 hours per day at the university, and this is the first break he's had in four months.

Van has concluded that the United States is in a short warming period similar to several that have occurred over the past thousand years. The current period followed a cooling period that began a decade ago. It is expected to continue through the first decades of the twenty-first century. Van's research into the resulting tropical storm patterns, melting of icebergs, and violent weather patterns has been both alarming and fascinating. He believes that these violent weather patterns will continue.

As Van continued his research on his limited but growing scientific understanding of these weather phenomena and storm patterns, as well as the tragic toll on human life, he explained his understandable worry to Ross about the level of preparation in the modern-day United States—especially the coastal areas in the east and far west. Van explained that ocean water levels could change, something for which we must prepare in many urban population centers. He also felt that the existing systems of long-term preparation—setting aside reserves for disaster and reworking building codes—had a long way to go to meet minimum needs. Ross was fascinated, and somewhat alarmed, as he listened to his friend. Van concluded with a lengthy description of his profound respect for the forces of nature.

Later that night, Ross lay awake for two hours thinking about Van and his exciting research project.

Issue Summary. Are you aware of the profound impact that natural disasters have had on the United States in the past century? Do you realize how the failure to prepare for these events has risked, and taken, thousands of lives? Are you confident that your leaders are taking the actions needed to protect life and property, as the inevitable disasters occur in the future?

Obviously, there are not enough resources to fully compensate for all risks. Therefore, priorities must be set. Priorities are difficult to justify for politicians; but they are a necessity for principled business leaders.

The United States has a long history of developing homes and commercial facilities in geographical areas that are highly vulnerable to disaster. For example, several of the nation's largest cities—San Francisco, Los Angeles, and St. Louis—sit astride or near major earthquake fault lines. Many cities are at substantial risk of hurricanes, floods, and ocean storms because they were built in low-lying areas. New Orleans, countless communities in Florida, and many beach communities on the east and west coasts of the United States are further examples. Unfortunately, more than 53 percent of Americans live within 50 miles of a coast where weather disasters are most likely to occur.

The federal government has taken the major financial responsibility for storm recovery and rebuilding in areas damaged by natural disasters. Unfortunately, the federal government is *broke*, so it may not be as effective in the future. Consider first the ancient and modern history.

Leaders Confront Disaster in Advance

Chapter 2 explained how Joseph prepared for disaster by storing food and provisions. Pharaoh had a frightening dream that he did not understand, and Joseph explained it to him: Egypt was headed for seven good years and seven years of famine. Joseph recommended that Pharaoh find a wise leader to manage the affairs of Egypt during the coming hard times. Pharaoh was so impressed with Joseph's clear thinking and good plan for surviving the difficult years that he immediately appointed Joseph to be the prime minister and head of government.

And so, Joseph swung into action. He immediately insisted that all of the farmers pay taxes in the form of a *one-fifth* share of their crops. Joseph stored this food in government shelters, so it was in good condition when it was needed to feed starving people. After the seven good years, the storehouses were full. And the seven years' drought soon followed.

Joseph was able to help the people during the years of hardship. He sold food to them, but only when they needed it. When they were unable to pay, he purchased their land and added it to the land already owned by Pharaoh. He also made sure that the currency of Egypt was stable and that the budget and economy were sound—even in the years of hardship. He continued as prime minister for many years, because he was a prudent and resourceful leader. Joseph saved Egypt from collapse. Where are the Josephs of today? How should businesses prepare for disaster?

The Challenge. Leaders at all levels and in all institutions must address the risk of loss due to disaster as an integral part of their ongoing responsibilities. Politicians are inclined to react to the onset of a disaster; they don't typically assess risks in advance or plan to counteract risks of disaster. They only spend money when these events occur, often far in excess of what is needed or usable at any one time.

Lesson for Principled Business Leaders. Leaders know that the forces of nature are far more powerful than any forces known to humans. Moreover, they know that:

- Priorities must be established for disaster response based upon the highest probability disasters.
- There is no substitute for a chain of command and interoperability of communications.
- There is no substitute for prior planning for disasters, based upon systematic risk assessments.
- There is no substitute for agreements between the levels of government on the specific duties and responsibilities at each level.

Preparing for Disasters   The History Channel recently reported (on the 100th anniversary of the San Francisco Earthquake, April 18, 2006) that repairs and recovery for a modern San Francisco earthquake would cost *$300 billion* at current prices. Recovery from the original earthquake cost $5 billion. They also reported that such an earthquake had at least a 50 percent probability of occurring.[1]

Notwithstanding the devastation of Katrina, the Federal Emergency Management Agency (FEMA) and the National Oceanic and Atmospheric Administration (NOAA) reported on August 12, 2006, in their annual pre-hurricane season briefing that 56 percent of the U.S. population do not consider themselves vulnerable to a natural disaster, 60 percent have no plan to cope with a natural disaster, and 13 percent would refuse to evacuate from their homes even if they were ordered to do so in an emergency.[2]

Principled business leaders must approach potential emergencies and disasters differently and systematically. But first, the definition and categories of emergencies follows:

> An emergency is any unplanned event that can cause deaths or significant injuries to employees, customers or the public; or that can shut down your business, disrupt operations, cause physical or environmental damage, or threaten the facility's financial standing or public image. Obviously, numerous events can be *emergencies*, including:

- Fire
- Hazardous materials incident
- Flood or flash flood
- Hurricane
- Tornado
- Winter storm
- Earthquake
- Communications failure
- Radiological accident
- Civil disturbance
- Loss of key supplier or customer
- Explosion

The term *disaster* has been left out of this document because it lends itself to a preconceived notion of a large-scale event, usually a *natural disaster*. In fact, each event must be addressed within the context of the impact it has on the company and the community. What might constitute a nuisance to a large industrial facility could be a *disaster* to a small business.[3]

Lesson for Principled Business Leaders. Business leaders must have a plan that includes the following basic elements:

1. It is broadly representative of the entire enterprise and has a cross-section of employees involved in the planning process and in the execution of the plan.
2. It includes all business functions in the planning process and in assigning responsibilities for execution.
3. It consists of a minimum of applicable internal plans and policies, including:
   a. Evacuation plan
   b. Fire protection plan
   c. Safety and health program plan
   d. Environmental policies and procedures
   e. Security policies and procedures
   f. Insurance programs and contact information
   g. Finance and purchasing policies and procedures
   h. Plant and facility closing policies and procedures
   i. Employee manuals
   j. Hazardous materials plans and manuals
   k. Process safety assessments
   l. Risk management plan
   m. Capital improvement program plan
   n. Mutual aid agreements
4. It contains the results of meetings with local public safety officials, emergency organizations, and local utilities.
5. It identifies all relevant local codes and regulations.
6. It identifies critical products, services, and operations in the business.
7. It identifies internal resources and persons responsible for their use.
8. It identifies external resources and contact information.
9. It contains the insurance review results and contact information.
10. It has a business vulnerability analysis, consisting of the following minimums:

   a. Listing of potential emergencies—historical, geographic, technological, human error, and physical

   b. Evaluation of possible and probable results of any potential disaster

   c. Estimated probabilities of human, property, and business impacts
of each disaster

11. It has a systematic response plan to address each potential disaster by
probability, including:

   a. Business response resources

   b. Outside response resources

   c. Training requirements

   d. Equipment requirements

   e. Mutual aid agreements

   f. Outside contractor arrangements

   g. Schedules and checklists of actions

12. It contains the instructions for management of emergency response
and recovery, including:

   a. Direction and control

   b. Communications

   c. Life safety

   d. Property protection

   e. Community outreach

   f. Recovery and restoration

   g. Administration and logistics[4]

Lesson for Principled Business Leaders. Businesses need not only
plans, but also reserves for the highest probability disaster events in their
market areas, because there may not be:

- Well-thought-out contingency plans that provide scenario planning
and prepared responses to the highest priorities and/or likely disasters.

- Coordinated levels of responsibility between and among state, county,
and local government entities. (The federal government is not able
to override the responses of local authorities and of managers of local
areas without prior agreements.)

- Reserves for disasters at the federal, state, or local government levels.
(Only leaders will insist that this be done.)

- Defined limits to the assistance that can be provided by a bankrupt
nation to respond to private property damage and local disasters without any pre-established reserves.

Stretch Goal for My Enterprise. Does our disaster recovery plan enable our enterprise to resume full operations within five business days at either our current or an alternative location in the event that our primary business location is totally destroyed?

Questions to Ponder. Are we aware of the potential disasters that may occur in our region and in the locations of affiliated businesses? Do we have communications and management relationships with the public safety organizations in our areas of operations? Do we have contingency plans for the top five potential disasters? Do we have a systematic plan for risk mitigation and risk management?

Action Steps

Business leaders must realize that natural and man-made disaster is a looming possibility for every enterprise, regardless of size, because of the significant impacts of disasters on markets as a result of globalization, high-speed communications, and electronic financial markets. They must prepare accordingly, and have:

1. An emergency assessment and response plan;
2. Plans to take advantage of alternative markets when disasters strike a given geographical area;
3. Access to present and alternative markets; and
4. Backup records and information technology (IT) operations capabilities away from its main location.

Key Measures of Success

Measurement Date	Item	Weakest Function(s)	Corrective Action Steps	Date to Complete
1. __/__/_____	Internal plans			
2. __/__/_____	Local codes/ contacts			

(continued)

Key Measures of Success (*continued*)

Measurement Date	Item	Weakest Function(s)	Corrective Action Steps	Date to Complete
3. __/__/_____	Vulnerability assessment			
4. __/__/_____	Response plan			
5. __/__/_____	Reserves			

Suggested Reading

Grose, Vernon L. *Managing Risk: Systematic Loss Prevention for Executives.* New York: Prentice Hall, 1982, 404 pp.

Klare, Michael T. *Resource Wars.* New York: Henry Holt and Company, LLC, 2002, 304 pp.

Redlener, Irwin, MD. *Americans at Risk: Why We Are Not Prepared for Megadisasters and What We Can Do Now.* New York: Alfred A. Knopf, 2006, 304 pp.

Schwartz, Peter. *Inevitable Surprises: Thinking Ahead in a Time of Turbulence.* New York: Gotham Books, 2003, 256 pp.

Controlling Inflation's Damage to Business

The government's deliberate policy of inflation is no less a fraudulent claim on real wealth. It is no less a form of thievery, though subtle. It is "legal" only because it is done by the government and its central banking mechanism—and it is against the law for anyone else to do.[1]

—Eddie Willers

New Accounting

R oss and his friend Doug often met for lunch. One Monday, however, Doug arrived at the deli with a troubled look on his face. He had been talking with the bank's comptroller earlier that morning about long-term value in the bank's portfolio of assets—loans and investments. The comptroller was due to retire in less than a month, so he was in an expansive, talkative mood. As they discussed the upcoming financial reports, he cautioned Doug not to be too impressed with the much-expanded assets being reported by the bank. Most of this was what he called *phantom wealth*.

Doug was puzzled until the comptroller suggested that Doug calculate the value of his home, which had supposedly risen in value over the previous five years by 30 percent, in terms of the value of gold. Gold, he explained, is the most reliable indicator of value. When Doug did this simple calculation, he learned that the original purchase value of his home had actually *decreased* in value, if measured in terms of the ounces of gold that it would take to purchase it today.

Surprisingly, Doug also realized that gold had increased in market value by more than 50 percent per ounce during the prior five years. So the investment upon which he'd been counting on for his long-term savings had actually *dropped* in value when measured against an absolute standard. Inflation, he learned, is really the practice of stealing his investments and savings' long-term value. Ross understood Doug's dismay all too well as they continued to talk.

Issue Summary. Inflation is the friend of borrowers and self-serving typical politicians. However, it is the enemy of savers, investors, and principled business leaders. The U.S. dollar has lost 96 percent of its value in the past half century; and its decline continues notwithstanding public pronouncements to the contrary because many special interests favor a weaker dollar. Inflation is often the means used by government to limit the impact of debt, while it spends more than its income year after year. Business leaders must lead the call for a change in direction and then demonstrate it.

Our Choices. Our approach to the creation of *phantom wealth* through the massive expansion of the money supply and the maintenance of low central bank discount rates has helped to transfer our wealth to Asia and Europe. Our insistence on deferring the bills for current expenses to coming generations will only handicap our children and their children as we saddle them with unconscionable debt. We can, therefore—by deception, delusion, and denial—lead our citizens to believe that there is no cost for our excesses and irresponsibility. Indeed, inflation is the vehicle that government can use to not only provide the illusion of financial success to this generation, but also enable it to incur massive debts today, which can in turn be repaid by our children with cheaper dollars of tomorrow. Isn't it time to change course? How should business respond?

Inflation is the means by which the government eliminates (inflates away) its debt, since it repays obligations with dollars of lesser value. Moreover, it is the vehicle that will accelerate the erosion in the value of the dollar for the millions of U.S. business leaders, savers, and investors—just as it has for half a century. Debasing a nation's currency is one of the worst wrongs that can ever be perpetrated. The United States is debasing its currency at a rapid rate, and it is in danger of destroying it, all in the interest of excessive public borrowing and serving special interests. Should business follow this path?

The Challenge. Economist Michael Hudson (MH) explained the hidden impacts of inflation on the consumer in a 2003 interview with independent journalist Standard Schaefer (SS), an exchange summarized by Schaefer in an article entitled *The Coming Financial Reality*. This account describes in detail Hudson's daunting picture of the combined impact of inflation and lower interest rates on the nation's economic future. The 44 adverse impacts, which are, in most cases, just as true today, follow:

1. With the war in Iraq winding down and interest rates dropping, neither the economic recovery of 1990 to 1991 nor the one of 2001 to 2003 saw an appreciable rise in employment. Moreover, the growth rates each time were lower than the last (situation in 2010—same).

2. The last seven economic recoveries were much stronger than the one of 2000 to 2001. Unemployment didn't benefit, and corporations benefited from yet another "jobless recovery" with even higher rates of profitability (situation in 2010—same).

3. The big financial papers tout the growth of employment, but it is only services employment that has benefited. The "refinancing boom" only helped retail sales with the related consumer credit jumps, all of which was aided by the Fed's aggressive money supply expansion (situation in 2010—worse with many retail sales down).

4. Federal deficits—with their accompanying tax cuts that hurt state budgets, accelerated public job losses, and lowered the pricing power of labor—kept wage rates low, opened the door to a coming wave of foreclosures, and set the table for continued weakness in employment (situation in 2010—worse).

5. Not only are corporations working to realize profits at the expense of the workforce, but politicians are also fighting more for their donors than for their voters (situation in 2010—same).

6. The Fed's family of borrowers has the lowest cost of funds in decades; but banks have not cut credit card rates, long-term mortgage rates, or commercial lending rates. Savers lose again (situation in 2010—same).

7. Low rates have even benefited the investor and non-financial borrowers by bumping up the level of their investment "gambles" and failing to help fixed capital formation (situation in 2010—same).

8. In Schaefer's words: "Like Japan, the U.S. economy has painted itself into a debt corner that is locking in low interest rates." As a result, less income supports more business and consumer debt: "A thousand dollars per month can carry twice as high an interest-only loan at 5 percent as it can at 10 percent" (situation in 2010—same).

9. Business and consumers did not use the lower interest rates to pay down debt; instead, they borrowed more and consumed more. So the people who fell for the "live better on more borrowing" approach only benefited the banks, while government ignored the opportunity to get its financial house in order (situation in 2010—same).

10. Since much of the new debt is in "floating rate" mortgages, banks can keep their depositors with better interest returns, rather than see the scale of withdrawals that killed the savings and loan associations (S&Ls) in the 1980s (situation in 2010—same).

11. Borrowers took the risk of loss if rates ever rose, since their debt carrying charges would "jump sharply, especially for real estate" (situation in 2010—same).

12. Those who have borrowed "to the hilt" will be forced to sell in a downturn. Many will find that they are in debt in excess of the value of their property (upside down; situation in 2010—same).

13. Those in control won't change this nightmare scenario, so they will allow the bubble to continue to build, which will set the stage for an even more devastating downturn (situation in 2010—same).

14. Pension funds are another loser, as defined benefit plans will be changed to defined contribution plans. Another common practice is to "financialize" peoples' earnings by buying their own stocks and bonds for their pension funds (situation in 2010—same).

15. With lower interest rates, pension contributions must rise, so most of the corporate earnings should go to pension funding—a serious problem in both Britain and the United States (situation in 2010—worse, if not dire).

16. With lower earnings, stock prices fall, pension fund values drop, and capital gains aren't available to pay benefits. Thus, they are forced to move to defined contribution plans. Unfortunately, only the top people with "golden parachutes" receive defined benefits (situation in 2010—mixed).

17. The companies without principled leaders often terminate employees before they are fully vested in their pension plans. Another way to avoid pension responsibilities is to merge with another firm, or to allow one's enterprise to be raided by a buyer whose pension terms are less generous. "The raiders [then] empty out the pension funds and use them for their own purposes, partly to pay off their financial backers and partly to pay bonuses to their leading officers out of the savings they have expropriated from the employees" (situation in 2010—same).

18. Lower interest rates also decrease income on Social Security and medical care funds. Bond purchases, stock purchases, and investing in an economy where there is limited production all combine to lower long-term purchases. Low interest rates make purchases of stocks and bonds less profitable (situation in 2010—same).

19. These factors also amplify the folly of privatizing Social Security, which would give rise to the vain hope of making up losses from the last bubble on the next one (situation in 2010—no longer being considered).

20. According to Hudson: "Every stock market bubble in history, starting with the South Sea and Mississippi bubbles in the 1710s in Britain and France, has been sponsored by government. The driving force has been the government's attempt to cope with debt obligations beyond its foreseeable ability to pay. Creating a bubble has been a way to solve their public debt problem—and to pay off political insiders at the same time, thereby killing two birds with one stone" (situation during the 2007 to 2009 meltdown—same and done again in 2010).

21. In Hudson's words: "Modern governments are not politically able to simply default on their debts—at least not debts owed to their own bondholders in their own currency. The problem has to be solved through the marketplace. The simplest solution is to get people voluntarily to swap their government bonds—or in today's case, their Social Security entitlements—for stocks that then can be permitted to fall in price, once the investment no longer is the government's responsibility" (situation in 2010—no longer being considered).

22. We no longer study economic history, debt, and similar essential factors in current practice. People seek to get rich in a new economic model that has no apparent downside, until it rises up to bite them, yet again. Meanwhile, we impose our debt on the larger world to our collective peril (situation in 2010—worse).

23. The financial sector has become a parasite—an organism long known for killing the host as it convinces the same host that it is feeding itself. Says Hudson, "Something like this is happening today as the financial sector is devouring the industrial sector. Finance capital pretends that its growth is that of industrial capital formation. That is why the financial bubble is called 'wealth creation,' as if it were what progressive economic reformers envisioned a century ago. Emperors of Finance have trumped Barons of Property and Captains of Industry" (situation in 2010—same).

24. Economists have defined a new concept of *wealth creation* that most people would refer to as a *rip-off*. While some would say there is no free lunch, ". . . the economy has become all about getting a free lunch." The goal "is property income, not the creation of new means of production" (situation in 2010—same).

25. Financial engineers call stock market bubbles *wealth creation*, an appealing concept to the two-thirds of homeowning Americans who believe they are benefiting from it. Borrowing against this higher value property is termed *value extraction*. "In fact, riding the wave of asset-price inflation—the real estate and stock-market bubble—has been the way in which most people have been able to get to be what they consider to be pretty rich." Unfortunately, this formula doesn't work for renters, ethnic minorities, immigrants, members of large families, people who get sick and need to pay for medical care, people who get fired or have their pension fund ripped off, or anyone who otherwise falls outside the norm (situation in 2010—same; downturn cut all asset values drastically).

26. Climbing house and stock prices *seem* like a way to build wealth at no apparent cost, which thereby redefines wealth as "financial market value" rather than the factor of production—capital (downturn from 2007 to 2009 proved this correct; same in 2010).

27. Investment bankers were thus able to feed "the bubble by the 'forced saving' that was withheld from the paychecks of employees," while the deregulated Securities and Exchange Commission (SEC) allowed these practices to continue (situation in 2010—same).

28. Savers could contribute only to pension plans managed by third parties or by their employers, who carried out their tasks to benefit themselves more than the people whose pensions they managed (situation in 2010—same).

29. Meanwhile, as Hudson says, "Alan Greenspan was committed to using monetary policy to prevent a stock-market downturn . . . until . . . Long-Term Credit Management (LTCM) got into trouble in 1997 to 1998, when he bailed out the banks that had put up the money that was gambled on derivatives." People wanted Greenspan to succeed for their benefit (situation in 2010—still true and continuing).

30. Enter the era of media-generated "psychological engineering," where good market days were called "profit-taking, and . . . always give a positive spin on every development, up or down" (situation in 2010—this practice continues).

31. A new "circular flow" was to have Europe and Asia recycle the U.S. payments deficit to finance the budget deficit so that Americans didn't have to save money any more. They could spend what they had, and let foreign central (banks) do the saving (situation in 2010—still true).

32. These same "free-market boys" stopped any discussion of other outcomes. Power trumped ideas, and the parasite took over (situation in 2010—practice continues).

33. Deflation has emerged not as price deflation but rather as "debt deflation." Growing debt must be fed by a growing share of the income, so the income is not available to buy goods and services (situation in 2010—same and getting worse).

34. Some consumers countered this cycle by using their income to pay mortgages while they simultaneously used credit cards and loans to pay day-to-day costs (situation in 2010—same and getting worse).

35. Real estate emerges as the favorite son, while industry declines (situation in 2010—same).

36. In the end, bankers get income and the homeowner gets the capital gain to make the financial bubble come full circle, until there is a downturn (situation in 2010—same).

37. Speculation becomes a faster way to fortune than investment (situation in 2010—same).

38. Meanwhile, the federal tax cuts drive tax increases at the state and local levels because of a myriad of waterfall effects to make up for the loss of revenues that have gone to creditors (situation in 2010—same).

39. Low interest rates also have international impacts. For example, they will force down the dollar exchange rate while the cheaper dollar drives up prices in the local market (situation in 2010—same).

40. Low U.S. interest rates also send the international signal that the United States is protecting only its interests and no one else's. Falling dollars cause rising euros, and European exporters get hurt (situation in 2010—same).

41. Says Hudson: "The U.S. knows that this policy package pits it against pro-labor and strong social benefits, causing them to reorder their priorities and transfer the economic surplus from labor to finance, as is occurring in the United States. So instead of the deficit 'crowding out' domestic U.S. saving, America is getting (got) the kind of free ride . . . [while] Europe and Asia are lending us the money at virtually no interest to buy as much as we want from them, for our paper IOUs of increasingly dubious quality" (situation in 2010—same).

42. There is also a lesson for private versus public control of monetary policy. Public control of the monetary system is inherently more stable, because the goal is long-term investment. Private control, however, has the goal of "financ[ing] short-term asset-price gains—that is, to inflate bubbles" (situation in 2010—same).

43. According to Hudson, "Every hyperinflation in history, especially in the Germany of the 1920s, stemmed from the government's being painted into a debt corner and trying to inflate its way out of debt" (situation in 2010—danger exists but the outcome is not yet certain).

44. Now we must ask "how America is going to avoid paying its debts, and how other countries are not going to pay their own public and private debts? It looks like the debts to labor will be wiped out in order to preserve the 'sanctity' of debts owed to the wealthiest layer of the population. Big fish eat little fish"[2] (situation in 2010—same).

The U.S. economic house is, quite clearly, not in good order; and at this point, there don't seem to be any prospects, possibilities, or emerging leaders committed to changing this reality. China has recently been joining the chorus of voices calling for reason; a representative comment from a professor of economics and Senior Wei Lun Fellow at Hong Kong University of Science and Technology follows:

> We need the Fed doves to help remove the lid on the long rates and break the wishful thinking that cheap financing is always around for property purchase, for fiscal budget deficit, and for current account deficit. The property market will cool off. With well-targeted CPI inflation rate eating into the value of the house and with dollar depreciating against all major currencies, the property market bubble will shrink over time. The U.S. households will finally begin to realize that they need to save for their retirement nest egg, or else, be prepared to face the reality that the equity they build into and the capital gains on their house won't be enough to keep them happy for the rest of their retirement life.
>
> The risk of allowing for inflation to resurface is that it may go out of control. But we trust that the Fed has had more experience in putting the inflation rate within the desired range. Will the moderate increase in long-term inflation rate have a negative impact on long-term health of the economy? There is no evidence suggesting this will be the case. A core CPI inflation rate between 2.25 and 3.25 percent will not put a dent in long-term productivity growth.[3]

China is increasingly outspoken in expressing its misgivings about U.S. monetary and fiscal policy. The reader can be sure that this pronouncement was fully authorized by the State and that it was made for specific purposes. China's substantial holdings of U.S. Treasury bills give it a platform not only to express itself fully, but also to be heard clearly.

Lesson for Principled Business Leaders. Inflation is creating a false image of economic welfare and asset worth. The dollar now has only 5 percent of the purchasing power that it had in 1965. The purchasing power will continue to erode—thereby devaluing pensions, investments, and intangible asset values.

Lesson for Principled Business Leaders. Confronting inflation by testing for real asset value is one indicator. This is done by calculating the value of any owned facility or equipment in ounces of gold, both at the time of purchase and at present. Some will find asset values have dropped sharply when measured by this standard.

Stretch Goal for My Enterprise. What is my current break-even sales volume? Can our enterprise lower its fixed costs and manage its variable costs in such a way as to ensure that it breaks even at a business volume of 50 percent of its 2009 revenue levels?

Stretch Goal for My Enterprise. Have I removed every cost other than those that drive my business in an effort to improve our financial stability?

Stretch Goal for My Enterprise. What additional steps should I take in order to preserve asset values (capital, facilities, equipment, supplies, inventory) in my business?

Questions to Ponder. Which factor has more potential to affect our business within the next five years—inflation or deflation? Why is this the case? Do we have reliable evaluations of each of our products so that we can break even at lower revenues? Do we have a product ranking based upon the cost to manufacture or purchase so that products with unacceptably low margins can be discontinued, as capital availability or credit limitations demand?

Action Steps

Business Leaders Must Realize That:

1. Inflation is the biggest looming obstacle to stable operations, effective financial management, and reliable long-term plans.

2. Fixed costs must be moved to variable costs in order to provide flexibility in operations when and if labor and commodity prices escalate in an environment of unchecked inflation.

3. They must have sound inflation contingency plans and be prepared to drop products that lose margin because of rapid rises in vendor, labor, or materials costs.

Key Measures of Success

Measurement Date	Fixed Costs (%)	Weakest Area(s)	Corrective Action Steps	Date to Complete
1. __/__/_____				
2. __/__/_____				
3. __/__/_____				
4. __/__/_____				
5. __/__/_____				

Suggested Reading

Bonner, William. *Empire of Debt: The Rise of an Epic Financial Crisis*. With Addison Wiggin. Hoboken, NJ: John Wiley & Sons, 2006, 384 pp.

———. *Financial Reckoning Day: Surviving the Soft Depression of the 21st Century*. Hoboken, NJ: John Wiley & Sons, 2003, 320 pp.

Karmin, Craig. *Biography of the Dollar*. New York: Crown Publishing Group, Random House, 2008, 272 pp.

Leeb, Stephen, PhD. *The Coming Economic Collapse*. New York: Warner Business Books, 2006, 224 pp.

Schiller, Robert J. *The New Financial Order*. Princeton, NJ: Princeton University Press, 2003, 384 pp.

CHAPTER 11

Avoiding the Liquidity Traps

Practices of the unscrupulous money changers stand indicted in the court of public opinion, rejected by the hearts and minds of men.

—Franklin D. Roosevelt's First Inaugural Address, 1933

Money, Money, Money

Ross and Doug decided to travel to New Zealand during their sixth winter after college. Their interest in the outdoors and the availability of less expensive air travel sealed the deal for them; and New Zealand was perfect at this time of the year. During their first night there, the pair visited a local pub and talked quietly with one of the older gentlemen, named Charlie Young, who happened to be from the Ministry of Finance. The conversation was especially fascinating for the two of them: one a U.S. banker and one an information technology (IT) professional.

Charlie had been a new accountant in the Ministry of Finance in 1984, when New Zealand nearly went under financially. Government employment rolls were bloated. Inflation was out of control. Public sector budgets were growing faster than the economy. Schools were only massive bureaucracies, and students were underperforming in most key subjects. Business was laboring under huge tax burdens, and the economy had slowed to a walk while inflation was consuming a growing share of each citizen's paycheck. Charlie could not have launched his public service career at a worse time.

But he had found himself in the midst of a wonderful economic revolution before the story concluded.

To Charlie's amazement, several new ministers had also been appointed by the prime minister; one of them, a man named Maurice McAdams, had brought about revolutionary change. Starting in the Ministry of Finance, McAdams had privatized many programs that somehow resulted in individual wage gains *without* massive job losses. He introduced competition into elementary and secondary education. Although he had no control over the Central Bank, he took steps to cut the demand for new debt and thus lessened inflationary pressures throughout the economy. Quietly and without fanfare, McAdams had revolutionized New Zealand's economy and averted bankruptcy for the nation. Ross and Doug wondered if such a sea change could ever happen in the United States. Is such profound transformation even possible in the modern United States, and could business leaders somehow help to bring it about?

Issue Summary. Excess liquidity and home-equity lending has been the nation's ATM for much of the past 20 years. This consumption and borrowing epidemic spread to many households. By the time it was over, Americans had piled up $3 trillion in added home-equity debt alone. They went on a spending binge until stagnant wages dictated that they use credit cards for living expenses and home-equity lines of credit (HOLECs) to pay off their credit card debt. It was an ugly downward spiral that came to a crashing halt in 2008. In fact, U.S. consumers continued to overspend right up to the time of the Wall Street collapse, with the systematic help of self-serving credit card issuers, bankers, and those who manage many of the western United States' central and commercial banks.

The subprime mortgage crisis of 2007 to 2009 was one direct result of excess liquidity, consumer borrowing, and use of home equity to finance current consumption—that is, until house values plummeted. Lenders were all too willing to use available liquidity to create high-risk loan packages that could then be sold to institutional buyers in large blocks with no recourse. The Street had gone wild.

A second tragedy arising out of the era of easy new money and liquidity was the deceptively high market values that housing prices reached, before the 2007 collapse. This overpricing was in part the result of high liquidity levels, intense lender competition to place new mortgages, high appraisals, and fraudulent loan applications. But the new money was available to support these staggeringly high prices, as Figure 11.1 illustrates.

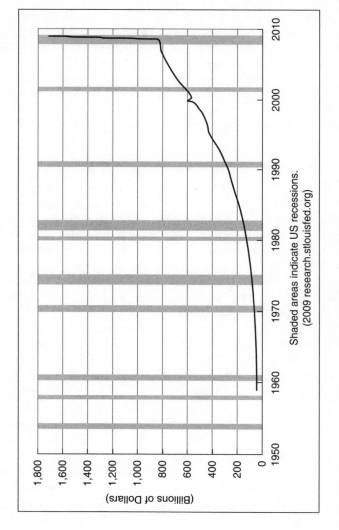

Figure 11.1 Board of Governors Monetary Base, Adjusted for Changes in Reserve Requirements (BOGAMBNS)
Source: Board of Governors of the Federal Reserve System.

U.S. Money Supply Growth—1950–2010

The United States has created more money in the past decade than it has in all of its history. This liquidity, or expanded money supply by the Federal Reserve, consists of new capital in search for a reasonable return on investment. These returns were increasingly difficult to obtain in an expanding economy of low interest rates, until the advent of the collateralized debt obligations (CDOs), no-fault mortgages, and credit default swaps (CDSs) arrived to provide those dizzying returns to investors. Then it all came crashing down—on the heads of taxpayers. Enter new, massive government borrowing; trillions in grants to the offending parties; and $18 trillion in lost wealth. Another bubble has burst, and another round of leadership failures has occurred. The same is true in the international sphere.

The History of Recent Financial Leadership Failures

Canadian economist[1] Michel Chossudovsky is a professor of economics at the University of Ottawa. Addressing the growing problems of poor financial practices on the world stage—because of its influence on large-scale money creation, central bank plundering, and the potential for a failed dollar in the future—Chossudovsky provided a daunting forecast of today's reality more than a decade ago. His concerns follow:

1. The post–Cold War economic crisis is of such magnitude that it is causing the rapid "impoverishment of large sectors of the World population." Ample evidence is provided by the massive losses in currency value worldwide, while it has plunged a number of economies into "abysmal poverty" (situation in 2010—worse).

2. The crisis has ranged far beyond Southeast Asia and the former Soviet Union, to force sudden and widespread drops in the standard of living in many countries. He saw the resulting outcomes as "more devastating than the Great Depression of the 1930s." The resulting economic dislocations can be expected, he asserted, to cause future regional conflicts, societal breakup, and even the "destruction of entire countries." He went on to describe the events as "the most serious economic crisis in modern history" (situation in 2010—accurate assessment).

3. Largely denied by the Western media, he noted that the social impacts of this economic crisis were systematically distorted, rejected, or downplayed to such a degree that even the United Nations disavowed the "mounting tide of World poverty," while the media trumpeted vain efforts to reduce poverty in the wider atmosphere of economic prosperity and health[2] (situation in 2010—accurate assessment).

4. The 1997 destruction of several of Asia's currencies was followed by massive losses in other currency markets, panic-selling of Japanese stocks, and collapse of the Russian ruble. Even the Dow Jones index lost 554 points on August 31, followed by $2.3 trillion in lost market value over a period of less than six months.[3]

5. Russia's currency collapse was the event that enabled a small group of Western banks to nearly take over Russia's financial system and the accompanying debt to default to Moscow's Western creditors (including the German Deutsche and Dresdner banks). He concluded that these events, along with the 1992 "IMF 'shock therapy,'" effectively transferred $500 billion in Russian military/industrial assets to Western interests.[4]

6. At the same time, the "worldwide scramble to appropriate wealth through 'financial manipulation' [was] the driving force behind this crisis" and the accompanying "economic turmoil and social devastation." He pointed out that even billionaire George Soros acknowledged how "extending the market mechanism to all domains has the potential of destroying society."[5] He observed that the forces of "market manipulation by powerful actors constitutes a form of financial and economic warfare [eclipsing] the need to recolonise [sic] lost territory or send in invading armies" (situation in 2010—the damage is done).

7. He wryly observed that "... the outright 'conquest of nations' meaning the control over productive assets, labour, natural resources and institutions can be carried out in an impersonal fashion from the corporate boardroom: commands are dispatched from a computer terminal, or a cell phone." This "Financial warfare ... also applies complex speculative instruments including the gamut of derivative trade, forward foreign exchange transactions, currency options, hedge funds, index funds, etc. ... with the ultimate purpose of capturing financial wealth and acquiring control over productive assets" (situation in 2010—accurate assessment).

8. Quoting Malaysia's Prime Minister Mahathir Mohamad, he noted, "This deliberate devaluation of the currency of a country by currency traders purely for profit is a serious denial of the rights of independent nations"[6] (situation in 2010—accurate assessment).

9. Adding to the indictment of Western financial interests, Chossudovsky pointed to the fact that "The appropriation of global wealth through this manipulation of market forces is routinely supported by the IMF's lethal macro-economic interventions which act almost concurrently in ruthlessly disrupting national economies all over the World" (situation in 2010—accurate assessment).

10. Concluding that "'Financial warfare' knows no territorial boundaries; it does not limit its actions to besieging former enemies of the Cold War era." Citing losses in Korea, Indonesia, and Thailand, he asserted that Asia's hard currency losses exceeded $100 billion—sums that ultimately found their way into private hands, leaving "mass poverty, destabilized national economies, and conditions for the 'subsequent plunder of the Asian countries' productive assets by so-called 'vulture foreign investors'"[7] in its wake (situation in 2010—the damage is done).

11. The price of this plunder in Thailand alone was the closedown of 56 domestic banks and financial institutions on orders of the IMF, and unemployment almost doubled overnight.[8] The price in Korea was similar (situation in 2010—the damage is done).

12. Adding insult to injury, he points out that the IMF's 1997 "mediation" caused the shutdown of some 200 companies per day; 4,000 lost worker jobs daily;[9] and an estimated 15,000 bankruptcies in 1998. Korea's losses included most of the nation's largest construction companies, "with combined debts of $20 billion dollars to domestic financial institutions"[10] (situation in 2010—the damage is done).

13. The forced IMF destruction was complete as the process opened the way for "strategic alliances with foreign firms (meaning their eventual control by Western capital) and devaluation . . . of Korean labour." As he put it, "It's now cheaper to buy one of these [high-tech] companies than buy a factory—and you get all the distribution, brand-name recognition and trained labour force free in the bargain."[11]

The destruction is complete. Michael Hudson then details the ultimate outcome—"The Demise of Central Banking."

The Demise of Central Banking

Hudson wryly describes the most tragic of all outcomes of the crisis—a de facto loss of national sovereignty in the form of denying states the ability to control their own money through the central bank. It occurs when "privately held money reserves in the hands of 'institutional speculators' far exceed the limited capabilities of the World's central banks. . . . who [are] . . . no longer able to fight the tide of speculative activity." This places monetary policy "in the hands of private creditors who [can] . . . freeze State budgets, paralyse [*sic*] the payments process, thwart the regular disbursement of wages to millions of workers (as in the former Soviet Union) and precipitate the collapse of production and social programmes [*sic*]." Hudson insisted that this process had affected central banks in China, Latin America, the Middle

East, Canada, and Australia, whose local authorities were powerless to stop it. Hudson also saw the process as the "'dress rehearsal' for the takeover of Japan's financial sector by a handful of Western investment banks ... including Goldman Sachs, Morgan Stanley, and Deutsche Morgan Gruenfell, among others who are buying up Japan's bad bank loans at less than ten percent of their face value." He also cited the political pressure of U.S. officials calling for Japan to sell its troubled assets at a discount. He saw industry takeovers as the next step.[12]

Lastly, Hudson saw the large banks and brokers as "both creditors and institutional speculators ... destabilising [*sic*]) national currencies, ... boosting the volume of dollar denominated debts, and then ... reappear[ing] as creditors with a view to collecting these debts." The same had happened in Indonesia, where "amidst street rioting and in the wake of Suharto's resignation, the privatisation [*sic*] of key sectors of the Indonesian economy ordered by the IMF was entrusted to eight of the World's largest merchant banks including [the former] Lehman Brothers, Credit Suisse-First Boston, Goldman Sachs and UBS/SBC Warburg Dillon Read."[13] The IMF effectively appoints "the World's largest money managers" to: (1) "set countries on fire" and (2) show up as "firemen (under the IMF 'rescue plan') to extinguish the blaze."

Hudson also admits that the central banks' futile efforts to protect themselves with "multi-billion dollar contracts [in the forward foreign exchange market] in a vain attempt to protect their currency" only opened the way for guarantees to the institutional speculators "that they would be able to collect their multi-billion dollar loot." Ironically, all of the money to finance these operations came from "G7 countries including the U.S. Treasury" who made "large lump-sum contributions to these IMF sponsored rescue operations leading to significant hikes in the levels of public debt."[14] He concludes:

> As a result of this vicious circle, a handful of commercial banks and brokerage houses have enriched themselves beyond bounds; they have also increased their stranglehold over governments and politicians around the World. The "big six" Wall Street commercial banks (including Chase, Bank America, Citicorp and J. P. Morgan) and the "big five" merchant banks (Goldman Sachs, [the former] Lehman Brothers, Morgan Stanley and [the former] Salomon Smith Barney) were consulted on the clauses to be included in the bailout agreements. In the case of Korea's short-term debt, Wall Street's largest financial institutions were called in on Christmas Eve (24 December 1997), for high-level talks at the Federal Reserve Bank of New York.[15] [These] global banks have a direct stake in the decline of national currencies [where, in one instance,] the Institute of International Finance (IIF), a Washington

based think-tank representing the interests of some 290 global banks and brokerage houses had "urged authorities in emerging markets to counter upward exchange rate pressures where needed.[16]

The IIF even called upon the IMF to "advocate an environment in which national currencies are allowed to slide."[17] American billionaire and former presidential candidate Steve Forbes asks, "Did the IMF help precipitate the crisis? This agency advocates openness and transparency for national economies, yet it rivals the CIA in cloaking its own operations. ... Did IMF prescriptions exacerbate the illness? These countries' moneys were knocked down to absurdly low levels."[18] Enter the big banks and investment firm "partners" of the IMF.

Christian Mulder, senior economist in the IMF's policy development and review department, examined the substantial risks that unregulated international capital movements created for unsuspecting targets of banks and speculators (special interests). He pointed first to the special interests' steady drumbeat of pressure to deregulate capital flows, including the movement of "hot" and "dirty" money.[19] The IMF Interim Committee rolled over to these demands more than a decade ago (1998) following superficial discussions with the G7 finance ministers,[20] notwithstanding the acknowledgment of IMF Managing Director Michel Camdessus that "a number of developing countries may come under speculative attacks after opening their capital account." The alternative to this risk, he added, was each nation's "adoption of 'sound macroeconomic policies and strong financial systems in member countries' (i.e., the IMF's standard 'economic cure for disaster')."[21] The sheep were headed for the slaughter.

Even more shocking, it was later learned that these IMF decisions to deregulate capital flows was made in secret just two weeks prior to numerous protests worldwide, organized to oppose the OECD's Multilateral Agreement on Investment (MAI), a document giving banks and multinational corporations the right to overturn both foreign investment statutes in the target country, and certain citizen rights in those same jurisdictions.[22] Is there no end to the hubris of wealth? None of these steps even required the added steps of an OECD or WTO agreement.[23] The door to the slaughter pen was slammed shut.

By now, you can clearly see the pattern of reckless disregard for international capital markets driven by transnational special interests, only compounded by the institutional arrogance of Western central banks, both of whom placed emerging economies at even greater risk than they already had. In a world awash with both debt and U.S. dollars, who wins? The private special interests win. Who loses? The U.S. taxpayer and the innocent workers in these emerging economies. It is another case of "Heads, I win; tails, the taxpayer loses." And we add innocent, grossly underpaid nationals struggling to eat to the growing list of victims. It is an astounding irony that the IMF calls this strategy a *rescue* process.

These are not the products of principled leaders. They are the stuff of unseen financial managers and widespread bureaucracies in the international institutions. In either event, they are a significant risk. How is this greater risk to be spotted? As Thomas Jefferson observed during the debate over The Recharter of the Bank Bill in 1809:

> I believe that banking institutions are more dangerous than standing armies. If the American people ever allow private banks to control the issue of their currency, first by inflation, then by deflation, the banks and corporations that grow up around the banks will deprive the people of all of their property until their children wake up homeless on the continent that fathers conquered.[24]

Lesson for Principled Business Leaders. Special interests have silently realigned both the national and the global financial systems to accommodate large bank control. Liquidity and easy credit are the stealth tools used for this purpose. Once the borrower is lured into this trap, the door slams shut with devastating impact. The borrowing enterprise is at risk. The borrowing central bank can be at risk for collapse. The smaller currencies devalue, and the long arm of the international regulatory banks reaches in to take control. Special interests stand by to cherry pick the victim banks, businesses, and investors—all in the name of *rescue*. Principled business leaders beware and be wise. You now know the danger signs.

Lesson for Principled Business Leaders. Business leaders know that the passion for liquidity is loaded with traps for them, the nation, and the wider world. They are well aware of the danger that these practices pose for enterprises, currency, and the future. They must lead the debate for change and for repayment of public debt. They must advocate for paying down the debt resulting from nearly a half-century of political mismanagement and excess liquidity because it eliminates consumer ability to be customers.

Lesson for Principled Business Leaders. Leaders must take on the challenge of achieving genuine fiscal reform, pursuing a more pragmatic monetary policy that limits liquidity, and restoring the value of the dollar. Public debt is now dominant, and debt retirement is the way to restore the financial future of the United States as well as the character and the strength of the dollar.

Lesson for Principled Business Leaders. Retiring debt in an era of excess liquidity is a leadership challenge. But it is a worthy goal. The Federal Reserve Bank can be expected to continue to pour liquidity into the financial system to entice borrowers.

Stretch Goal for My Enterprise. What steps can I take to ensure that my enterprise is not weakened by taking on excess debt while interest rates are low? What steps are being taken to cap interest exposure in the event of sudden interest rate increases?

Stretch Goal for My Enterprise. Is my enterprise able to maintain a current ratio of 2:1 (current assets: current liabilities) for up to five years or until economic and business conditions substantially improve? Is our cash invested to offset the dollar's continuing decline in value?

Questions to Ponder. Is my enterprise careful to assess liquidity traps and/or a jump in the rate of inflation as low interest rates persist? Are there steps that can be taken to limit the adverse impacts of inflation or deflation? Do we know all optional sources of credit for our business and what open credit is available? Have we taken every step necessary to limit financial exposure of excess liquidity that we cannot afford? Have we disposed of any unneeded assets in order to limit financial exposure? Have we cut every cost that does not *drive* our business? Have the capital and production plans been structured so as to postpone optional purchases in time of high interest rates, to cap interest exposure, and/or to take advantage of low interest rates for needed purchases?

Action Steps

Principled Business Leaders Must Be Aware That:

1. Excess liquidity can be a deadly lure into business debt and financial products that fail when conditions change and volatile markets erupt unexpectedly.

2. Central bankers who use money creation to manage inflation are actually creating other problems that may ambush unwitting business owners and managers.

3. Excess liquidity used for increased borrowing may be a silent killer of low-margin products, businesses, and markets.

Suggested Reading

Bonner, William. *Empire of Debt: The Rise of an Epic Financial Crisis*. With Addison Wiggin. Hoboken, NJ: John Wiley & Sons, 2006, 384 pp.
_____. *Financial Reckoning Day: Surviving the Soft Depression of the 21st Century*. Hoboken, NJ: John Wiley & Sons, 2003, 306 pp.

Dent, Harry S., Jr. *The Great Depression Ahead: How to Prosper in the Crash Following the Greatest Boom in History*. New York: Free Press, Simon & Schuster, 2009, 400 pp.

Diamond, Jared. *Collapse: Why Societies Choose to Fail or Succeed*. New York: Penguin Books, 2005, 592 pp.

———. *Guns, Germs, and Steel: The Fate of Human Societies*. New York: W.W. Norton & Company, 1997, 512 pp.

Duncan, Richard. *The Dollar Crisis: Causes, Consequences, Cures*. Singapore: John Wiley & Sons (Asia) Pte Ltd., 2005, 324 pp.

CHAPTER 12

Maintaining Sound Business Pensions

Be the future you want to see.

—Mahatma Ghandi

Give proper attention to those widows who are really in need.

—I Timothy 5:3

The Awakening

Ross Gregory thinks back to that morning after his 2011 graduation. He recalls vividly how his parents woke him early the next morning to say good-bye before leaving on their trip to the West Coast in their new motor home. As they departed, his parents mentioned that there was one more letter for Ross that they had not included in the gift pile from the prior evening.

It was a note from Social Security informing them that the Department of the Treasury had been forced to postpone repayment of IOUs left over from the War in Iraq. Foreign treasury bill notes that had been promised from 2011 to 2013 were due, but there was no money to pay them. This meant that, due to lack of funds, there would be no Social Security payments for Ross's parents for the next 10 years, until 2023.

To this day, Ross is frustrated; he knows that both of his parents had paid Social Security taxes for their entire work lives, and on the first year of their eligibility, they were left high and dry. Ross was shocked then; he is still shocked to this day. And as if that weren't bad enough—there was a second blow.

Ross's parents' employers had been very successful for many years. But as jobs began to move overseas, they revealed that their retirement funds, which had been largely invested in their own companies' common stock and in other U.S. equities, had declined in value to such an extent that they are now worth only half of the amounts contributed, including accrued interest. What had been established as a defined benefit retirement plan became a 50 percent defined contribution plan.

Ross's parents departed on their trip with just enough money to support them for the coming months while the financial mess was being untangled—by Ross. They were on the road for nearly four years when the situation began to improve; and it was only the small jobs they found in cities along the way that enabled them to travel for so long. Finally, Ross's parents received a letter telling them that their pension fund would begin paying 30 percent of their promised retirement benefits. This was made worse by the fact that, by then, the dollar had eroded so badly in the international markets. Even worse, their gas prices had risen sharply because the United States was paying in gold and euros to buy oil. Ross still flinches when he thinks of the unfulfilled promises to his parents.

Issue Summary. Employers are currently staring at one-time pension losses of $2.2 trillion for 2007 to 2009. The combination of the subprime meltdown, the unmanageable national debt, bank bailouts, stimulus bills, ongoing wars, and expanding government have devalued U.S. pension assets at the same time that market forces wiped out a substantial portion of the nation's private wealth.

Our Congress has made sure that their pay and benefits have kept pace with inflation. However, they have passed on the bill for not only their pay raises, but also for all of the added federal initiatives and earmarks they sent home. Unfortunately, tax receipts have grown much more slowly than federal spending, so the debt is piling up at staggering rates.

Low interest rates, excess debt, and a falling dollar have also combined to erode the value all private (and public) pension and retirement plans, most of which had just become fully solvent when the tech bubble burst in 2000. They never recovered. The *dot.bomb* stock market meltdown, the 9/11-attack market meltdown, and the 2007 to 2009 subprime meltdown crippled tens of thousands of private, commercial, and government pensions. The continuing devastating impacts of one meltdown after another have done massive damage to the life savings of many and to the pension funds of many states, counties, and municipalities.

To make matters worse, the federal pension guarantee programs have been running a growing deficit in plan premiums. A steady stream of payouts since 2002 to bolster failed plans has left the PBGC (Pension Benefit Guaranty Corporation) grasping for both new premium income and new ways to lower its future risks. Ross Gregory is not the only one who will be stunned in 2023. Each of our children will be shocked as well when the bill comes due.

Today's pensions may be tomorrow's only source of income for many retiring baby boomers and other seniors. A pile of IOUs has replaced much of the Social Security Trust Fund, because its cash resources were used by the Federal Treasury to pay for 40-plus years of budget deficits and overspending. Unfortunately, these IOUs are non-negotiable and cannot be sold to return the funds to the Social Security Trust Fund. The dates when experts estimate that the Social Security Trust Fund will be insolvent range between 2017 and 2040. (Factors such as liquidity, inflation, and others drive this wide variance in estimates.)

Commercial and public service pension underfunding in the past decade took its toll as the heady world of an expanding economy and the raging stock markets of the 1990s were replaced by a burst tech bubble; the bankruptcies of companies like Enron, Bear Stearns, and Lehman Brothers; and the subprime meltdown. And the core problems remain unresolved. PBGC, which insures more than 100,000 private pension funds and several thousand multi-employer pension funds, is also underfunded and underinsured. Similarly, federal insurance programs for guaranteed student loans, rural electrification loans, ship-building loans, small business loans, disaster loans, and flood insurance are all in line for more funding to meet growing actuarial demands. Joining them, the Veteran's Administration insures the individual home mortgages of veterans, and the Federal Housing Administration (FHA) insures consumer mortgages.

The potential obligations are staggering. First, business leaders need to consider the private pension dilemma.

Where Are Private Pensions?

Charles Morris, author of The Century Foundation report *Apart at the Seams: The Collapse of Private Pension and Health Care Protections*, provides valuable insight on "A System Under Stress." Morris nostalgically recalls the long-standing goal of many in the post-war workforce to join a big company with a defined benefit pension plan—one that promised lifelong monthly benefits for the worker and his or her spouse. It was truly the perfect end to a long work career. Then came the collapses.

First there was Studebaker in 1963, which defaulted on its pension commitments. Within a decade, then-Senator Jacob Javits of New York led the fight to pass the Employee Retirement Income Security Act (ERISA) of 1974, which he hailed as the ultimate security for the worker. PBGC was created by ERISA to insure these promised benefits.

Among other things, ERISA mandated employers to set aside reserves to meet their pension obligations. By mid-2005, Morris reports that private employers had reserved $1.8 trillion in pension assets against defined benefit pension obligations estimated at that time to be $2.2 trillion. Preferring high-grade bonds at the outset, employers soon learned that common stock could grow in value, while it decreased their annual funding obligations. A good solution in the strong equity markets of the 1990s, this approach hit big snags in bad market years—especially after 2000, when market drops demanded more funding, as falling profits limited employers' ability to contribute. "The negative swing in corporate pension fund positions has been roughly $750 billion since 1999—from a $300 billion surplus to an estimated $450 billion deficit as of mid-2005."[1]

The list of major companies in serious default (pension obligations at or greater than the company's market value) was staggering. Delta Airlines, for example, had pension obligations 13 times its market value; General Motors, 4.7 times higher; Ford, 2.7 times higher; Lucent, 1.9 times higher; and U.S. Steel, 1.4 times higher. It is no surprise that some of these names are now extinct, and others are either in or headed for receivership. Pension obligations are at the center of their financial stress.

Companies have found various ways to approach the problem, most notably seeking one or another means to decouple them from their defined benefit pension funding obligations. One is borrowing; another is increasing the funding from profits (thereby cutting reported profits and stock value); a third is selling out to another company (as a way to get rid of the pension plan); a fourth is the strategic bankruptcy; and the list continues. All of these are products of modern financial engineering, and employees live in continuous anxiety about the possible loss of long-promised benefits. Morris assesses the losses: "Collectively, it appears that United, Delta, and Northwestern [sic] airlines, and the auto parts maker Delphi will be relieved of some $32 billion in pension liabilities through the bankruptcy process."[2] (Last-minute Congressional legislation in 2007 saved the three airlines from dumping their pensions on the PBGC.)

Clearly, the defined benefit plan is a thing of the past. Only 20 percent of private sector workers now participate in defined benefit pensions, and "that number will drop to the vanishing point over the next ten years or so."[3] Only federal, state, county, and local employees routinely belong to defined benefit plans. But many of those public plans are also in funding trouble.

Where Are Public Pensions?

These government employee pension plans are facing staggering funding obligations. Morris notes, "the unfunded liabilities of state and local defined benefit plans are even higher than in the private sector."[4] Pension contributions often outpace many other government budget items, including education. Many states are turning to bond issues to enable them to catch up on pension funding. And their accounting standards and disclosure rules are being tightened, as well.[5] Employers are also aware of these realities.

The icon of U.S. technology, IBM, saw the signs of change as markets dipped in early 1999. Within weeks, the corporate giant had moved tens of thousands of its senior employees from the IBM defined benefit plan to a "personal pension account," saving an estimated $200 million of contributions in the first year alone. More recently, it has also systematically lowered the average age and annual wages of its professional staff through regular layoffs (9,000 in 2009 alone), while it hires aggressively (47,960 new hires outside the United States in 2009) in lower wage international markets.[6] Then there is another important dimension to this pension dilemma—health and dental benefits for both private and government employees.

Termed *other employee benefit plans* (OEBP), state and local plans are also required to fund these health care benefits "on an actuarially sound basis" for active workers. The retiree benefits, termed *other post-employment benefit* (OPEB) obligations, pay retiree health, dental, and similar obligations. The Government Accounting Standards Board (GASB) recently published stringent pension accounting guidelines for state, county, and local plans, effective December 15, 2006, with accounting instructions for such plans. Paid from current revenues, these obligations have a material impact on government balance sheets and their financial and bond ratings. Again the funding and accounting must be done "on an actuarially sound basis."[7] The 2007 to 2009 meltdown has decimated many of these pension plans, making the challenge all the greater—especially since up to 60 percent of state, county, and local employees are eligible to retire in 2010!

Estimates of this added liability range between $700 billion and up to 10 times the current liability for retiree health care because of the coming wave of state, county, and local retirements. The task becomes all the more complicated when one considers the differences between contractual responsibilities (pensions) and other non-contractual benefits (i.e., health care). These GASB regulations are similar to the rules that the Financial Accounting Standards Board (FASB) had already placed on private firms in 1992 (SFAS 106).[8]

Several compliance strategies have been developed, many of them with a view toward removing cost burdens from the employers. E. McNichol, writing on the state fiscal crisis, describes the most popular of these steps—moving the responsibility to the employee—in a paper for the Center on Budget and Policy Priorities.

> Shifting more costs to retirees can be an option, along with trying to limit future OPEB obligations by changing benefit packages for new employees. One strategy that is popular (and essentially required) for addressing OPEB costs is to set up a trust fund. A trust fund meets the new accounting standard requirement that an irrevocable source is identified for meeting OPEB obligations. It also has the advantage of allowing governments more flexibility in the use of investment options. Like pension funds, OPEB trust funds would permit investments in equities and other potentially higher yielding investment vehicles. A potentially attractive option that a trust fund may allow is the ability to issue OPEB bonds to cover part or even all of a government's OPEB liability.[9]

A senior economist from the Federal Reserve Bank of Chicago cautions that OEPB bonds can have a hidden cost when they are sold—higher interest rates required to cover federal taxes:

> Like pension bonds, these are essentially an arbitrage strategy, where the bond issuer anticipates that the investment yield they will receive from the bond assets will exceed the interest that will be paid to bond holders. Also like pension bonds, the OPEB bonds are not free from federal taxes so they must carry slightly higher interest rates than tax-free investments.[10]

The National Governors Association and the National Association of State Budget Officers examined the private sector impacts of these OEPB funds with some daunting conclusions.

> OPEB is still a major concern for the private sector. It is estimated that for the 337 companies in the S&P 500 that have OPEB obligations, the funding ratio is around 27% (versus 88% for pensions). For the 282 companies with the most complete financial records, the unfunded liability in 2005 was estimated at $292 billion versus an unfunded pension liability of $149 billion. OPEB liability is concentrated in Ford and GM. Their unfunded liability alone is $94 billion, representing 32% of the S&P 500's total. (These two companies also have 13% of the total pension under-funding.) Telecom is the other industry where OPEB is a significant issue.[11]

Both public organizations and private enterprises must make pension planning and funding a high priority for the sake of maintaining high employee confidence and morale.

Lesson for Principled Business Leaders. Business must first give an honest accounting of the current state of their promised pensions to all covered employees. Principled leaders seek to care for employees fairly.

Lesson for Principled Business Leaders. Businesses must assess their ongoing costs, and consider added funding options, including higher employee contributions. The recent financial meltdown took away nearly half of the value of many pensions; it is now time to rebuild them. Business must lead the way by example.

Lesson for Principled Business Leaders. Business may also wish to lead the advocacy of a national debt repayment strategy. This would not only restore Social Security and rebuild underfunded public pension funds but might also advocate for all public pension funds to be funded on an actuarially sound basis (rather than pay pensions from current tax revenues).

Stretch Goal for My Enterprise. Are our pension obligations structured in such a way that we can fulfill our obligations for pension contributions if or when our gross revenues drop by 50 percent?

Questions to Ponder. Do our employees take full responsibility for their pension plans, or do they trust *us* in our fiduciary responsibility for pension plan management? Have we provided guidelines to our fiduciaries to ensure the best possible management of our employee pension plans? Is there full transparency in reporting the status of pension plans? Are our employees able to allocate pension assets in a prudent manner in the current economic environment? Are pension assets allocated to common shares of our enterprise in an imprudent manner? Is there excess risk in our pension policy and asset allocation policies?

Action Steps

Principled Business Leaders Must Realize and Change Policies as Needed in Light of the Fact That:

1. Pensions are at great risk in volatile financial markets and in the weakening dollar environment. They must plan and act accordingly to preserve value and fulfill promises to employees.

2. Defined benefit plans increase employer risk in volatile financial markets. Defined contribution plans lower employer risk and can share contribution responsibility with employees.

3. Employees must contribute as large a share as possible to private, defined contribution plans in order to better manage the fixed cost burdens of enterprises.

4. OEBP obligations require diligence by both the employer and the employee, ensuring that prevention, healthy lifestyle, and regular health examinations are all part of a total process.

5. Investing employee pensions in one's enterprise increases the employer's fiduciary responsibility. Enron and others destroyed the trust of millions of innocent employees who had invested in this way.

Key Measures of Success

Measurement Date	Funding Level (%)	Target Pension Funding Addition Amounts ($)	Source of Funds	Date to Complete
1. __/__/_____				
2. __/__/_____				
3. __/__/_____				
4. __/__/_____				
5. __/__/_____				

Suggested Reading

Cooper, Jim. *Financial Report of the United States*. Nashville: Nelson Current, Thomas Nelson, Inc., 2006, 263 pp.

Hacker, Jacob S. *The Great Risk Shift: The Assault on American Jobs, Families, Health Care, and Retirement and How You Can Fight Back*. New York: Oxford University Press, 2006, 272 pp.

Parker, Thornton. *What if Boomers Can't Retire? How to Build Real Security, Not Phantom Wealth*. San Francisco: Berrett-Koehler Publishers, Inc., 2002, 288 pp.

Wattenberg, Ben J. *Fewer: How the New Demography of Depopulation Will Shape Our Future*. Chicago: Ivan R. Dee, 2004, 241 pp.

Business and Our Nation's Financial Stability

Banks found new ways to use money, when the old ones worked so well.

—Warren Buffett

Changing Course

Ross is beginning to wonder why so many generations suffer the same bubbles and reversals, one after another. There must be some insiders driving this whole thing, he thought. During a conversation with his father, he was reminded that three generations of Americans had made no headway in retiring their public debts and that families had been living on credit for much of the same period. Ross and his father both agreed that there was obviously something more to the situation than meets the eye. The special interests had been driving the culture of debt, and they had run the whole economy into the ground in the process.

Obviously, some major modifications are needed to restore the nation's finances. Without a significant course change, all consumers, young and old, would be working for the government at one level or another for most of their lives. Meanwhile, interest costs, energy costs, and (next) food costs would be out of control. Then again, Ross thought, maybe there *is* a way to get at this.

Why couldn't business leaders come together to demand a course change? The United States can take two big steps to improve its finances, infrastructure, and environment in short order. First, we start paying off all public debt. Then, we restore all of the Social Security, Medicare, Medicaid, and pension plans that are underfunded. We do this by charging a transaction fee on all money transactions and applying the proceeds of this fee to retiring public debt—90 percent for federal debt and 10 percent for state and local debt. The idea of how quickly this would free us of public debt excites Ross. Once restored, these trust and pension funds can invest in public infrastructure restoration investment grade bonds issued by cities, states, counties, and local authorities so that the funds receive income on their money and stay abreast of their obligations. Borrowers would guarantee repayment.

Then, business leaders can recommend that every young American between the ages of 18 and 24 spend two years in public service and that the Congress make some form of public service mandatory for all young adults. They would be paid the minimum wage, and they would devote 4,000 work hours over a two-year period to environmental projects, service projects in schools, or other public institutions; or in international work projects to help the nation's allies abroad. This would solve two problems. First, it would demonstrate a serious intent to improve our environment and infrastructure nationwide. Second, it would help to alleviate the losses of the 60 percent of public servants at the state, county, and local levels who started retiring in 2010.

Ross is truly invigorated. America *can* be restored. *Wow!*

Paying Off Our National Debt and Unfunded Liabilities

Let's take a closer look at Ross's ideas. Table 13.1 outlines a 15-year plan to retire all federal, state, county, and local debt while it restores underfunded pension plans, builds an infrastructure development fund, and builds reserves at every level to restore the finances of all 84,000 units of government in the United States.

Ross's plan is based upon the realization that the yearly total amount of all financial transactions in the United States is $850 trillion. Most of this volume is comprised of currency purchase and sale transactions ($3 trillion per day, leaving approximately $100 trillion in transactions for the balance of the economy). Ross's plan anticipates some downturn in overall economic activity, particularly in currency trading, due to the 2 percent fee on transactions. Notwithstanding the lower transactions levels, the nation is able to retire its federal debt in two years. Moreover, the plan restores the Social Security Trust Fund to solvency in three years, and it builds enough reserves to pay all current unfunded federal liabilities in 10 years after debt repayment is completed. (That's right; laws have been passed that can't come close to being funded in full for another decade!)

Table 13.1 Repayment of U.S. Debt in U.S. Dollars ($ Billions)

Year	Annual Transactions	Annual Fee Income	Federal Income Share 90%	State/Local Income Share 10%	Federal Interest per Year at 4.3%	Federal Debt Balance	Federal Unfunded Liabilities Balance	Social Security Debt Balance	Medicare Unfunded Liabilities Balance	State/Local Debt Balance	State/Local Unfunded Liabilities
Annual payment Principal amount	850,000.0	2%			480.3	12,100.0	5,000.0	15,000.0	85,900.0	2,200.0	2,200.0
YEAR-END BALANCES OUTSTANDING											
2011	500,000.0	10,000.0	9,000.0	1,000.0	480.0	3,580.0				1,200.0	
2012	525,000.0	10,500.0	9,450.0	1,050.0	77.0	782.0	(1,160.2)	13,839.8		150.0	
2013	551,250.0	11,025.0	9,922.5	1,102.5				3,917.3			1,247.5
2014	578,812.5	11,576.3	10,418.6	1,157.6					79,398.68		89.88
2015	607,753.1	12,155.1	10,939.6	1,215.5					68,459.12		(1,125.63)
2016	638,140.8	12,762.8	11,486.5	1,276.3					56,972.58		(2,401.91)
2017	670,047.8	13,401.0	12,060.9	1,340.1					44,911.72		(3,742.01)
2018	703,550.2	14,071.0	12,663.9	1,407.1					32,247.82		(5,149.11)
2019	738,727.7	14,774.6	13,297.1	1,477.5					18,950.72		(6,626.56)
2020	775,664.1	15,513.3	13,962.0	1,551.3					4,988.77		(8,177.89)
2021	814,447.3	16,288.9	14,660.1	1,628.9					(9,671.28)		(9,806.79)
2022	855,169.7	17,103.4	15,393.1	1,710.3					(25,064.34)		(11,517.13)
2023	897,928.2	17,958.6	16,162.7	1,795.9					(41,227.05)		(13,312.98)
2024	942,824.6	18,856.5	16,970.8	1,885.6					(58,197.89)		(15,198.63)
2025	989,965.8	19,799.3	17,819.4	1,979.9					(76,017.27)		(17,178.56)

Furthermore, all known state, county, and local debt is also paid off in two years. Then state, county, and local pension underfunding liabilities are restored in four years, and financial reserves for future liabilities are created thereafter. All of the nation's 84,000 units of government can be solvent by 2014. The alternative is for states, counties, and localities to raise taxes every year to avoid being on the brink of bankruptcy.

There is also a benefit to the federal income tax fund, in that the transaction fee will first pay all current interest on the federal debt. As a result, and because interest on the federal debt will have been paid by the transaction fee, the federal budget will receive an income boost of nearly $500 billion in the first year to lower its deficit and to provide funds for appropriated programs. A second benefit is that debt relief will allow Congress to take the time it needs to seriously address health care, Medicare, Social Security, defense, environmental cleanup, infrastructure rebuilding, and the myriad of other priorities that face the twenty-first century United States, while the transaction fee returns the nation's economy to solvency.

A third benefit to the business community and to government at all levels is that funds (guaranteed AAA investment grade bonds from the various trust funds) can be available to invest in secure, investment-grade bonds that will be used to rebuild local water systems, electric grids, renewable energy projects, wastewater treatment systems, and aging infrastructure of many types. States, counties, and localities will at last be in command of the resources to rebuild their infrastructure, as long as their credit ratings are strong and there are buyers for their bonds. Investments in bonds will be limited to one-third of total project costs; they will be in first lien position; and repayment will be guaranteed by the borrower.

Fourth, and most importantly, the business community will at long last have a sound economic platform upon which it can begin to rebuild individual markets and the nation's economic strength. The danger to the U.S. dollar will have been eliminated, and the nation's credit at home and abroad will again enjoy the confidence of the investment world.

If business does not take the lead in bringing about these changes for the better—notwithstanding the short-term impact on some transactions in the currency markets—it will be constantly bombarded with new taxes in every state, county, and locality where it operates as governments struggle to balance their budgets. And the Federal Reserve will be able to stop growing the money supply and weakening the dollar.

Role of the Federal Reserve Bank in the Debt Spree   The Federal Reserve Bank has been at the center of the spending binge for the past 20 years. It has continuously expanded the money supply, resulting in interest rates being low during most of this period. Consumers have overspent liberally because credit was so easy to obtain and inflation was low.

Unfortunately, many consumers are now involuntary servants to banks and credit card companies, and they have limited credit to purchase from businesses. This *must* change, and business has to lead the charge. Both sales and employment will expand when consumers are again solvent.

Role of Business in Demonstrating Energy Leadership and Renewal
Consumers and business alike have been the beneficiaries of relatively inexpensive energy for four decades. Americans and businesses built a lifestyle around cheap energy. Low energy prices enabled them to ignore calls for conservation, as U.S. consumers set new world records for per capita consumption. Unfortunately, cheap energy is no longer a reality. Transportation, a foundation for business and consumers, is the biggest user of energy. So business must find innovative ways to lower its share of per capita energy consumption. Imported oil is the first target. The United States can no longer be the dominant force in world oil consumption. Business must lead this change.

Role of Business in Renewing Government, Renewing the Environment, and Renewing the Nation's Infrastructure   These three causes can become a hallmark of the modern-day United States. While they have received much lip service, no real service and no real accomplishments have occurred for nearly a half-century. All three causes need *real service* in the twenty-first century. This need can be an opportunity for business, once the desired outcomes are carefully defined in each cause.

- If renewing government includes replacing the 60 percent of total state, county, and local employees who are to retire starting in 2010, business can help with recruitment, training, process design, and systems modernization and streamlining.

- If renewing the environment is a true priority, business can aid with project formulation, project support, project management, and logistics. It can also help out with supervision of brownfield cleanup, reforestation, and countless other environmental innovations that use the 18- to 24-year-old workforce.

- If renewing the infrastructure is a true priority, business can again support project formulation, project support, project management, and logistics. Business can also assist with engineering designs and program management.

For all three causes, the workforce needed to carry out the work has typically been the constraint to achieving real change. No solution has been advanced that realistically undertakes these enormous needs, and money spent has been only a token. If renewing government and education, the environment, or the nation's infrastructure is truly a priority, then the United States needs to call on those who have the passion, the energy, and the time to do the work: our nation's young adults (18 to 24 years). They have been the most outspoken in calling for renewal; they will be able to match words with deeds. And they have the most at stake for the future. Business can recruit them, train them, and manage them if government is unable to do so. It is time for *everyone* to be counted. Young adults in the 18- to 24-year range have a central role in this turnaround—two years of public service. That is their contribution to match public debt payoff—debt that they inherit if it is not retired.

Lesson for Principled Business Leaders. If business does not lead the call for a 2 percent transaction fee to repay all of the nation's public debt, it will be facing an endless demand for new taxes, a shrinking market to serve, and the loss of its economic platform for the long term.

Lesson for Principled Business Leaders. If business does not lead the call for mobilization of all young adults in the United States to accomplish much-needed renewal work in many sectors, it will experience a steadily shrinking consumer market, an endless series of new taxes, or a constant dribble of much money to special interests, while renewal needs go unmet.

Lesson for Principled Business Leaders. Business has much to offer in aiding the accomplishment of the often-mentioned but never achieved goals for the nation's renewal in education, government, environmental cleanup, infrastructure, and sense of community for noble purposes. The challenge is to find the right match between community needs and enterprise capability.

Stretch Goal for My Enterprise. Is our enterprise ready and able to lead the call in our community to retire all public debt at all levels?

Stretch Goal for My Enterprise. Is our enterprise ready and able to provide recruitment, training, job placement, logistics support, program management, project management, accounting, or other services in combination with young adult staff persons to advance the causes of renewal of education, government, environmental cleanup, or infrastructure within its distinctive competences?

Stretch Goal for My Enterprise. Is there a larger role that our enterprise can undertake in the broader community (federal, state, county, or local level) to promote: (1) best practices on a systematic basis; (2) improved self-regulation, licensing, training, or higher standards; or (3) improved regulation from industry associations or government? What role can our enterprise fulfill in these important steps?

Questions to Ponder. What crisis will it take to mobilize business to step forward and provide leadership for the renewal of the United States?

When will business bring best practices to the nation's most nagging, unresolved problems?

Action Steps

Principled Business Leaders Must:

1. Take a leadership role in demonstrating a new ethic in sound financial management.
2. Lead the call to repay U.S. public debt instead of fighting to secure benefits at the expense of taxpayers.
3. Take a much greater role in industry self-regulation or face the possible loss of their economic platform in the coming years of highly volatile financial markets.
4. Convince Americans that the nation cannot borrow its way out of financial turmoil and into prosperity.
5. Bring realism and candor to eliminate debt, deception, delusion, and denial in every area of institutional and national financial leadership.
6. Insist on sound, adequately funded public pensions at the federal, state, county, and local levels.

Key Measures of Success

Measurement Item	Date	Balance ($ Billions)	Amount Paid Down ($ Billions)	Target Date to Retire
1. Enterprise debt				
2. Federal debt				
3. Social Security debt				
4. Federal unfunded debt				
5. Medicare unfunded debt				
6. State/local debt				

Suggested Reading

Hacker, Jacob S. *The Great Risk Shift: The Assault on American Jobs, Families, Health Care, and Retirement and How You Can Fight Back.* New York: Oxford University Press, 2006, 272 pp.

Kunstler, James Howard. *The Long Emergency—Surviving the Converging Catastrophes of the Twenty-First Century.* New York: Atlantic Monthly Press, 2005, 320 pp.

Peterson, Peter G. *Running on Empty.* New York: Farrar, Straus and Giroux, 2004, 239 pp.

Vanden Heuvel, Katrina. *Meltdown: How Greed and Corruption Shattered Our Financial System and How We Can Recover.* New York: Nation Books, 2009, 336 pp.

Managing Vital Resources

Water—Business and a New Direction

All the water that will ever be is, right now.

—*National Geographic*, October 1993

The Awakening

Ross's friend Larry Fitzgerald works for the local water department with Anita Pierson, another former classmate of his. Larry works in the operations group, and Anita is in accounting. While both love their work, they also know that there are a lot of problems within this sector of local government. As the three of them talk over dinner, they begin to understand that the water problem in the United States goes far beyond their own backyard.

First, there are the local issues. Since their hometown is nearing its 100th birthday, the town water distribution system is breaking down monthly with pipe bursts, undiscovered underground leaks, and countless urgent local system repair demands arriving daily. Larry also reports that the city has had no success in switching from chlorine to more modern disinfection technology. Local chlorine distributors have made it clear that chlorine is the only way the city will go.

Anita reports on the plant condition and overdue maintenance and modernization plans. A recent bond issue failed to pass the voters, and an international company has been lobbying the City Council to buy the entire system in exchange for a major investment in modernization. The last vote turned down the proposition by a margin of one. All of the employees are very anxious for their jobs and for their inability to find a single acquisition that paid off for the local consumers.

The three local water systems that sold out in their state still have not been modernized after nearly 10 years. Nonetheless, local rates were raised immediately, and service quality dropped substantially. There is not a single success story—except, that is, for the buyers. Unsurprisingly, Larry and Anita do not see a solution with that approach. But what about the rest of the nation?

Ross describes some research that he has done on the larger environmental issues relating to water—research that has led to some deeply troubling findings. He explains that, despite the Clean Water Act of 1972, more than 20,000 waterways and streams in the United States are still polluted in one or more ways that affect the habitat, human use, and local human health. He learns that the cleanup process is decades behind and that enforcement of the cleanup statutes is spotty at best. Ross has also discovered wide gaps between the work of the federal, state and local governments on unresolved water rights issues, particularly in the western United States. He is also shocked to discover that the underground aquifers in many coastal areas are badly drawn down or tainted by saltwater. Moreover, the nation's biggest aquifer in the Midwest is badly drawn down—something that is even further complicated by the use of water to produce ethanol for energy use. Unfortunately, it takes 40 precious gallons of water to produce 1 gallon of ethanol. The three friends wonder who is responsible for this imbalance. And when Ross examines the water issues in Tucson, Arizona—one of the great growth areas of the United States—he is shocked to learn that the aquifer has been drawn down from its nineteenth century level of 12 feet below mean sea level to 524 feet below mean sea level. Tucson may be running out of water, he concludes.

Ross, Larry, and Anita agree to talk more during the coming week, but Ross can't help leaving with a deep sense of dismay.

Issue Summary. Water is one of a few defining issues of the twenty-first century. The United States has a growing water problem because of high demands in water-starved regions, rapidly dropping water tables, and extensive saltwater encroachment in many coastal regions. Unfortunately, water conservation is a low priority. Key allocations of water are also inefficient, because they are based on the principle of *first come/first served* and local politics; and the small fees don't compensate for the lost resource.

Water is also one of the two key resource issues that will determine the course of twenty-first century international relations; the other is energy. The water/energy balance is also a seldom discussed, but critical, determinant of future economic growth in the United States.

The World's Water Picture in Brief

One of many reference web sites on water puts this vital resource in perspective, as it points out that while "70% of Earth's surface is water ... 97.5% is saltwater and (a precious little) 2.5% is fresh water." Less than 1% of this 2.5% amount of freshwater is accessible (the majority is frozen in ice caps or exists as soil moisture). According to the site, "We currently use about 50% of the world's readily available water."[1] It goes on to note:

> Nearly 70% of that fresh water is frozen in the icecaps of Antarctica and Greenland; most of the remainder is present as soil moisture, or lies in deep underground aquifers as groundwater not accessible to human use.[2]

> [Surprisingly,] less than 1% of the world's fresh water (~0.007% of all water on earth) is accessible for direct human uses. This is the water found in lakes, rivers, reservoirs and those underground sources that are shallow enough to be tapped at an affordable cost. Only this amount is regularly renewed by rain and snowfall, and is therefore available on a sustainable basis. Since antiquity, irrigation, drainage, and impoundment have been the three types of water control having a major impact on landscapes and water flows. Since the dawn of irrigated agriculture at least 5000 years ago, controlling water to grow crops has been the primary motivation for human alteration of freshwater supplies. Today, principal demands for fresh water are for irrigation, household and municipal water use, and industrial uses. Most supplies come from surface runoff, although mining of "fossil water" from underground aquifers is an important source in some areas. The pattern of water withdrawal over the past 300 years shows the dramatic increases in this century.[3]

America's water appetite, however, exceeds almost any in the world. A recent Russian study on water usage levels by world region indicates that citizens of North and Central America, including Americans, "use 1,861 cubic meters of water per year or:

- 45% more water per capita per year than Europeans (1,280 cubic meters)

- 760% more water per capita per year than Africans (245 cubic meters)
- 359% more water per capita per year than Asians (519 cubic meters)
- 389% more water per capita per year than South Americans (478 cubic meters)
- 261% more water per capita per year than the former Soviet Union (713 cubic meters)[4]

The United States has much work to do in managing its overuse of water and in rebuilding its aquifers. For example, the highest population growth states in the east, southwest, and west also have the largest and growing water shortages and water runoff losses. Additionally, "With 28 percent of the U.S. population, the arid West accounts for 80 percent of the average water consumed."[5] The same budget provided funds for a National Water Census to evaluate the condition of aquifers, reservoir storage, surface and groundwater flows, water quality, and water use. It also launched a competitive grant program for water conservation and basin studies. The total funding recommended was $21 million.[6] (Chapter 17 contains infrastructure renewal estimates that call for $1.28 billion just to rehabilitate canals and rivers and $1,314.6 billion to rehabilitate and modernize dams, levees [291 of which are in failing condition], and locks. The U.S. government is officially making a 0.002 percent down payment on its water resources recovery.) Perhaps there is an opportunity for business to lead the way through *public-private partnerships*.

Public-Private Partnerships (PPPs)—Pathway to Business Contributions

In addition to taking the steps that can be taken within enterprises to manage resources, business leaders may wish to consider forming or joining a public-private partnership to address needs that are beyond their immediate business. An issue like water is important to both the enterprise and to the community, especially for large-volume water users. It can also be important if the community water supply system or the wastewater treatment systems are outdated, insecure, or in need of modernization. A PPP may be a catalyst for many businesses to become involved in finding solutions to water shortages.

Washington's Center for Strategic and International Studies (CSIS) has been quite successful in developing and implementing a PPP business model, which worked quite well in the international arena. George Handy, a distinguished former military officer, managed the CSIS program from

1992 to 2006 very effectively. He offers eight key factors for success, which are summarized below:

1. **Define clear outcomes.** Action commissions function best when they work directly on affordable issues that have clear, practical solutions with a good potential near-term impact.

2. **Develop a work plan that drives partnerships and not difference.** Successful commissions sought projects in which (a) government had a clear interest in a successful outcome; (b) government was willing to hear and, if possible, implement sound recommendations; (c) business and private investors could point to as obstacle(s) to growth; and (d) businesses were willing to invest resources and/or expertise.

3. **Conduct open solutions-oriented discussions.** The working group process was open and transparent, with all viewpoints presented. However, discussion on the underlying problems was minimized, and was instead focused on developing and agreeing upon practical solutions that would work in the country in question.

4. **Emphasize proven best practices.** Avoid meeting time or group discussions devoted to personal opinions or individual bias. Instead, highlight local and global best practices that can be adapted to regional needs and conditions.

5. **Communicate to link people, successful outcomes, and new ideas.** Successful commissions had detailed, accurate, understandable, and timely communications that emphasized partnership successes, openness, and effective use of participants' time. Good communication often leads to consensus-based solutions.

6. **Involve prestigious leaders and experienced professionals.** Working groups benefited from the volunteer contributions of established local professionals, because there was a mutual desire for practical, shared solutions. The resulting recommendations had strong local support and could often be applied globally. Government responded positively when high-profile professional and business leaders collaborated.

7. **Develop projects that solve issues of concern to both business and government.** Recommendations often began with small, measurable steps as the basis to pursue larger, long-term objectives. Government also benefits, as does business, when small steps of progress can be publicized.

8. **Give credit often and accurately.** Seek to recognize government, when appropriate, to speed additional steps toward long-term solutions.[7]

Lesson for Principled Business Leaders. Business can no longer be a bystander in either domestic or international water issues. At present, many water users are overly demanding, and conservation is a low priority. Business must be a leader in water conservation, and in demanding water infrastructure modernization. Homeowners will follow the example once they recognize its importance.

Lesson for Principled Business Leaders. Business has an opportunity as an independent but interested partner (when the business case exists) to lead or to join a PPP whose purpose is to lead the transformation of local and regional water programs and water conservation.

Lesson for Principled Business Leaders. Business can demonstrate innovation in water conservation, water reuse, and process water management when water is a vital component of its own operations.

Stretch Goal for My Enterprise. Can our enterprise become a leader in demonstrating prudent water management in its own operations? Can we join with others to participate in a PPP aimed at modernizing local systems in the communities where we work? Can we make water a pivotal resource issue alongside energy to lead an enlightened enterprise for the twenty-first century? Am I prepared to take a leadership role in addressing the water issue in my community and in my enterprise? Am I prepared to pay more for water in order to achieve modernization of our local water system?

Questions to Ponder. How strategic is water to the future of our enterprise? What are the best practices that good managers implement in the use and conservation of water? Who is setting an example that our enterprise can emulate in the future? Can our enterprise cut its water use in half in one year, and what would it take to do so?

Action Steps

Principled Business Leaders Must Adapt to New Realities in the Resource That Is Most Often Taken for Granted by Developing New Policies, Which Recognize That:

1. Water is one of the world's scarcest resources.

2. Effective water conservation and use is essential for enterprise users of water.

3. New technologies for desalinization, irrigation, and rainfall collection may be good market opportunities for businesses.

4. Modernization of enterprise and community water infrastructure is a high national priority for this decade.

Key Measures of Success

Water Issue	Goal (Gals.)	Priority Function (s)	Person (s) Responsible	Date to Complete
1. Water conservation				
2. Water reuse				
3. Process water reuse				
4. Water partnership(s)				
5. Water development				

Case Histories

3M: Reusing Wash Water in a New Jersey Plant

In Belle Mead, New Jersey, in the United States, a 3M facility developed a process to reuse the wash water generated when making colored roofing granules.

In the past, the Belle Mead facility sent their wash water off-site for disposal. Today, Belle Mead's new system recycles the wash water back into the process, eliminating the use of fresh water in colored granule production. This new system reduced over 200,000 gallons of annual off-site wash water disposal without increasing manufacturing cost or affecting color quality.

Source: Global Environmental Management Initiative.

3M: Upgrading a Pure Oxygen Wastewater Treatment System in Illinois

Upgrading the oxygen treatment system at a 3M wastewater treatment facility has brought increased efficiency, capacity, and annual savings.

The 3M Cordova, Illinois, facility in the United States treats process wastes on-site at its wastewater treatment facility. The facility treats its organic waste biologically by introducing oxygen into aeration basins. Oxygen had been provided by an air blower system, but 3M replaced the blower system with a pure oxygen system in 2001. Liquid oxygen is transported from off-site, vaporized, and injected into the activated sludge treatment system.

The new system has decreased energy and chemical usage, reduced emissions of volatile organic compounds, and increased the treatment efficiency and capacity of the wastewater treatment system. The annual savings resulting from the system replacement project is $85,700.

Source: Global Environmental Management Initiative.

A National Young Adult Action Plan to Preserve Vital Resources

The last seven chapters discussing the nation's economic peril have largely ignored a second mega-tsunami that our country is facing in its near-term future—massive demographic shifts. This pattern results from lower current birthrates; retirement of 77 million baby boomers which began in 2007; retirement of 40 percent of all federal and 60 percent of all state, county, and local employees starting in 2010; and substantial workforce dislocations occasioned by the economic meltdown of 2007 to 2009. The 44 million unqualified legal or illegal immigrants and 5 million expired visa holders in the United States at present cannot fill these massive voids, nor should they.

Moreover, government at all levels is somewhat helpless to address these changes because it is *broke*. Benefit systems will be strained. Investment markets will be further depressed, as retirement funds are withdrawn and seniors exit the workforce. Tax revenues will also drop, and stresses on government will grow. And the major issues of vital resource management in Part III of this book will go unresolved, unless the federal government takes a second strategic step.

The United States must confront the continuing demographic tsunami with a workforce tsunami of its own—its 18- to 24-year-old young adults—a group with a passion for clean water, clean energy, a better environment, and a rebuilt infrastructure. Appendix B indicates that there are nearly 40 million of these young adults in the United States as of 2008. Again, how can they help?

Each of these young adults will provide two years of mandatory paid universal public service at some point between the ages of 18 and 24 as a first step. They can work after high school, after college, or even during a college break. They will be paid the minimum wage, and they will have a GED before they finish if they do not already have a high school diploma. This national service corps will replace some coming losses of public servants at the federal, state, county, or local levels. They will enable states, counties, or localities to compensate for worker losses. They will also enable government to lower their already bloated short-term costs and overspending. They will help a *broke* nation get solvent.

Most importantly, the national service corps will do some very important work in the United States—cleaning up brownfields, rebuilding or securing critical infrastructure, cleaning riverbanks, helping teachers in classrooms, or doing other urgently needed jobs. Moreover, this mandatory work experience will give every young American a consistent set of public service values, job skills training where needed, a drug-free start on adult life (since they would need to be drug-free to complete the service), and job skills that they can use in the years to follow.

Young workers would have the choice to live at home and work for an agency of their choice in the community; or they could go abroad, help families in remote villages or underdeveloped communities, and thereby win back some friends for the United States. Gifted corps members can serve at any level or position for which they are qualified, removing the argument that time spent in service postpones a useful career. Public service can be a great asset to each participant because it can use the best of the individual's talent to achieve a greater contribution. These young workers are essential to addressing the water, energy, environmental, and infrastructure problems in the United States.

However, preservation and protection of America's vital resources is but one engine of necessity for the formation of a national service corps. A second is the short-term need to fill the millions of entry-level positions in government, education, international relations, and security that will be left open by retiring baby boomers. Moreover, the service corps is the means by which new generations can move toward an ethic culture of service to others and to the nation.

Lastly, the corps is the source of entry-level workers to maintain and restore parks, public lands, and devastated forests for states, localities, and the federal government. Not only will these workers acquire skills, they will also become real citizens who are giving to the future generations and not taking for themselves.

This program will lead to a new ethic of citizenship. As a condition of full citizenship, the service corps will require that every American between the ages of 18 and 24 work for two years (4,000 hours) for a federal, state, county, or local agency at the minimum wage. The Social Security Administration will administer the financial and services accounting aspects of the program. The using agency will pay the workers and set the terms of work. Supplementary education will be available, as will language training, health training, drug rehabilitation, and citizenship training apart from the work requirements. This training will be provided by the sponsor organization as part of the service contract. The United States' management of its vital resources will rise to a new level because of the commitment of its young adults. The potential of the national service corps for achieving good in the future of the United States will be further explored in Chapters 15 through 18.

Suggested Reading

Barlow, Maude. *Blue Covenant*. New York: The New Press, 2007, 208 pp.

Kemp, William H. *The Renewable Energy Handbook*. Ontario, Canada: Aztext Press, 2005, 592 pp.

Klare, Michael T. *Resource Wars*. New York: Henry Holt and Company, LLC, 2002, 304 pp.

Business Solutions to Energy Gridlock

I'd put my money on the sun and solar energy. What a source of power! I hope we don't have to wait 'til oil and coal run out before we tackle that.

—Thomas Edison, inventor (1847–1931)

The Puzzle

It was the third summer after Ross Gregory's 2011 graduation when Ross and Bill Best, an urban planner and longtime friend, decided to travel to Scandinavia during Ross's first two weeks' vacation from the information technology (IT) company. Norway, Sweden, and Denmark were on the schedule. They landed first in Oslo.

Oslo fully lived up to its wonderful old world reputation. The pair explored the city for three days and saw exhibits dating back nearly 2,000 years while simultaneously enjoying modern Norway. The country provided some fairly astounding surprises, however.

Norway was modernized well beyond their expectations. The country had also revolutionized its education system; its 15-year-old student population was in first place in education achievement among all Organization of Economic Cooperation and Development (OECD) countries. Additionally, Norway was and still is energy independent. However, Bill and Ross were equally puzzled to find that despite this energy independence, Norway charged the equivalent of $21 per gallon of fuel. How could this be?

When they asked a local citizen about the outrageous fuel prices, they were told that Norway has two major objectives incorporated into the country's energy pricing and tax system.

First, they sought to limit energy consumption in vehicles, and they believed that price is the best regulator. In addition, limiting local energy use enabled them to export more crude oil and distilled fuels to other purchasers at a good price. Second, the government of Norway invested more than half of the $21 per gallon fuel price in a retirement fund to support the large population of elderly people in Norway. By 2006, Norway had already accrued a $250 billion fund to support its seniors. By 2014, Bill and Ross learned, the fund had grown to a staggering $1.2 trillion. Norway, Ross realized, is in very sound financial condition.

The nation's energy independence combined with its excellence in elementary and secondary education enabled Norway to be fully prepared for its twenty-first century future. Ross and Bill were both very impressed as they contrasted Norway and the United States on their respective education and energy strategies. Norway was energy independent, but it charged a very high price for fossil fuels. The United States was not energy independent, but it charged a relatively low price for fossil fuels. They wondered why the United States, which was *not* energy independent, still provided substantial subsidies to the fossil and biofuels industries to stimulate production and to maintain lower fuel prices. Further, they were astonished to realize that the United States allowed its citizens to consume nearly twice (169 percent) the energy per capita as the per capita usage levels of all but two OECD countries, including Norway. On the education front, Norway had been first in several subjects such as reading, science, and math for some years. The United States remains ranked fifteenth against other OECD countries in reading and science, and it is ranked twenty-sixth in math.

Bill and Ross departed Norway bewildered at these stark differences. How was their own country, a supposed world leader, preparing for the twenty-first century? They concluded that the United States is simply not prepared for the decades to come.

Issue Summary. Business can lead the way in addressing another of the three most important issues in the nation's future: energy. Based on past patterns of use, the United States has an unrealistic expectation that it should be able to consume vastly more energy per capita than all but two Western nations, when much of it is imported. Although energy shortages were acknowledged as the "moral equivalent of war" by President Jimmy Carter nearly three decades ago, the United States' long-delayed response has been to:

1. Establish a cabinet-level department to monitor the decline;
2. Test biomass and clean energy alternatives;

3. Keep new nuclear power and spent fuel disposal alternatives on the shelf;

4. Monitor but allow the continued decline of our electrical grid and transmission system;

5. Build more, larger vehicles for its growing car market;

6. Defer the imposition of lower fuel consumption standards in the interest of short-term profits; and

7. Allow the financial strength of the oil industry to increase, while the refining infrastructure deteriorates.

Is this truly an energy strategy? Meanwhile, the average American continues to use nearly *twice* the total energy per capita annually as his or her Western counterparts in Europe and elsewhere. Our country uses 25 percent of the world's energy output per year, while it exports vast sums (as high as $700 billion per year) to its foreign suppliers. The 2009 drop in fossil fuel prices following the worldwide economic crisis offered brief budget relief to exhausted middle-class consumers, but it didn't bring real changes. Is this a challenge that business should embrace on a strategic level?

Peak Oil

In 1956, Dr. M. King Hubbert predicted that U.S. oil production would peak sometime between 1965 and 1970. It actually peaked in 1971. A second, famous geologist, Oklahoman Professor Kenneth Deffeyes, worked as an oilman with Shell and then joined the faculty at Princeton. An avid student of oil fields, Deffeyes studied these locations and lectured bankers and brokers on the subject of peak oil. Claiming to be the only non-Saudi to ever study the reservoir rock samples from Saudi Arabia's Ghawar oil field (widely acknowledged as the largest conventional oil field in the world), Deffeyes used the same approach as Hubbert and predicted that worldwide peak oil production would occur in 2005 in his 2001 writings.

In 2001, using the exact same techniques Hubbert used to predict peak U.S. oil production in the 1950s, Deffeyes predicted global peak oil production would occur on December 16, 2005. He made his prediction in 2001 in a book titled *Hubbert's Peak: The Impending World Oil Shortage*. Deffeyes later quipped, "It turns out I was a few weeks off. With the benefit of the most recent data, we now know the actual peak occurred sometime in mid-January 2006."

Only the U.S. Geologic survey disagrees, and claims that the United States has not developed its remaining reserves. Deffeyes saw 2010 production dropping by 10 percent against its 2005 levels, and 2035 production dropping by half against 2005 levels. He also saw prices dropping to between $30 and $40 per barrel, but for entirely different reasons than those that followed the 2007 to 2009 subprime meltdown.

Of course, the impacts vary by industry, ranging from the highest impact on aviation, agriculture (because of the high energy content of fertilizers and pesticides), autos, and others.[1] All of Deffeyes foresight has proven true to this point, nonetheless. Peak oil is history. So what's next?

World Energy Demand

The U.S. Department of Energy indicates that:

1. World energy consumption will grow by 50 percent between the 2005 base year and 2030 (463 quadrillion Btu—2005; 563 quadrillion Btu—2015; 695 quadrillion Btu—2030).
2. The highest demand growth will be outside the OECD countries (85 percent versus 19 percent).
3. Liquids and other petroleum fuels (crude oil, lease condensate, natural gas plant liquids, and refinery gain) use will grow from 83.6 million barrels per day in the 2005 base case to 95.7 million barrels per day in 2015 and 112.5 million barrels per day in 2030, when other fuels replace a portion of this demand.
4. Transportation uses 74 percent of the liquids worldwide and industrial demand accounts for virtually all of the remainder.
5. OECD countries will continue to use 40 percent of the liquids and non-OECD (with most of the growth in emerging economies) countries will use the balance.
6. Unconventional sources (oil sands, extra heavy oil, biofuels, coal-to-liquids, and gas-to-liquids) only provided 2.5 million barrels per day in the 2005 base case and are expected to grow to 9.7 million barrels per day by 2030—an 8 percent share of total world supply.
7. Worldwide natural gas consumption is expected to increase from 104 trillion cubic feet in the 2005 base case to 158 trillion cubic feet in 2030.
8. World coal consumption is expected to increase from 123 quadrillion Btu in the 2005 base case to 202 quadrillion Btu in 2030. (China accounts for 74 percent of this increase, while the United States and India, both of which have substantial coal reserves, each account for only 9 percent of this increase.)

9. World net electricity production triples from a base of 17.3 trillion kilowatt-hours in 2005 to 24.4 trillion kilowatt-hours in 2015 and to 33.3 trillion kilowatt-hours in 2030.

10. Renewable fuels (wind, solar, hydro) grows from 35 quadrillion Btu in the 2005 base case to 59 quadrillion Btu in 2030.[2]

America's Energy Demands

Appendix C details the United States' current and anticipated power demands between now and 2030. It also details the needed investment in four key sectors. The implications for business are huge.

By studying Table 15.1, you will notice that the U.S. electric power demand is expected to grow by as much as 36 percent over its 2007 (latest USDOE Energy Outlook level) by 2030. This growth (whether it is in the midrange [20 percent; columns (b) and (c)] or in the high range [36 percent; columns (d) and (e)]) will require staggering investments in new capacity in the four primary plant types, as indicated.

The lower estimate of growth by 2030 envisions a 20 percent increase in the demand for electric power. This translates to constructing 1,913 new power plants at an estimated cost of $1.3 trillion (U.S. dollars, 2015). The high growth estimate envisions a 36 percent increase in the demand for electric power or the addition of 2,324 new plants at a cost of $1.5 trillion.

Where Is America's Energy Future? Chapter 13 has already provided a financing strategy for the United States to meet its future energy needs, and for the modernization of its grid and infrastructure. Business cannot wait, however, for the country to decide its energy future; it must act now.

Table 15.1 Meeting America's Primary Power Demands

	Current Plants (a)	2030 Mid Plants (b)	2030 Mid ($ Billion) (c)	2030 High Plants (d)	2030 High ($ Billion) (e)
Nuclear plants	104	116	180.0	116	180.0
Coal plants	1,470	1,680	210.0	1,820	350.0
Natural gas plants	5,439	6,043	543.6	6,043	543.6
Renewable plants	815	1,902	326.1	2,173	407.4
Totals	7,828	9,741	1,259.7	10,152	1481.0

Source: US Department of Energy (plant requirements).

Where Is Your Energy Future? How can business help to meet this need that is so essential to economic welfare? Where is the capital to make these investments in light of the high taxes on business? How can energy providers manage the risk of such staggering investments? Business growth capacity, cost profiles, and expansion to new markets will all be controlled in some way by energy. Consider Asia's big economies: While the United States debates its energy options, China will build 40 nuclear power plants prior to 2020. India is following a similar course.

Managing Energy Since energy is both a strategic and a tactical issue for business, it must be managed accordingly. Business leaders are compelled to address energy from five standpoints—having a sound energy plan, examining energy for transportation, taking conservation measures, analyzing the energy content of all unit costs for products and services, and reviewing carbon footprint exposure—and measuring success one day at a time.

Transportation Energy The biggest energy cost is transportation. Addressing this most pressing expense may lead to innovating business solutions, including:

1. Retrofitting local delivery vehicles to use rechargeable electric drive systems.
2. Purchasing hybrid vehicles for both local and long distance light hauling.
3. Purchasing lighter, less-expensive electric passenger vehicles for urban use.
4. Purchasing natural gas–powered vehicles for over-the-road use.

Energy Conservation The next strategic step for business is managing and measuring conservation. The wide range of solutions for industrial and commercial space heating and air-conditioning conservation includes high-efficiency insulation, automatic switches, modified work schedules, off-site work arrangements, conservation incentives for managers, energy benchmarking, work process management, and others. Someone needs to be in charge of energy conservation, and the performance of this individual should be measured.

Energy Unit Costs A third key energy management step is assessing energy unit costs (energy cost per item produced, per service performed, or per work hour). Multiplying unit energy costs by product or service units sold will quickly expose the biggest overall energy users in your product line. Unit cost measurements will also highlight the places where future energy cost growth and cost exposure will be greatest. Products or services with higher unit energy costs should be the first to be reviewed, modified, or eliminated. If not now, it is only a matter of time before this will be done.

Future Carbon Footprint Cost Exposure   From a strategic viewpoint, businesses can measure the enterprise's carbon footprint and install technical monitoring systems to see which current uses are within an acceptable range of cost, emissions, and technology. High-carbon footprint items should be the first ones to be addressed. High users are vulnerable to any future carbon tax, an exposure that could markedly change business economics.

Energy Supply Options   Prudent business leaders will also examine opportunities for the use of renewable and alternative sources of energy. Table 15.2 illustrates the unit costs for each category of conventional and renewable sources. These estimates have taken into account costs for engineering and planning, mechanism components, equipment assemblies, marketing costs, permits, installation costs, distance to a grid connection, security, maintenance, fuel (if applicable), disposal of hazardous waste (if applicable), general environmental impact, and decommissioning (if applicable).

Clearly, renewable energy can meet some, but surely not all, of the United States' future energy needs. Unit costs, fuel sourcing, and the availability of adequate amounts of investment capital will drive practical business solutions to meet those needs—provided that there is a cohesive national energy strategy and regulatory framework to encourage a business response. This is not the case at present.

Lesson for Principled Business Leaders. Business leaders must actively manage energy cost and supply exposure or step aside for motivated energy-savvy managers.

Lesson for Principled Business Leaders. Market forces are already pushing energy supply and cost exposure issues to the top of the business agenda.

Lesson for Principled Business Leaders. Energy management responsibility has risen to the level of the CEO as it affects long-term planning, transportation, conservation, carbon emissions exposure, capital planning, market planning, product planning, and renewable energy options.

Lesson for Principled Business Leaders. Energy is joining the environment in posing business risks at home and abroad that demand focused management attention.

Table 15.2   Renewable Energy: Unit Cost Options and Opportunities

Category of Energy Cost	Cents per KwH	Strengths	Limitations	Notes
Coal	3.9–4.4	Plentiful supply	Environmental/ political	Now half of U.S. supply. Emissions control is costly.
Natural gas	4.8–5.5	Ample domestic supplies	Fuel is biggest cost	Fuel supplies are ample. Most modern plants are gas.
Nuclear	11.1–14.5	Big risk Capital cost	Fuel disposal problems	Fuel disposal problems remain. Political sentiment is opposed. Nuclear is moving offshore.
Wind	4.0–6.0	Ample fuel	Steel cost 30% reliable	Now 1.4% of global supply. Now 2.1% of U.S. supply.
Geothermal	4.5–30.0	Ample fuel New designs	Depth 95% reliable	Now 0.23% of U.S. supply.
Hydroelectric	5.1–11.3	Ample fuel	60% reliable	Now 19.9% of U.S. supply.
Solar	15.0–30.0	Ample fuel	Silicon supply	Currently 0.8% of U.S. supply.
Tide	2.0–5.0	Predictable	Capital Location Technology	Tidal fence.
Atmospheric cold Megawatts	0.03–1.0	Low upkeep	Technology	Dual pipeline system maximizes pressure gaps.
Thermal electric	3.0–15.0	Efficiency	Cheap	Energy conversion chip. More efficient than solar. Cheaper than solar.
OTEC*	6.0–25.0		No plants	Two plants being built.

*Ocean Energy Thermal Conversion
Pure Energy Systems: PesWIKI Directory: Cents Per Kilowatt Hour

Stretch Goal for My Enterprise. Can we envision an energy management strategy that will enable our enterprise to cut its average energy unit costs by one-third? Half?

Stretch Goal for My Enterprise. Does our energy management plan improve our enterprise's competitive position in selected products, services, markets, or locations? What steps must I take to ensure that our competitive position is improved from the energy standpoint?

Stretch Goal for My Enterprise. What resources and/or leadership time are we able and/or prepared to commit to rationalizing our business' energy challenges? To lower per capita consumption? To lead the effort for infrastructure modernization in our region?

Questions to Ponder. Which of our lines of business, products, services, locations, or facilities are most exposed to energy supply and cost problems? What steps must we take to address them?

Questions to Ponder. Do you know the energy/carbon footprint of your enterprise? What steps have you taken to lower per capita energy consumption in your business? In your home? Do you know that the United States must cut its per capita energy consumption by nearly half to reach the levels of consumption that are common in Europe and in all but two OECD countries? Do you know the potential applications of renewable energy in your enterprise? Do you know of transportation alternatives that use a greater share of renewable energy sources?

Action Steps

Principled Business Leaders Must:

1. Take full responsibility for:
   a. Energy management
   b. Energy usage levels
   c. Energy conservation
   d. Transportation innovation
   e. Energy content of products and services
   f. Measurement of energy unit costs
   g. Strategic management of energy supplies

2. Take any one (or all) of a combination of a number of optional actions to reduce their consumption of energy and ration long-term energy consumption, including:
   a. Space heating

b. Air-conditioning

c. Work processes

d. Innovative employee work arrangements

e. Energy education

Principled Business Leaders Must:

1. Take the lead in advocating lower per capita consumption, while they encourage public leaders to follow their lead. These advocacy steps may relate to tax policy, commercial buildings, consumption levels, transportation energy use, and industry best practices for energy. It is time for major changes in energy use.

2. Consider participating in PPPs, industry associations, and community groups to manage area energy programs.

Principled Business Leaders May:

1. Take an active, national role in advocating for prompt, effective action to:

a. Expand domestic energy supplies

b. Remove costly subsidies

c. Renew the nation's energy infrastructure (inefficient power transmission grid and others)

d. Reduce the excess use of fossil fuels

e. Expand the use of renewable energy sources

f. Markedly improve the electric production and transmission system in both the community and in the nation

2. Provide leadership to establish and build the fund for renewal of the United States' energy infrastructure through the transaction fee (Chapter 13).

Principled Business Leaders Must:

1. Know their carbon and energy footprint at the enterprise level in order to prepare for future regulatory charges.

2. Continuously monitor and manage energy use and conservation for the benefit of shareholders and their income statements.

3. Set the best example of responsible energy use at every level for enterprise profitability.

4. Reward innovation and performance in energy use and conservation to lower fixed costs at the enterprise level.

5. Monitor and support regional efforts at infrastructure modernization.
6. Actively support removal of subsidies for infeasible energy strategies.
7. Make energy management a cornerstone of principled leadership.
8. Consider available alternative fuels (electricity, natural gas, etc.,) for transportation assets and/or delivery vehicles in an effort to lower overall energy consumption.

Key Measures of Success

Energy Action Point	Energy Goal	Weakest Function(s)	Corrective Action Steps	Date to Complete
1. Energy conservation plan				
2. Transportation energy use				
3. Product/service energy unit costs				
4. Energy market limitations				
5. Energy supply options				

Case History

Nuclear Power Development in China

China's committee on state-owned enterprises is currently considering a proposal by a proposed joint venture of U.S. nuclear scientists and two Chinese organizations to assist them with the construction of 40 nuclear power plants that are scheduled for construction before 2020. Friendly use of nuclear power under appropriate agreements will be a constructive element of improved China-U.S. relations. Other international cooperation can continue from the successful nuclear power development program between China and the United States.

Suggested Reading

Heinberg, Richard. *Power Down*. British Columbia, Canada: New Society Publishers, Friesens Inc., 2005, 288 pp.

Kemp, William H. *The Renewable Energy Handbook*. Ontario, Canada: Aztext Press, 2005, 600 pp.

Klare, Michael T. *Resource Wars*. New York: Henry Holt and Company, LLC, 2002.

Leeb, Stephen. *The Oil Factor*. With Donna Leeb. New York: Warner Business Books, 2004, 256 pp.

McKillop, Andrew, and Sheila Newman, Eds. *The Final Energy Crisis*. London: Pluto Press, 2005, 336 pp.

Savinar, Matt. *The Oil Age Is Over: What to Expect as the World Runs out of Cheap Oil, 2005–2050*. Kearney, NE: Savinar Publishing, 2004, 183 pp.

16

Environment—Renewal and Redirection

Our environmental problems originate in the hubris of imagining ourselves as the central nervous system or the brain of nature. We're not the brain, we are a cancer on nature.

—Dave Foreman

Taking Action at Last

Ross returns home to attend his 10-year high school reunion. One decade out of school, his work is going well and he has had two promotions. *Not a bad story to pass on to my classmates*, he muses.

The first night's gathering was a great success. All but 50 of his class of 300 were there. He found his old friend Emily Sackett Parker coming in with Christopher Lee, and having known each other since high school, they fell into instant conversation. Emily and Chris both have jobs with the Federal Bureau of Land Management (BLM), and were picked up in a new program to launch a massive reforestation effort in the Midwest. Ross was astonished to learn from them that the nation has only 4 percent of its original forests and that most of the loss has taken place in the lower 48 states.

BLM had sold the Congress on a 20-year nationwide initiative to replant up to half of the lost forestland by 2030. Nearly 20,000 student interns from the national service corps are doing the work in six regional locations. Keith and Chris were each coordinating work in one of the six locations. They loved the work and saw so much good coming from the carbon dioxide recovery that was already occurring as a result of the this effort. Ross was a bit envious. What a great project to be a part of!

Issue Summary. The United States' environmental record is a story of intermittent successes, punctuated by regular steps back. In the early stages, we led the world in environmental damage; and while we have made progress in exposing our environmental problems, we are far from achieving virtually *any* of our proclaimed goals. The world perceives us as a people of arrogance and overbearing refusal to seriously address many environmental problems, especially those where special interests are in the lead.

The Environmental Challenge

Environmental issues are a huge public policy challenge because they are (1) complex, (2) highly technical, and (3) overwhelmingly perplexing to the average citizen and to all levels of government because of the well-organized, well-funded, and often enraged interest groups. Because of the technical complexity, it is often only specialized scientists who can fully comprehend the problems. Notwithstanding this, scientists often disagree on remedial actions and policy issues, so the stalemate continues without clear resolution. As Goethe once observed, "Most men only care for science so far as they get a living by it, but they will worship error when it affords them a subsistence."

Environmental issues bring together both competing interests and differing values that range from accusations of business for producing products and services that are not beneficial to the environment, up to and including outright opposition to further economic development at any level. The most frequently mentioned array of environmental challenges includes but is not limited to:

- Global warming
- Air quality
- National lands
- Species preservation
- Treatment of waste
- Nuclear waste
- Water quality
- Chemicals in air and food
- Genetically modified foods

Global Warming   The widespread beliefs surrounding climate change, with its accompanying incidences of glacier melt, growing worldwide storm intensity, and problematic greenhouse emissions, are driving most current environmental debate. Advocates point to the heightened (and presumably more enlightened) agreement in Europe in environmental remediation and the ill effects of consumption growth.[1]

Global warming is the term for the "steady rise in average global temperatures"; and advocates of this issue cite the facts that: "a) The ten warmest years on record have all occurred since 1983; b) 1998 was the warmest year on record; and c) Seven of the hottest years have occurred since 1990."[2] Global warming results from the concentration of *greenhouse gases* like carbon dioxide and methane in Earth's atmosphere, which have resulted in part from the use of fossil fuels. Greenhouse gases "act like the glass on a greenhouse—they let the sun's heat in but they stop it getting out."[3]

Carbon dioxide from energy use is the primary culprit, followed closely by methane gases produced by agriculture, landfills, and animal emissions. Of the two sources, methane is the least damaging, because it disperses more quickly than carbon dioxide. The federal government anticipates that emissions will increase 57 percent by 2025 and most of the growth will come from developing countries. Remediation methodologies to minimize carbon dioxide emissions suggested by the 1997 conference on climate change held in Kyoto, Japan (*Kyoto Protocol*), include:

- Energy efficiency and conservation
  - Raise vehicle fuel efficiency from 30 to 60 mpg.
  - Reduce vehicle use and annual car mileage by half.
  - Improve building efficiency/cut emissions by 25 percent.
  - Modernize coal plants to burn more efficiently.
  - Move from coal to natural gas where possible.
- Carbon dioxide capture and storage
  - Exploit means to capture/store carbon dioxide.
  - Restore devastated forest lands to limit carbon dioxide.
- Nuclear power
  - Resume use of nuclear power when feasible.
  - Resolve the spent fuel storage issue.
- Renewable electricity and fuels
  - Expand use of feasible solar and wind technologies.
  - Allow individuals to sell extra power to the grid.
  - Modernize the electric grid for access to wind/solar.

- Land use
  - Reverse the deforestation practice.
  - Improve soil management and renewal practices.
  - Use higher efficiency water-use technologies.

The Kyoto Protocol agreed upon at this conference was signed by 183 countries, including the United States. The United States did not ratify the treaty, however, so it was not bound by the Protocol.[4]

However, despite persistent statements to the contrary, there is not uniform agreement among scientists that global warming is the reality advocates suggest. Restoring ozone concentrations in the atmosphere has been progressing as a result of the prompt worldwide efforts to eliminate the use of *chlorofluorocarbons* (CFCs).[5]

Air Quality　While our overall air quality has improved as a result of the Clean Air Act, improved emission standards, and cleaner-burning gasoline, 400 U.S. cities continue to experience a large number of unhealthy days because of low air quality.[6]

The U.S. Environmental Protection Agency (EPA) measures air quality using eight standards—one-hour ozone, eight-hour ozone, carbon monoxide levels, nitrogen dioxide levels, sulfur dioxide levels, coarse particulate matter levels (2.5 to 10.0 micrometers in size), fine particulate matter levels (2.5 micrometers or smaller), and lead levels. These measures have all been combined into an overall Air Quality Index (AQI) that converts the measurements to a 500-point scale indicating hazard levels. Plant emissions of sulfur dioxide remain a problem in many areas.[7] Auto emissions standards were lowered further in late 2008. Coal-burning power plants remain a major source of air pollution, and lobbyists for older plants work hard to limit the impact of new standards on these plants.[8]

National Lands　The United States has only 4 percent of its original forests. Ninety-six percent of those original forests are now gone. The federal national forest system contains three-fourths of that remaining 4 percent. Seven hundred million acres of the nation's largely undeveloped federal land is located in the western part of the country.

The BLM was formed in 1946 to manage 246 million acres of these national lands—177 million acres in the lower 48 states and 87 million acres in Alaska (including the 1.5-million-acre Arctic National Wildlife Refuge[9]), 60 million acres of which are unprotected wilderness.[10] Unfortunately, reforestation has been a low priority for the nation's environmentalists, despite the key role of forests in removing carbon dioxide from the atmosphere.

Wetlands   Past legislation has been largely aimed at converting wetlands to agricultural or residential use. This was a mistake, however, because wetlands protect water quality, serve as a storm and erosion buffer in coastal areas, and are a source of outdoor recreation. Happily, the rate of wetland loss was decreased by 80 percent between 1986 and 1997,[11] although management issues remain.

Rain Forest Destruction   The United States has not been a leader in the preservation of rain forests and national lands, despite its now century-old establishment of Yellowstone National Park—an early national policy to preserve natural lands.[12] Although much effort has been expended to slow and eventually stop rain forest destruction, particularly in Brazil, where the rate of loss was considered highest in the world, the pace has only slowed. Ironically, rain forests are a major inhibitor of greenhouse gases, but their preservation remains a low priority for international action.

Endangered Species   The United States launched its efforts to protect endangered species when it passed an act by that name in 1973. Plants were similarly protected in a related piece of legislation. However, despite these protective acts, the number of endangered plants and animals has increased marginally, while 11 species have been taken off the list altogether. Nearly half (41 percent) of the species have at least stabilized. Because of landowner disputes over endangered species, little or no funding has been provided for the work since 1992. The critical factor, habitat loss, prompts some landowners to rid themselves of the designated habitats to avoid being subject to the act. As one source explained, "Because of the [landowner opposition] controversy, there has been no specific funding of the Endangered Species Act since 1992 although funds have been authorized for its procedural implementation during each subsequent fiscal year."[13]

Waste Disposal   Disposal of solid and liquid wastes is covered by the Resource Conservation and Recovery Act of 1976. The statute aims to protect human health from the possible hazards of waste disposal by setting regulatory standards for processes such as conserving energy and natural resources, reducing waste generation, and managing wastes in an environmentally sound manner. Although state, county, and local governments most often regulate landfills, the EPA also sets minimum standards for the management and operation and the exclusion of hazardous waste in landfills. The act was responsible in part for a leveling off of individual waste generation levels since 1980, nearly a third of which is paper. Recycling has also emerged as a serious alternative.[14]

Brownfields   The Government Accountability Office estimates that there are 400,000 to 600,000 *brownfields*—areas with low-level or low-suspicion levels of damaging waste deposits at former industrial or chemical sites in the United States.[15] Hazardous waste exposure or potential health effects cause a site to be reclassified as a *Superfund site*, covered by the provisions of Resource Conservation and Recovery Act (RCRA) in 1978.[16] The fact that 30 years have not witnessed cleanup of this group of 39,000 hazardous sites nationally is a testimony to special interests, avoidance of accountability, and "heads, I win; tails, the taxpayer loses" implementation.[17]

Superfund Program   So much money has funded this failed program that the Congressional Budget Office (CBO) said in 1996 that the program was to be terminated. The EPA expected to spend a total of $31 billion cleaning the first 1,354 sites on the National Priorities List (NPL), $17 billion of which was after 1995. More recently, the CBO estimated that the total cleanup bill might reach $130 billion, when all potential sites were known. Ironically, two of the biggest offenders are the U.S. Departments of Energy and Defense.[18]

Nuclear Power   Once an attractive alternative to fossil fuel, the 1979 accident at Three Mile Island has stymied further development of nuclear power. Early in 2009, the Tennessee Valley Authority—one of the nation's pioneers in nuclear power—announced that it would restart its reactor at Browns Ferry, and that it would complete work on two reactors at its Bellefonte site, all of which had been idle for more than two decades. The United States now has 104 active nuclear plants that provide 21.4 percent of the nation's total electricity. Although nuclear power virtually eliminates greenhouse emissions, opponents use three issues to oppose further use of nuclear energy: potential plant accidents, the danger of a terrorist attack on a plant, and the unresolved issues related to storage and disposal of spent fuel.[19]

Wastewater   Many of the nation's most serious water quality problems have been addressed at a level aimed at avoiding this serious health danger. The Clean Water Act in 1972 provided federal support and a 1988 deadline for sewage plant construction. Eighty-six percent of all cities met the deadline, while the many in the remainder were put under judicial or administrative watch schedules for compliance. Most of the remaining jurisdictions are small cities with limited capability for plant upgrade. Unfortunately, remedying industrial pollution has not been solved, and few states enforce the required permit system.[20]

Clean Water   A review of the EPA indicators for clean water address water quality in terms of whether it is:

1. Safe to drink;
2. Safe to eat fish and/or shellfish from that source;
3. Safe for swimming;
4. Suitably protected as a watershed;
5. Suitably protected coastal and ocean water area;
6. Suitably protected wetland;
7. Suitably protected Mexican border water quality;
8. Suitably protected Great Lakes;
9. Suitably protected Chesapeake Bay; and
10. Suitably protected Gulf of Mexico.

For each indicator, the latest available record suggests that:

- 91 percent of U.S. community water is safe to drink;[21]
- 485,285 river miles and 11,277,276 lake acres are under an advisory for fish/shellfish safe to eat;[22]
- 3.2 million lake acres were unsafe for swimming in 2002 (an increase from 2000);[23]
- 453 of 2,262 protected watersheds met 80 percent of criteria;[24]
- Protect coastal/ocean waters have only reached a "fair" status by EPA measures;[25]
- 850,000 acres of the 3-million-acres goal of protected wetlands have been restored since 2004;[26]
- The goal of protecting 1.5 million Californians from Mexican sewage water dumped into the Tijuana River has been "stalled"[27] (work has recently begun to build a new secondary treatment plant);
- The safety of the Great Lakes scored 21.9 on a target scale of 40 in 2005;[28]
- The Chesapeake Bay has achieved some progress on the goal of improving and submerged aquatic vegetation;[29]
- The Gulf of Mexico has scored 2.4 of 5.0 in preventing pollution in 2004.[30]

The EPA summarizes its progress as flat on one item, awaiting data on four items, down on four items, and up on three items.[31] Maybe it is time to bring business innovation and a national service corps of young adults to bear on the nation's environmental challenges.

Chemicals The Pesticide Act directs the EPA to restrict the use of pesticides in air and food to prevent unreasonable adverse effects on people and the environment. The Federal Insecticide, Fungicide, and Rodenticide Act prohibits the sale of any unregistered or unlabeled pesticide without approval. The Pollution Prevention Act requires owners and operators of manufacturing facilities to report annually on source reduction activities. EPA data suggest that chemical releases remain substantial, particularly in the mining states of Alaska and Nevada.

Pesticide residues are also quite common in food products. The U.S. Food and Drug Administration (FDA) found residues in more than 25 percent of samples, many of which were within acceptable FDA limits. Imported fruits and vegetables pose the greatest risk. The Centers for Disease Control and Prevention (CDC) found certain pesticide residues in a significant percent of the population.

In this category of risk, persistent organic pollutants (POPs) are the greatest concern. POPs include PCBs, DDT, and 10 other chemicals; and all 12 of them resist the normal processes of degradation. Identified as *endocrine disruptors*, POPs can interfere with body hormone function, while they accumulate and remain for as long as decades before breaking down. They are also found in the food chain and in animal products (meat, fish, and milk), where they ultimately cause human exposure.[32]

Genetically Modified (GM) Foods Emerging as an issue in the last decade, this group of foods is the product of advances in biochemical science, which produce food varieties that have been *genetically engineered*. GM scientists are able to modify plant DNA to realize plant input traits (to aid growers, processors, and marketers) and output traits that allegedly benefit consumers with nutritional and food quality improvements. Input traits may include pest and disease resistance, herbicide resistance, and other techniques designed to increase crop yield. Because of more predictable yields, these products have quickly gained acceptance among growers. Over 80 percent of U.S. soybeans and nearly 50 percent of U.S. corn is presently based on genetically engineered products. Globally, the percentage of acreage devoted to these crops continues to climb.[33]

Energy Pollution Virtually every means of energy production and use involves some form of pollution of our environment. Moreover, each source of energy pollutes differently and to varying levels. Coal and oil burning, for example, both produce carbon dioxide, nitrous oxides, and dust particulates (microparticles), thereby contributing to atmospheric global warming, smog, and/or lung ailments. Nitrous oxides are most prone to create smog and haze.

Nuclear power is also an energy polluter, giving off radioactive waste from spent fuel or reactor coolants, potential radiation leaks into the air, and heat emissions into local water sources. The first two not only pose great health hazards but are also extremely difficult and costly to remediate. Heat in local coolant water gives rise to substantial algae growth and kills marine life. The thousands of tons of existing radioactive nuclear waste sit in sealed drums around the nation awaiting an opening in legislative gridlock that has kept it on local sites for decades.[34]

Lesson for Principled Business Leaders. The days of "heads, I win; tails, taxpayers lose" for business neglect in environmental matters are, or certainly should be, over. Even if your enterprise is not guilty of environmental destruction, principled business leaders must demand and facilitate constructive action to remove the environmental blight that still exists in many communities.

Lesson for Principled Business Leaders. Business innovation can be a source of environmental remediation on a broader basis in order to lower unit costs, speed the work, and bring greater competence to the work—in partnership with the national service corps workforce. It is time to expand the work.

Stretch Goal for My Enterprise. Are there environmental issues that our business is aggravating? Are there environmental issues that our business can assist to resolve? Are there environmental issues that threaten the future of our business?

Stretch Goal for My Enterprise. What environmental project can our enterprise assist in resolving? For example, is there a brownfield in my immediate area in need of restoration? Is there a public-private partnership that I can join to get it done? Shall I take leadership of such a project? Is there economic potential for my business in this endeavor?

Questions to Ponder. How long will business leaders tolerate environmental gridlock with hundreds of billions of their tax dollars being spent without satisfactory results? How can business leaders bring innovation to the resolution of environmental problems in the nation, rather than abdicate this task to trial lawyers and special interests? What steps can even the smallest enterprise take to begin to remove one of the 400,000 to 600,000 brownfields, restore the missing 96 percent of the nation's forests, modernize the water and wastewater infrastructure, clean the ailing streams and rivers, restore the millions of acres of wetlands, or resolve the nuclear gridlock that is resulting in annual increases in power costs? What is the responsibility of business to address these problems?

What role should special interests have in partnership with business to rationalize our environmental problems? Can business take the lead in providing leadership on environmental issues?

What steps am I taking to relate my business interests to a future cleaner environment? How do my business's best practices address environmental issues? How are we at a disadvantage?

What is my role in addressing the environmental gridlock and dismal record of accomplishment? What environmental quality do I plan to leave for my children and their children after them?

Action Steps

Principled Business Leaders Must:

1. Incorporate environmental management issues into every relevant business process.
2. Make environmental management a cornerstone of business leadership.
3. Bring innovation to resolution of environmental issues, as they have done in every generation and to every major issue that has faced them.
4. Make a paradigm shift in assessing their environmental responsibilities.
5. Set an environmental example that is a model for the world.

Key Measures of Success

Environmental Action Point	Environment Goal	Weakest Function(s)	Corrective Action Steps	Date to Complete
1. Clean air				
2. Clean water				
3. Products/services related environmental issues				
4. National lands				

Environmental Action Point	Environment Goal	Weakest Function(s)	Corrective Action Steps	Date to Complete
5. Species preservation				
6. Treatment of waste				
7. Chemicals in air and food				
8. Genetically modified foods				

Suggested Reading

_____. *Collapse: How Societies Choose to Fail or Succeed*. New York: Penguin Books, 2005, 575 pp.

Diamond, Jared. *Guns, Germs, and Steel: The Fate of Human Societies*. New York: W.W. Norton & Company, 1997, 512 pp.

CHAPTER 17

Infrastructure Renewal—Business Can Lead

Our nation's infrastructure needs are tremendous, and they're growing.

—Bill Lipinski

Blackout

Ross is on his first business trip—a half-day rail trip from his Maryland home to Boston through New York on the Northeast Rail Corridor. Electrified Amtrak trains speed along in both directions. Passing through the small towns that surround the city of Baltimore, the scattered green of the 'burbs gives way to the spectacular scenery along the Chesapeake Bay. He talks quietly with his boss, Zach Kern, who is along on the trip to provide some high cover. Wilmington is not far ahead.

As the train speeds through the Aberdeen station going north, there is a sudden lurch and then a screeching stop. All of the lights in the snack car where he is sitting go out, and only the early eastern sun that streams in through the window illuminates their table. The minutes go by for what seems like a short eternity. Finally, an announcement is made. Overhead electric power on the line has been interrupted, and the cause is undetermined. Ross thinks about his first meeting in Boston, set for 2 o'clock that afternoon.

Another hour passes—still no lights, still no power. It is now 10:00 A.M. Train generators are not available. Then comes another announcement: The entire Northeast corridor has had a power grid blackout. Power from Canada's Quebec Hydro is now limited to supporting upstate New York, western Massachusetts, Vermont, New Hampshire, and Maine. New York City is blacked out. Philadelphia is blacked out. Wilmington is blacked out. And the power grid in the Baltimore region is blacked out. The train will be stopped outside of Aberdeen for an indeterminate time. Ross's heart sinks. No passengers are allowed to leave the train. Ross can only think about his upcoming Boston meeting with the William Family Trust partners—Austin, Garrett, and Grace—three very demanding clients.

Four hours go by. The snack shelves are now empty. It is 1:00 P.M., and Ross phones ahead on his cell to delay the meeting. He thinks that he can make it the next day. By 6:00 P.M., there is another announcement, indicating that power has been restored to the south and that the train will return to Baltimore to discharge all of the passengers. That takes another three hours and the ride home takes until 1:00 A.M. What a day, and what a waste of time! How could this have happened?

Unfortunately, Ross's meeting had to be postponed for two weeks because the rail grid power was not restored for nearly a week. When he called the power company, he learned that the Northeast Rail Corridor is situated on the most vulnerable part of the entire U.S. power grid. Investment in the entire system has been continuously dropping for 40 years, and the growth in demand has been relentless. As a result, Ross's unrealized trip was the eighth time that the grid had gone down. Although it was the first blackout since his graduation, it didn't help his cause in getting the Boston account, and Ross ended up losing the bid.

The Size of the Challenge

Infrastructure is defined as the critical elements of the physical and operational systems of the nation that are vital to its sustained performance and smooth functioning for the benefit of U.S. citizens. This definition is commonly cascaded into a series of functional divisions of the economy, including:

- Banking and finance
- Chemical
- Commercial facilities

- Commercial nuclear reactors, materials, and waste
- Dams
- Defense industrial bases
- Drinking water and wastewater treatment systems
- Emergency services
- Energy
- Food and agriculture
- Government facilities
- Information technology
- National monuments and icons
- Postal and shipping
- Public health and health care
- Solid waste disposal
- Telecommunications
- Transportation systems[1]

Table 17.1 provides budget estimates for the modernization by category of infrastructure. School buildings have been added to the modernization budget, even though they are not classified as critical infrastructure.

How Many Jobs Are Needed?

Table 17.2 summarizes the job requirements to renew and modernize the United States' infrastructure and to clean up most of the nation's environmental problems. The work done will accomplish both the modernization and the environmental remediation needs outlined in Chapter 16.

Next Steps

America's infrastructure is outdated. Robust economic growth is impossible when the outdated infrastructure is a limiting factor. Moreover, added employment for new infrastructure development is impossible when there is no capital for new infrastructure. How can this reality be changed to opportunity?

For example, the overage water purification and delivery systems in many of our 30,000 municipalities is but one element of the challenge. The outdated electric power grid is a second; outdated water treatment plants are a third. Many of the 70,000 poorly maintained Interstate Highway System bridges and millions of miles of roadways are a fourth. Outdated passenger rail systems rights of way and commuter rail lines are a fifth. These are designated as *critical infrastructure*.

Table 17.1 Modernization Investment for America's Infrastructure

Sector	Chapter Note	Are They Secure?	Number	Estimated Replacement Value ($ Billions)	Modernization Investment ($ Billions)	Public/Private*
Banking and finance bank organizations	2	Yes	8,000			
Bank branches		No	40,000	80.0	20.0	Public
Chemical	3	Yes	15,000	4,500.0	1,500.0	Public
Commercial facilities	4	No	7,200,770	7,200.8	3,600.4	Public
Commercial nuclear reactors, materials, and waste[4]	5	Yes	104	520.0	156.0	PPP
Dams and levees						
Dams	6	No	75,000	2,250.00	1,125.0	PPP
Levees (291 failing miles)			100,000	1,000.0	112.5	Private/G
Locks (30—19th century)			257	154.2	77.1	Public
Defense industrial base[5]	7	Yes	1,200	240.0	180.0	PPP/G
Drinking water—public treatment systems	8	No	53,000	1,060.0	530.0	Public
Private treatment systems		No	21,400	428.0	214.0	Private
Wastewater treatment		No	16,000	320.0	160.0	PPP/G
Emergency services	9	No	60,000	90.0	30.0	Public/G
Energy plants- conventional generating plants	10	No				
Coal plants		No	1,470	7.4	3.7	PPP

(continued)

Table 17.1 (*continued*)

Sector	Chapter Note	Are They Secure?	Number	Estimated Replacement Value ($ Billions)	Modernization Investment ($ Billions)	Public/Private*
Geothermal plants		No	224	1.3	0.1	PPP
Hydroelectric conventional		No	3,992	47.9	16.0	PPP
Natural gas plants		No	5,439	54.4	16.3	PPP
Other gas		No	105	0.6	0.2	PPP
Other biomass plants		No	1,229	7.4	1.2	PPP
Petroleum		No	3,743	93.6	44.9	PPP
Pumped storage		No	151	4.5	0.9	PPP
Solar thermal/photovoltaic		No	38	0.7	0.2	PPP
Wind power		No	389	5.8	1.6	PPP
Wood derived		No	346	1.7	0.3	PPP
Other			42	0.1	0.0	PPP
Total conventional plants		No	17,168	225.5	85.5	PPP
Transmission grid	11	No		500.0	500.0	
Food and agriculture	12	No	2,600,000	1,300.0	520.0	Private
Government facilities	13	Yes	94,000	141.0	47.0	G
Information technology	14	No	41,945	629.2	209.7	PPP
National monuments and icons	15	No	1,500	30.0	15.0	G

#	Infrastructure					Strategy*
16	Postal and shipping	Yes	47,741	47.7	11.9	G
17	Public health and health care	No	762,451	571.8	190.6	PPP
18	Solid waste disposal	No	20,000	80.0	20.0	PPP
19	Telecommunications	No	100,000	1,000.0	500.0	PPP
20	Transportation systems—airports	Yes	13,715	685.8	274.3	P/PPP
	Bridges	No	590,111	2,360.4	885.2	G
	Canals (miles each)	No	2,000	0.20	0.1	P/PPP
	Highways	No	4,000,000	400.0	200.0	P
	Rivers (miles)	No	25,483		1.27	P
	Offshore oil platforms (miles)	No	4,000	800.0	200.0	
	Pipelines, oil (miles each)	No	377,189	75.4	28.3	
	Ports	Yes	149	14.90	7.5	P
	Railroads (miles each)	No	94,801			G/PPP
	Total critical infrastructure		11,879,362	24,914.4	10,464.2	
21	Schools—primary and secondary	Yes	91,957	367.8	92.0	G/P/PPP
	Grand total—each infrastructure		11,971,319	25,282.2	10,556.2	

*Strategies for modernization are Public (shareholder owned), Private (all privately owned establishments), PPP—Public-Private Partnership, G—Government

189

Table 17.2 Infrastructure Modernization/Environmental Cleanup Workload

Infrastructure Type	Notes	Units	Unit of Measure	Work Days per Year (Each)	Total Work Days per Year (000s)	Person Work Years (000s)	Value of Work ($ Millions at 20,000 per Work Year)
Brownfields	22	600,000	each	1,000	600,000	2,400	48,000
County lands	23	4,000,000	acres	400	1,600,000	6,400	128,000
County parks	24	100,000	each	400	40,000	160	3,200
County roads	25	3,000,000	miles	100	300,000	1,200	24,000
County energy retrofit	26	100,000	each	100	10,000	40	800
County facilities	27	100,000	each	100	10,000	40	800
County, other	28	50,000	each	100	5,000	20	400
Dams and levees							
Dams	29	75,000	each	1,000	75,000	300	6,000
Levees	30	100,000,	miles	200	20,000	80	1,600
Locks	31	257	each	500	128.5	0.514	10
Forest fire lanes	32	1,000,000	miles	200	200,000	800	16,000
Forest replanting	33	10,000,000	acres	100	1,000,000	4,000	80,000
Local energy retrofit	34	150,000	each	100	15,000	60	1,200
Local maintenance	35	300,000	each	100	30,000	120	2,400

36	Local lands	2,000,000	acres	100	200,000	800	16,000
37	Local parks	50,000	each	200	10,000	40	800
38	Local roads	4,000,000	miles	100	400,000	1,600	32,000
39	National monuments/icons	1,500	each	1,000	1,500	6	120
40	National parks projects	50,000	each	400	20,000	80	1,600
41	Schools—primary/secondary	91,957		1,000	91,957	367.828	7,357
42	State energy projects	300,000	each	100	30,000	120	2,400
43	State parks	50,000	each	200	10,000	40	800
	Transportation systems						
44	Airports	13,715	n/a				
45	Bridges	590,111	n/a				
46	Canals (miles)	2,000	miles	1,000	2,000	8	160
47	Highways	4,000,000	miles	400	1,600,000	6,400	128,000
48	Rivers (miles)	25483	miles	1,000	25,483	101.93197	2,039
	Total work days per year				6,296,068		
	Total persons per funds (000s)				25,184	25,184	503,685

While public school facilities aren't part of the critical infrastructure, the outdated and poorly maintained facilities are a disgrace to many communities. What happens to twenty-first century education? In short, the nation's first-generation infrastructure is either worn out or rapidly wearing out. Other economic priorities have come first for 50 years. Now is the time to change course. The infrastructure deficiencies are those brought on by age, overuse, technology changes, population growth, demographic changes, aging of baby boomers, and many others. These realities impact business, education, energy, health, housing, law enforcement, security, transportation, and every economic sector. But there is hope for a turnaround in this situation—if there are leaders ready to confront these challenges.

Lesson for Principled Business Leaders. Repairing the nation's outdated infrastructure may well be a catalyst for the creation of thousands of new craft jobs for young Americans. It is also a potential source of thousands of new and expanded enterprises. Third, it is a basis for a vastly expanded vocational and trade school enterprise preparing for millions of new construction trade jobs of all types. Business can bring leadership to this modernization effort. Further delays are unwarranted, since capital can be made available through the transaction fee. (See Chapter 13.)

Lesson for Principled Business Leaders. The national service corps can be the source of entry-level workers to maintain and restore parks, public lands, and devastated forests for states, localities, and the federal government, provided that the workers are properly trained, supervised, and managed. Only business can provide this leadership and management. If this is done correctly, not only will workers have acquired skills, they will also have become real citizens who are giving to the future generations and not taking for themselves. It will be a new ethic of citizenship.

Stretch Goal for My Enterprise. Is renewal of the nation's infrastructure a market into which my enterprise can enter? Are our distinctive competences appropriate to this market? Are there public-private partnerships that my enterprise should join to assist in this work? Are the nation's infrastructure needs great enough for me to get involved? Can I make a difference in my community and in its infrastructure?

Stretch Goal for My Enterprise. Is the condition of infrastructure a limiting factor for my enterprise in the future? Will our business's growth be limited because of infrastructure limitations? Are there options for relocating, changing employment patterns, or modifying products or services that should be considered because of infrastructure limitations? Am I looking at this reality in a systematic and practical manner?

Questions to Ponder. What is the impact of the declining infrastructure on my business? How does this affect my costs, deliveries, expenses, or customer access? Is infrastructure modernization a big enough need for me to take a personal role in its taking place? Are there areas of business innovation that my enterprise can add to help meet this need? Are there limitations on my enterprise because of outdated and inefficient infrastructure?

Action Steps

Principled Business Leaders Must:

1. Bring innovation and cost management to infrastructure protection and rebuilding, where the business case exists to become involved.
2. Carefully plan future expansions and resource use in light of infrastructure shortcomings and modernization needs.
3. Manage their own infrastructure, where it applies, to meet or exceed best practice standards in the interest of lowering costs and improving sustainability.
4. Apply ISO 9000 standards to internal infrastructure management and modernization to lower fixed costs and improve execution.

Key Measures of Success

Infrastructure Evaluation	Review Person	Weakest Function(s)	Corrective Action Steps	Date to Complete
1. Enterprise limitations				
2. Market limitations				
3. Product/service limitations				
4. Critical constraints				
5. Outside involvement				

Suggested Reading

Bennis, Warren, and David A. Heenan. *Co-Leaders: The Power of Great Partnerships*. New York: John Wiley & Sons, 1999, 320 pp.

Kunstler, James Howard. *The Long Emergency: Surviving the Converging Catastrophes of the Twenty-First Century*. New York: Atlantic Monthly Press, 2005, 320 pp.

Redlener, Irwin, M.D. *Americans at Risk: Why We Are Not Prepared for Megadisasters and What We Can Do Now*. New York: Alfred A. Knopf, 2006, 304 pp.

Principled Business Leadership and Our Global Challenges

CHAPTER

18

Business and Renewed International Relationships

It may be long before the law of love will be recognized in international affairs. The machineries of government stand between and hide the hearts of one people from those of another.

—Mahatma Ghandi

Expensive Friends

Ellis Miller had been Ross Gregory's good friend since grade school. Ellis finished high school at the top of the class. She was also valedictorian at the state university in international affairs and a cheerleader—no small accomplishment. When Ellis returned home from two years in the Peace Corps in Africa, Ross immediately called her to meet for coffee.

Ellis had not changed a bit. As she ran her finger across the top of the cup, she animatedly described her love for the people with whom she had lived in Zimbabwe. She could give the African names of each family, and she told story after story about the gratitude of the families for any small thing that she did to help them.

The village people that Ellis had come to know faced so many difficult struggles on a daily basis, ranging from HIV/AIDS sickness in many families to the arduous four-mile walk that each mother had to make twice a day to the nearest well for water. Ellis had been a nurse, a social worker, an advocate, a part-time mother, and, yes, even an engineer at one time or another during her stay. She explained that of all of the burdens with which she saw these people struggling, the one for clean water was the most troubling. After six months in the village, she had written to one of her very gifted former professors, Dr. Laine Wilson, to seek help on the water issue. Ellis knew that a well would transform the village.

Dr. Wilson suggested that Ellis get in touch with a non-profit organization in Houston that enlisted U.S. volunteers to donate two weeks to bring water to villages around the world with simple shallow wells. Ellis was ecstatic at the possibility. She wrote to them the same day.

It took two months for Ellis to receive a response to her letter. But after all of the forms were completed, a team was scheduled to come to Ellis's village in the fall of her first year. Within six days the village had a well, the people had a two-day celebration, and Ellis became the hero of 200 grateful African villagers. The experience transformed her stay. Although she was the honored guest in the village, Ellis didn't stop with the work on the well. She went on to design a one-room school for the village. With her parents' help, Ellis raised $200 to buy materials for the one-room school. Ten village men worked for a month getting the materials delivered and building the school. Ellis was its first teacher. The village was ecstatic and held another celebration. Dr. Laine Wilson, Dr. Heather Stout, and Dr. John Becker even traveled to the village to join the celebration and to see the well.

Ellis explained to Ross that upon her return home, she realized that there was something very wrong with the United States' approach to international relations. The nation needed to be in the *friend-raising* business around the world. This wasn't as much about programs as it was about *people*. Friend-raising isn't merely comprised of large sums of aid money; it's about making the right investment to meet a well-defined local need. It is people living and sharing each other's culture. It is discovering basic needs, and then helping to meet them.

Ellis described to Ross how the United States has spent billions in Zimbabwe and other countries, supporting temporary governments who could turn against us in an instant. The United States, she believes, needs to be in the people business—and not the money business—when it comes to international relations. Ross is more puzzled than ever.

Issue Summary. Some people have concluded that the United States' litany of unwise choices on international assistance have benefited too few people in the receiving nations. Valuable tax funds were poured into international programs that gained no friends, improved no living standards for the neediest in the world, and gained no prestige for the nation. The cause?

International relations has not been a function of building upon shared core values, but rather a function of serving special interests—most often at the expense of the *truly* needy.

We must explore the international relations issue from three standpoints—the needs of our international neighbors; the United States' ability to really serve them and to be a good neighbor in the international sphere; and our sagging moral authority in today's international environment.

U.S. foreign policy generally followed a consistent path beginning in 1930 and extending through 1945. Termed the Roosevelt *Good Neighbor Policy*, the approach is a far cry from what has followed it during the past 65 years. The Good Neighbor Policy had two practical elements. First, there was an explicit moral and policy framework, the *ethic*, within which it functioned. Second, it had a prescribed economic framework that guided it.

A Global Good Neighbor Ethic for International Relations

The International Relations Center in Silver City, New Mexico, published a very thoughtful *Special Report* in May 2005 examining the nation's approach to international relations in the past half-century. They observed, "Seldom, if ever, has U.S. foreign policy been as confusing or as divisive as it is today. The occupation of Iraq, the deepening trade deficit, saber-rattling abroad, and disdain for international cooperation have left the American public uncertain about what exactly the U.S. government is doing overseas, and why."[1]

More recently, we note the opportunistic and aggressive strategy of China and other East Asian nations to use the post-Iraq/Afghanistan era to build their portfolio of international commodity suppliers; to strengthen their national goodwill in countless commodity-rich nations; and to acquire strategic assets in the Caribbean, South America, Africa, and South Asia. Theirs is a grand vision for the twenty-first century.

Meanwhile, the U.S. public struggles to see a cohesive strategy in the nation's foreign policy. Since the 1890s, we have pursued an insatiable outreach effort more for the purpose of "expanding the U.S. dominion abroad—and less about its own independence, democracy, and freedom."[2] This course has been expensive, and it has reaped for us some dedicated antagonists. Moreover, the strategy has done precious little in meeting human need, the recent Africa AIDS medicine program excepted. Is there not a way to bring clean water to needy people? Is there not a way that small sums of money can bring new jobs to those locked in poverty? Is there not a way that real help for needy people can be delivered? Is there a way to become good neighbors? Is there a future role for business?

Roosevelt called it a new approach to international relations. Announced in his March 1933 inaugural address, the policy was centered around the idea of "the neighbor who respects his obligations and respects the sanctity of his agreements in and with a world of neighbors." It was a sharp turn in the long-standing U.S. practice of "policing other countries, restructuring foreign economies, and installing new governments."[3]

Such a change in direction may be timely. The current time of transformation presents an enormous opportunity. Advocates offer seven principles, as follows:

1. The first step toward being a good neighbor is to stop being a bad neighbor.

2. Our nation's foreign policy agenda must be tied to broad U.S. interests. To be effective and win public support, a new foreign policy agenda must work in tandem with domestic policy reforms to improve security, quality of life, and basic rights in our own country.

3. Given that our national interests, security, and social well-being are interconnected to those of other peoples, U.S. foreign policy must be based on reciprocity rather than domination, mutual well-being rather than cutthroat competition, and cooperation rather than confrontation.

4. As the world's foremost power, the United States will be best served by exercising responsible global leadership and partnership rather than seeking global dominance.

5. An effective security policy must be two-pronged. Genuine national safety requires both a well-prepared military capable of repelling attacks on our country and a proactive commitment to improving national and personal security through nonmilitary measures and international cooperation.

6. The U.S. government should support sustainable development, first at home and then abroad, through its macroeconomic trade, investment, and aid policies.

7. A peaceful and prosperous global neighborhood depends on effective governance at national, regional, and international levels. Effective governance is accountable, transparent, and representative.[4]

This set of principles departs from the Cold War era mentality with which "foreign policy elites mobilized public and government support for international intervention by stirring up fear and hatred of the Soviet Union and communism."[5] From the Cold War ethic, we then moved to the *peace dividend*. From that era, events quickly moved the nation to address "'non-traditional threats' such as climate change, drug trafficking, failed states, and global health pandemics."[6] Has our hubris caught up with us? Good Neighbor Policy advocates suggest that it has, observing "But a new public consensus is emerging that, by its actions and arrogance, the U.S. government is stirring up dangerous discord and precipitating disintegration in international relations. In doing so, current U.S. leaders are jeopardizing America's future."[7]

Can these seven principles work for the twenty-first century United States? What is needed to establish an orderly set of new arrangements that emphasize economic promise for the nation's free enterprises, while they address the larger human condition in a world marked by extremes in poverty, values, and economic potential. Perhaps the United States can first demonstrate its real values. Those supporting the Good Neighbor Policy made a number of helpful recommendations.

> As such, [the arrangements] must be based not on arrogance and materialism but on civic pride and generosity; not on a unilateral sense of "mission" but on a collaborative role as global partner. The U.S. citizenry needs and deserves a new foreign policy that clarifies rather than confounds values—one that breaks through the barricades established by outdated political labels of conservative vs. liberal, realist vs. idealist, or isolationist vs. internationalist. We have moved beyond the age when international relations were the exclusive domain of governments. The global neighborhood we live in is shaped by flows of people, ideas, germs, trade, and investment—exchanges in which states are sometimes marginal actors at most. Although critical aspects of foreign policy are still the primary purview of states, we are all active stakeholders. We have learned the simple truth of [Ralph Waldo] Emerson that "the only way to have a friend is to be one."[8]

It may be time for a change, especially if the United States is *broke*. Enter business, and enter the nation's young adults. Exit arrogance, deception, delusion, denial, unilateralism, egocentrism, and hubris. There is a growing impatience with our arrogance and unilateralism.

> U.S. unilateralism and disregard of global treaties (the Kyoto Environmental Protocols, the Anti-Ballistic Missile Treaty, the Treaty to Ban Landmines, the Biological Weapons Convention, the Convention on the Rights of the Child, the Biodiversity Treaty) is causing a range of problematic emotional reactions around the world,

including resentment, fear, hatred, anxiety, terror, dread, envy, humiliation, intimidation, anger, rage, insult, and a healthy desire for a respectful responsiveness which, if not met will naturally drive others, in desperation, towards a desire for revenge. This endangers U.S. citizens. We are losing some of the admiration and good will that we have had in the past.[9]

Has hubris taken over? Has it become a strategy of *egocentrism* with four menacing vices? Consider examples of this egocentrism and the possibility that our international beneficence has been misdirected.

"Policies, strategies, language are organized around one's own security needs and sense of rightness."

"There is no consciousness about how these are experienced and received by other actors."

"We make incorrect assumptions about the psychology of the other, i.e., assuming deterrence will work."

"Imposing demands and ultimata is counterproductive in culture(s) where defiance to greater power is valued."[10]

The United States has poured an average of $25 billion per year for the past half century into foreign aid ventures in the form of direct aid and assistance through international organizations. Writer David Ignatius states, in a penetrating review of the book *The White Man's Burden: Why the West's Efforts to Aid the Rest Have Done So Much Ill and So Little Good*, how author William Easterly has "assembled overwhelming evidence of how little has been accomplished with the hundreds of billions of dollars in aid money, the thousands of advisory missions, the millions of reports and studies." He goes on to note "that 22 African countries spent $342 billion on public investment from 1970 to 1994 and received another $187 billion in foreign aid over that period. But the productivity gain from all this investment was *zero*. As an example of the Planners' folly, [Easterly] cites the $5 billion spent since 1979 on a publicly owned steel mill in Nigeria that has yet to produce any steel."[11]

As a final note of condemnation of current strategies, he credits Easterly for pointing out that, "the IMF's structural-adjustment lending—in which indebted countries get more money on the condition that they agree to Planners' free-market reforms—simply hasn't worked. One big reason is that the IMF, like the World Bank, is always fudging its failures, finding excuses for why past aid and advice haven't worked, discovering reasons to pump in even more assistance."[12]

Is it time for change? Is this an opportunity for business innovation? Alternatively, could public-private partnerships (PPPs) offer better solutions?

Public-Private Partnerships—Key Factors for Success

Having successfully managed 296 specific projects, 181 high-level conferences, and some 99 measurable outcomes as a result of six international PPPs in a period of 15 years (1992 to 2006), the Center for Strategic and International Studies (CSIS) in Washington developed a business model and *10 key goals for the successful PPP*. In order to be successful, a PPP must:

1. **Make a contribution to economic stability, national transformation, and economic competitiveness.** Stable economic policies, when consistently enforced, have had a significant impact on business and investment growth in countries in transformation.

2. **Realize genuine "value-added" through small, measurable actions steps aimed at overall change and growth.** The action steps were most effective when they resulted in measurable, near-term improvements and served to develop confidence and trust among the partners and contributed and opened the way to larger, complex, or sensitive challenges.

3. **Emphasize priorities that counter corruption and help to build a healthy business environment.** Opposing corruption and promoting a healthy economic environment encourages government efficiency and transparency, reforms, and ethical business conduct—all of which are essential to successful economic transformation.

4. **Improve local business access to capital, information, and law enforcement.** Affordable capital demands that banks, financial instruments, and the local market operate harmoniously.

5. **Pursue high technology and knowledge-based opportunities, where possible.** Local development and economic growth will have great appeal, if new technology applications and knowledge-based opportunities are included in the product and service mix. Added technical training and employee supervision make the resulting jobs all the more attractive to local job seekers.

6. **Engage government in bringing technology and high-potential new businesses.** The CSIS experience in Central and Eastern Europe provided a good opportunity to include government in the market development process and financing, where appropriate. Universities and other businesses (e.g., venture capital firms) were often helpful to the process.

7. **Promote infrastructure growth.** Matching market development with the parallel need for infrastructure modernization is essential to

successful economic growth and market development. Real national leadership and targeted investment is equally important to success.

8. **Strengthen cooperation with country neighbors.** Market development is aided by good relationships with neighboring countries.

9. **Support national self-determination.** Business-government cooperation in implementing practical, near-term actions enables the business community to contribute to policy development, national goal setting, and project implementation and enforcement.

10. **Facilitate systematic measurement of national growth indicators for citizen welfare, health, and education.** Meeting economic goals, improving competitiveness, and realizing sustainable profitability all contribute to economic foundation-building and other reforms.[13]

These key goals and the CSIS record of success both help to make the case for a *Good Neighbor Policy*.[14]

Our Choice

It is disappointing to realize that the funds and efforts that so many Americans have generously given to other nations in the past half-century have done so little to win lasting friendships or sustained economic improvements. But prior decisions have been driven by short-term considerations; they do not reflect a strategic mind-set. Is it time for a course change?

Lesson for Principled Business Leaders. International assistance without a human touch is ineffective. The United States best makes friends abroad one person at a time. It may be time for a new pragmatism and approach to friendship building. Businesses with international operations must be a part of this ethic, refusing to exploit or degrade international citizens while making friends.

Lesson for Principled Business Leaders. Expanded international cooperation in key sectors, such as energy, environment, water resource development, and fighting terror, may be in order, where the business case exists.

Stretch Goal for My Enterprise. Is there a business case for an alliance between my enterprise and the national service corps for international work? Can my enterprise provide training, logistics support, supervision, or other support without sacrificing revenue, profits, or market position? Would such an effort open new markets?

Stretch Goal for My Enterprise. Is there an international opportunity for innovation, technology sharing, market development, or international business alliances that present a PPP opportunity for my enterprise, as it helps to fulfill the seven "Good Neighbor" principles in this chapter? Am I prepared to step forward to implement it?

Questions to Ponder. How can principled business leaders play a more constructive role in the nation's international relationships? Should business actively engage with communities and citizens in other nations as a means to promote dialogue and understanding?

Action Steps

Principled Business Leaders Must:

Consider appropriate actions in international markets in light of the following:

1. Business innovation can be an aid to international relationships through the introduction of new products and methods in a highly visible way.
2. Business must be a responsible citizen and it must demonstrate the same level of care of employees, resources, and infrastructure in international markets that it does in the United States.
3. International PPPs may help to open new markets, new opportunities, and new innovation to meet market needs for enterprises, when the business case exists.

Key Measures of Success

Review Focus	2011 Goal	Biggest Opportunities	Most Significant Needs	Date to Complete
1. Current markets				
2. New markets				
3. Product opportunities				
4. PPP opportunities				
5. Other opportunities				

Suggested Reading

Easterly, William. *The White Man's Burden: Why the West's Efforts to Aid the Rest Have Done So Much Ill and So Little Good*. New York: Penguin, 2006, 436 pp.

Friedman, Thomas L. *From Beirut to Jerusalem*. New York: Anchor Books, 1995, 576 pp.

Godwin, Peter. *When a Crocodile Eats the Sun: A Memoir of Africa*. New York: Little, Brown & Company, 2007, 341 pp.

Huntington, Samuel P., PhD. *The Clash of Civilizations and the Remaking of World Order*. New York: Simon & Schuster Paperbacks, 1996, 367 pp.

Kirsch, Jonathan. *A History of the End of the World*. New York: HarperCollins Publishers, 2006, 352 pp.

Lewis, Bernard. *The Middle East*. New York: Scribner, 1995, 433 pp.

Business and the Limits to Empire

War is only a cowardly escape from the problems of peace.

—Thomas Mann

The World's Policeman

Ross Gregory recalls last week's luncheon with a military recruiter in the park. Quite by chance, they had run into each other on the street. The sergeant had just received his new assignment, and he wanted a listening ear. Ross agreed to go with him to get a bite to eat in the local deli. It was a sunny but very cold day.

The sergeant began to tell Ross about his assignment negotiations. The discussions have been underway for most of the fall, and the sergeant had received his orders that very day. He is now headed out on leave. His last assignment before recruiting was in Afghanistan; his next one is in the Republic of Georgia.

Ross listened carefully to the options for military assignments and quickly concluded that the United States has military personnel at more than 700 bases in 150 countries worldwide. He wonders how all of these commitments can be fulfilled with a military force that was cut in half in the 1990s. It is no wonder that overseas deployments tripled. Although the sergeant tried to put a positive spin on it all, he quietly admitted that he would retire at the first opportunity—something Ross was dismayed to hear.

The Challenge

Is the United States walking into the same snares as Rome? Author Legion XXIX's observations on the rise of Rome's military and its challenges in managing its empire are summarized as follows: Founded on the shore of the Tiber River, Rome's location was purely a function of the place where the Tiber could be crossed with ease. The city grew to govern the lives of 60 million people—one-fifth of the world's population at the time. Governing included taxes, obedience to Roman law, and adoption of its language, religions, and customs throughout the Empire. "Rome was quite literally the Super Power of the Ancient World," notes the author. The population of Rome in the first century AD was 1.0 million. It was more than 1,700 years before London would reach this pinnacle of urban population.[1]

Etruscan and Greek culture embedded itself in Rome; gladiator fights and chariot racing were Etruscan pastimes. Roman art, architecture, and literature were largely borrowed from the Greeks. Ruled by two consuls elected annually by the Senate, the logo "S*P*Q*R . . . *Senatus Populusque Quiritum Romanorum*" stood for the "Senate and People of Rome."[2]

Rome was first conquered by the Gauls in 390 BC. The city was pillaged by a force that included both the French and the Etruscans who had been thrown over some years earlier. This military defeat was exacted on the Roman Army—a force comprised of conscripted farmers and civilian landowners—later known as Legio (Legion), from the Latin root word for *conscription* or *chosen*. Providing their own weapons and body armor, these early Roman soldiers reflected their personal wealth and social status. The Gaulic conquest, however, drove the Romans to resolve to never be invaded again. They then set out to rebuild their militia with more professional soldiers. Again, comprised of farmers and landowners, and responsible for their own armor and weapons, these "professionals" served between the spring and fall harvest seasons until long campaigns soon imposed new burdens on them.

By 268 BC, virtually all of Italy was ruled by Rome. Carthage and Carthaginian-controlled Sicily were the next to be conquered. The long campaign against Carthage was especially noteworthy because it was the superpower of that day. It was also a seafaring nation, and Rome had no navy. Spurred by the Carthaginians to build a navy, Rome modeled its armada on the wrecked hull of a Carthaginian war galley. Carthage was finally beaten in 146 BC by a more powerful Rome after three lengthy Punic Wars covering more than a century.

This campaign further convinced Rome that it needed a professional army. Built upon standard pay and benefits, the army soon became a viable career for the poor who could now volunteer. Consol Marius, the acknowledged father of the Roman Army, also established rigorous training programs, a formal military lifestyle, standards, and proven rules of combat.

The Roman Army became history's first professional army paid from the taxes levied on citizens. By 100 BC, it had grown to 130,000 legionaries. One in every eight citizens was a soldier. They served for six years, and retired after 20 years of service to a piece of land awarded by Rome.

Rome's strategy of conquest went ahead full force—subduing Gaul (present-day France, conquered by Julius Caesar) in 51 BC; Egypt in 30 BC; and Britain (conquered by Claudius) in 43 AD. Conquest brought with it a heavy price of governing. A series of civil wars deeply divided the army, "pushing the Republic more and more toward dictatorship."[3]

Caesar was one offender, having returned to Rome with his legions in 49 BC without Senate permission. Those who opposed Caesar went to Greece, where they formed an opposition army under the command of Caesar's archrival, Gnaeus Pompeius Magnus (Pompey the Great), whom Caesar later defeated at Thrace. Pompey then fled to Egypt and was murdered. Caesar pursued Pompey's army to Egypt, soon defeating the pharaoh. It was in Egypt that Caesar met Cleopatra and placed her on the throne in early 47 BC. Caesar defeated the remains of Pompey's army at Thapsus, south of Carthage, in 46 BC.

Caesar then followed Pompey's sons to Munda in southern Spain, where he defeated them in 45 BC. The last of his enemies were defeated, so Caesar returned to Rome naming himself sole ruler and "dictator for life" in 44 BC. Caesar was himself murdered on the Ides (15th) of March by his opponents in the Roman senate. This event launched nearly two decades of struggle for power and Caesar's adopted son, Octavian, emerged to become Augustus Caesar, Rome's first proclaimed Emperor in 27 BC.

Rome ended as a republic and became an empire. Over the ensuing four hundred years, "the Roman Empire was ruled by 86 Emperors, some wise and just; others insane and corrupt."[4]

Reaching its height under Emperor Trajan in 117 AD, the Roman Empire controlled all of southern Europe, Britain, Asia Minor, Syria, Egypt, and North Africa. Rome was more than an empire; it was also a culture that established cities, managed trade, and created a uniform tax system. The Empire built more than 50,000 miles of roads, bridges, aqueducts, and sewers—many of which are still in use. One language, currency, religion, and passport linked Northern and Central Europe with the Middle East and Africa.

Constantine the Great developed substantially on this legacy. Installed as emperor in 312 AD, Constantine halted persecution of the Christians. He also established freedom of religion and worship with the Edict of Milan, and set norms for religious observance of the Sabbath, prayer in the army, the abolition of gladiator combat, and the end of execution by crucifixion.

He also defeated Licinius, the Emperor of the East, in 323 AD, to unite the Eastern and Western elements of the Roman Empire.

Notwithstanding Constantine's religious leadership, paganism was still the religion of many in Rome's government and many citizens. Rome's influence waned so much that Constantine moved the capitol from Rome to Byzantium in 326 AD. Byzantium was renamed Constantinople, an event that had the practical effect of dividing the Empire between Christians and pagans. This weakness was well known by Rome's enemies, who were all too eager to exploit this division.

Constantine's decision to move the capitol to Byzantium would ultimately be one of the many causes of the fall of the once mighty Roman Empire. As Legion XXIV observed,

> In many ways, United States history has paralleled that of the Roman Republic. Both were founded by colonists and ordinary people. Both came to greatness thru military power and political influence. And just like our Country, Rome has also suffered thru civil wars and political unrest. The Year 69 AD was particularly severe, when no less than four Emperors came to power thru conspiracy and assassination. Like our Civil War of the 1860s, the civil war of 69 AD saw fathers fighting sons and brother against brother, as army legions fought one another in contests of changing loyalty to those who coveted the emperor's throne.[5]

> Like all great empires, Rome reached the height of its power, and then over a long period of time, began to collapse. It became increasingly expensive for Rome to maintain the large armies that it needed to protect its borders from invasion. After 117 AD, when Emperor Trajan called a halt to the expansion of the Empire, the once-conquering Legions had now become an army of occupation and were kept busy building towns, roads, and aqueducts; as an "idle" legion's energies were likely to turn toward thoughts of returning to Rome and installing their Legato as Caesar. The legions also became increasingly staffed by foreign born soldiers and mercenaries, drawn from the conquered provinces. By 400 AD, less than 5 percent of Rome's soldiers were Italian, compared to 70 percent at the time of Christ. This led to decreased nationalism and allegiance to the Empire.[6]

Other signs of weakness emerged, including:

1. Legions feuded over who was the true emperor.
2. The fighting edge was lost by long-idled legions.
3. Foreign trade and commerce languished.

4. The many cultures and vast population of the empire were ungovernable.

5. Government bureaucracy was bloated and corrupt.

6. Non-Roman immigrants and invaders crossed Rome's borders and disrupted civil life.

7. The great city of Rome, impervious to invasion for nearly 800 years, finally fell—first to the Visagoths in 410 AD and later to the Vandals in 450 AD.

In the words of Legion XXIV, "To the average Roman citizen, life was hard, war was a constant threat and slaves were just another piece of property. And in spite of their sophistication in government, business and the arts, Romans had a crude taste for violence and cruelty. For almost a thousand years, Roman society represented both the best and the worst of human civilization."[7]

The Western Empire collapsed in 500 AD, while the Eastern one survived for another 800 years as the Empire of Byzantium—the ruling power in Eastern Europe. It was only the fall of Constantinople to the Moslems and Ottoman Turks in 1453 that brought the final end to what had been the Roman Empire. One thousand seven hundred years of Rome and its empires would influence art, language, culture, architecture, law, and history for years to come.[8]

Philosopher Hugh Elton examines the Romans and their failures in "Collapse of the Roman Empire—Military Aspects." Modern historians, he says, explain the collapse of the Western Roman Empire in the fourth and fifth centuries in one of two ways. One group follows an institutional approach, which finds the reasons in the long-term and looks closely at internal structures. A second group has adopted a political approach and looks at short-term causes of collapse. His lengthy analysis concludes, "If there was a single reason for the collapse of the western Empire, it was poor leadership, not military failure."[9]

Irishman Kirkpatrick Sale further amplified these gradual failures as they relate to America in "Imperial Entropy: Collapse of the American Empire."

It is quite ironic: only a decade or so after the idea of the United States as an imperial power came to be accepted by both right and left, and people were actually able to talk openly about an American empire, it is showing multiple signs of its inability to continue. And indeed it is now possible to contemplate, and openly speculate about, its collapse.

The neocons in power in Washington these days, those who were delighted to talk about America as the sole empire in the world following the Soviet disintegration, will of course refuse to believe in any such collapse, just as they ignore the realities of the imperial war in Iraq. But I think it behooves us to examine seriously the ways in which the U.S. system is so drastically imperiling itself that it will cause not only the collapse of its worldwide empire but drastically alter the nation itself on the domestic front.

All empires collapse eventually: Akkad, Sumeria, Babylonia, Ninevah, Assyria, Persia, Macedonia, Greece, Carthage, Rome, Mali, Songhai, Mongol, Tokugawaw, Gupta, Khmer, Hapsburg, Inca, Aztec, Spanish, Dutch, Ottoman, Austrian, French, British, Soviet, you name them, they all fell, and most within a few hundred years. The reasons are not really complex. An empire is a kind of state system that inevitably makes the same mistakes simply by the nature of its imperial structure and inevitably fails because of its size, complexity, territorial reach, stratification, heterogeneity, domination, hierarchy, and inequalities.

In my reading of the history of empires, I have come up with four reasons that almost always explain their collapse.[10]

First, environmental degradation . . . erosion of topsoils and beaches, overfishing, deforestation, freshwater and aquifer depletion, pollution of water, soil, air, and food, soil salinization, overpopulation, overconsumption, depletion of oil and minerals, introduction of new diseases and invigoration of old ones, extreme weather, melting icecaps and rising sea levels, species extinctions, and excessive human overuse of the earth's photosynthetic capacity.

Second, economic meltdown . . . excessive resource exploitation . . . peak oil extraction. . . . The dollar will be so battered that the oil states will no longer want to operate in that currency and will turn to the euro instead, and China will let the *yuan* float against the dollar, effectively making this nation bankrupt and powerless, unable to control economic life within its borders much less abroad.

Third, military overstretch . . . forced to extend their military reach farther and farther . . . coffers are exhausted . . . communication lines are overextended et al.

Finally, domestic dissent and upheaval . . . collapsing from within . . . attacked from without . . . repression of dissent . . . escalation of fear in the name of "homeland security" . . . a unique combination of entertainment, sports, television, internet sex and games, consumption, drugs, liquor, and religion that effectively deadens the general public into stupor.

. . . it's also hard to believe that a nation so thoroughly corrupt[s] as this—in all its fundamental institutions, its boughten parties, academies, corporations, brokerages, accountants, governments—and resting on a social and economic base of intolerably unequal incomes and property, getting increasingly unequal, will be able to sustain itself for long.

... I think a combination of several or all of them will bring about its collapse within the next 15 years or so.

Jared Diamond's recent book detailing the ways societies collapse suggests that American society, or industrial civilization as a whole, once it is aware of the dangers of its current course, can learn from the failures of the past and avoid their fates. But it will never happen, and for a reason Diamond himself understands.

As he says, in his analysis of the doomed Norse society on Greenland that collapsed in the early 15th century: "The values to which people cling most stubbornly under inappropriate conditions are those values that were previously the source of their greatest triumphs over adversity." If this is so, and his examples would seem to prove it, then we can isolate the values of American society that have been responsible for its greatest triumphs and know that we will cling to them no matter what. They are, in one rough mixture, capitalism, individualism, nationalism, technophilia, and humanism (as the dominance of humans over nature). There is no chance whatever, no matter how grave and obvious the threat, that as a society that we will abandon those.

Hence no chance to escape the collapse of empire.[11]

With all this in mind, what should principled business leaders do? They should first take a look at the use of security resources. They will be startled to learn that the nation has and plans to continue to spend *more* for security than it receives in net revenues (after the deduction of Social Security and other mandatory program receipts). Table 19.1 explains the 2010 to 2014 federal budget and this overspending strategy.

In short, the nation plans to spend $6.9 trillion for all forms of security and debt interest (because every other federal budget dollar must be borrowed to allow *all* net tax dollars to be spent for security) against a net income of $4.5 trillion over the five-year period—a deficit of $2.4 trillion dollars! It's no wonder the Social Security Trust Fund is *broke*! No enterprise could survive with this financial strategy. What should principled business leaders do?

Lesson for the Nation. The past and planned future practice of spending more than all of the nation's net revenue just for security is a model of deception, delusion, and denial. It is time for pragmatic business leaders to take a hard look at security leadership, financial accountability, and best practices in security—with a view toward advocating for the public

Table 19.1 Security Costs as a Share of the U.S. Budget, 2010–2014 ($ Billions)

Department	2010	2011	2012	2013	2014	2010–2014
Gross revenues	2,333.0	2,685.0	3,075.0	3,305.0	3,480.0	14,878.0
Less mandatory programs	2,037.0	2,039.0	1,973.0	2,097.0	2,230.0	10,376.0
NET REVENUES	296.0	646.0	1,102.0	1,208.0	1,250.0	4,502.0
Defense (w/o Iraq / Afghanistan)	755.0	753.0	766.0	783.0	800.0	3,857.0
Defense— contingency	65.0	148.0	153.0	157.0	162.0	685.0
Homeland Security	41.1	42.0	41.6	41.1	40.6	206.4
Interest— national debt	164.0	283.0	378.0	434.0	474.0	1,733.0
State department (50 percent share)	26.1	28.2	30.3	32.6	34.8	152.0
Veterans affairs department	53.0	54.5	56.0	57.6	59.2	280.3
TOTAL SECURITY	1,104.2	1,308.7	1,424.9	1,505.3	1,570.6	6,913.7
NET SECURITY DEFICIT	(808.2)	(662.7)	(322.9)	(297.3)	(320.6)	(2,411.7)
NET BUDGET DEFICIT	(1,258.0)	(929.0)	(557.0)	(512.0)	(536.0)	(3,792.0)

Office of Management and Budget, President's Budget, May 2009.

good new strategies, innovation, and accountability in our biggest area of unchecked excess.

Lesson for the Nation. Business leaders can detect the many signs that the United States is making some of the same errors that the Romans and other civilizations have made. Great armies consumed enormous resources. Military ambitions were too great. Environmental issues were unresolved and not seriously addressed. Territorial responsibilities were enormous. Financial constraints were ignored, while other resources were unnecessarily overexploited. Economic meltdown occurred—and is occurring. Should we take these factors into account as we consider larger world ambitions? Our resources? Our economic situation? Our vision for the future? Can principled business leaders advocate a different approach?

Lesson for Principled Business Leaders. If economic and military excesses do not force a course change, energy issues surely will. What immediate energy management steps have I taken in my enterprise to improve its economic welfare and sustainability? How can I limit the use of non-renewable resources and imported energy that may be sapping the nation or my enterprise?

Lesson for Principled Business Leaders. Business, more than any other institution, is comprised of pragmatists. Pragmatic and principled business leaders can objectively examine the limits on the United States' economic and resource assets. Pragmatic business leaders can readily detect leadership failures in these arenas and compare those failures in present U.S. practices. How can our enterprise set an example of prudence that will impact our industry and the nation?

Lesson for Principled Business Leaders. Leaders do not tolerate conditions or spending appetites that surpass resources, and business always has a plan that matches revenues with expenses to achieve profit. Does our enterprise have a good plan to sustain its profitability?

Stretch Goal for My Enterprise. Does my enterprise business plan reflect the emerging limitations on credit, natural and man-made resources, and growing global competition? Should it be revised to do so?

Questions to Ponder. What is the impact of the United States spending more than its total net revenue on all matters relating to defense and security? Can a business follow similar financial practices and survive? Should principled business leaders become involved in rationalizing our security interests and resources? What is the role of business in assisting the nation to measure its commitments against its resources? What leader can call this imbalance to the nation's attention? Am I willing to pass this problem on to the next generation?

Action Steps

Principled Business Leaders Must:

1. Manage international risk in a systematic way because there may not be federal resources to protect against international risks.
2. Partner with government to bring continuous innovation and cost reduction to international defense and assistance programs, where the business case exists.

3. Join public-private partnerships to share the international commitments, where the business case exists.

4. Demonstrate prudent business management by insisting upon industry self-regulation and oversight.

Key Measures of Our Success

Issue	Region(s)	Greatest Risk(s)	Corrective Action Steps	Date to Complete
1. Global risks				
2. Regional risks				
3. Resource risks				
4. Economic risks				
5. PPP opportunities				

Suggested Reading

Barnett, Thomas P. M. *The Pentagon's New Map: War and Peace in the Twenty-First Century*. New York: G.P. Putnam's Sons, 2004, 435 pp.

Black, Jim Nelson. *When Nations Die—America on the Brink: Ten Warning Signs of a Culture in Crisis*. Wheaton, IL: Tyndale House Publishers, 300 pp.

Diamond, Jared. *Collapse: Why Societies Choose to Fail or Succeed*. New York: Penguin Books, 2005, 575 pp.

———. Guns, *Germs, and Steel: The Fate of Human Societies*. New York: W.W. Norton & Company, 1997, 512 pp.

Friedman, Thomas L. *The World Is Flat: A Brief History of the Twenty-First Century*. New York: Farrar, Strauss, & Giroux, 2005, 616 pp.

Huntington, Samuel P., PhD. *The Clash of Civilizations and the Remaking of World Order*. New York: Simon & Schuster Paperbacks, 1996, 367 pp.

Kirsch, Jonathan. *A History of the End of the World*. New York: HarperCollins Publishers, 2006, 352 pp.

Klare, Michael T. *Resource Wars*. New York: Henry Holt and Company, LLC, 2002, 304 pp.

Martin, James. *The Meaning of the 21st Century: A Vital Blueprint for Ensuring Our Future*. New York: Riverhead Books, 2006, 512 pp.

Roberts, J. M. *The New Penguin History of the World*. New York: The Penguin Group, 2002, 1264 pp.

Overcoming Technology Losses

Once a new technology rolls over you, if you're not part of the steamroller, you're part of the road.

—Stewart Brand

Counting the Cost

Ross continues his studies on national issues. It is only a matter of time before he picks up a copy of a recent book on technology losses that the U.S. military has suffered over the past three decades. He is surprised to realize that defense contractors are in a basic conflict of interest. On one hand, they want to be paid to develop and field weapons for the United States. On the other hand, they want to add to their profits by selling these same systems to international buyers—some of which aren't U.S. allies.

Ross also sees a pattern of losses on sensitive weapons systems designs, ship designs, and others that seem to have found their way out of national laboratories and commands and into the hands of international governments. He is dismayed, because he knows that these technologies are the product of nearly three decades of work by an army of the nation's best scientists. What is the value of this work? Estimates range as high as $5 trillion. That's a full generation of scientific and technical work.

The Issue. The United States has experienced a massive loss in military technology and intellectual property over the past two decades. As a result, our nation must rebuild its technology base in order to regain its prior lead. The nation cannot forfeit its technology lead in military weapons and communications because of its global responsibilities. The development challenges provide great opportunities for innovative businesses.

Opportunities for Business Innovation

Past technology losses can open the way for new innovation. The National Academy of Sciences lists the priorities for new defense and commercial manufacturing technologies in 2010 and beyond in Table 20.1.

The technologies needed to produce the next generation of military and commercial technologies are outlined in Table 20.2.

A third and supporting axis of development to meet future defense needs will or may already have come from the commercial sector. Table 20.3 describes these advances and their potential applicability to defense.

How should principled business leaders respond to these opportunities and challenges?

Lesson for Principled Business Leaders. Twenty-first century technology development needs constitute an enormous market for innovation—process and product. Are there technology needs that your enterprise can meet?

Lesson for Principled Business Leaders. Business effort and public taxes funded much of the military technology development that has been lost in the past 30 years. Principled leaders must safeguard innovation and willingly self-regulate on matters of technology sharing.

Lesson for Principled Business Leaders. Principled business leaders would make no assumptions about our technological lead, our financial security, or our capacity to reestablish our foundation for the future. Deception, delusion, and denial won't restore the United States' lost technical assets. Principled business leaders must demand accountability and advocate for vast improvements in safeguarding military and other technology.

Stretch Goal for My Enterprise. What new technologies and process innovations can our enterprise offer to help the nation meet its twenty-first century technology needs in defense and in manufacturing?

Questions to Ponder. What role will innovation and new technologies have in future products, services, or product lines for our enterprise? How can product development, pricing, branding, and future marketing strategies be changed to further exploit existing technologies of my enterprise? What new technologies are most needed in our market? Our industry?

Table 20.1 Defense (and Non-Defense) Manufacturing Capabilities Required for 2010

Technology Area	Manufacturing Capability
Weapons system platform technologies	
Aircraft weapons systems	Repair techniques for aging systems
	Non-intrusive, real-time monitoring techniques for flight loads and damage
	Design techniques and processing methods for high strength-to-weight materials, particularly composites
	Design concepts and processing methods that reduce the costs of composite structures
	Electronic systems able to withstand high g loads and severe vibrational environments
	Affordable processing methods for launch equipment with reduced drag and signature
	Weapons systems capable of launching weapons at high speeds and under high g loadings
Surface and subsurface sea combat vessels	Design concepts that minimize weight and volume of vessel systems and reduce life-cycle costs
	Automated, intelligent monitoring and control systems
	System-level design approaches to reduce acoustic signatures and cost and increase shock resistance
	Design simulations to enable accurate performance versus cost trade-offs
Land combat vehicles	Maintenance and upgrade technologies for aging systems
	Integrated product and process development
	Virtual prototyping
Weapons technologies	
Expendable munitions	High-yield, robust fuse production process
	Methods for precise filling of explosives in munitions
	Automated filling of explosives in munitions to increase safety, improve process yield, and ensure performance
Missiles and torpedoes	Methods for miniaturizing system components
	Low-cost production processes
	Composite materials for advanced propulsion systems

(continued)

Table 20.1 (*continued*)

Technology Area	Manufacturing Capability
	Methods to reduce cycle time and non-recurring costs in production processes
	Overall system designs based on common subsystems
Guns	Methods to reduce cycle time and non-recurring costs
Mobile weapons systems	Methods for packaging electrothermal chemical technology
	Designs for high-efficiency plasma igniters and high-energy density propellants
	Designs for high-efficiency rails
	Designs to minimize weight and size of components
Cross-cutting technologies	
Low observability technology	Precise, automated methods for applying low observability coatings
	Process control sensors that can operate in hostile processing environments
	Affordable manufacturing techniques, processes, and tools that can form complex shapes with high stealth and aerodynamic/hydrodynamic performance
	Process models based on finite-element analysis of materials characteristics during forming
	Conformal mold line technology
	Methods for design trade-offs to minimize signatures created by gaps and edges
	Radar-absorptive materials and structures that are strong, lightweight, able to withstand extreme heat, formable into complex shapes, and affordable
	Designs for lightweight, effective infrared shielding
Sensors	Designs for high-performance radomes and infrared windows that are affordable and easy to manufacture
	Designs for electro-optical systems that are affordable, are easy to install, and have minimal drag and signatures
	High-density packaging for functional elements using monolithic microwave integrated circuits
Electronics	Automated validation tools to replace flight testing
	Commercial software systems to replace proprietary systems
	Methods to bridge existing networks using field programmable gate arrays, new wiring, and commercial protocols

Table 20.1 (*continued*)

Technology Area	Manufacturing Capability
	Avionics packaging with increased structural reliability and reduced connector problems for aging systems
	Built-in test diagnostics for aging systems
	Modular components to facilitate maintenance of aging systems
	Intelligent health monitors for aging systems
	Commercial hardware to replace military specification cards and improve reliability
	Commercial programmable network protocols to replace existing buses and networks and reduce costs
	Software engineering tools to facilitate upgrades and cope with rapid obsolescence of electronic technology
	Lightweight chip-on-board platforms that feature electronic miniaturization
	Platforms with reliability in terms of thermal shock resistance, thermal cycling fatigue, temperature and humidity tolerance, and mechanical shock and vibration resistance
	Materials, components, and processes that can be used in harsh military environments
	High-precision, high-reliability connectors, back planes, and traces
	Interruption-free connector systems
	Optical interconnections for ultra-high data rates
	Manufacturing processes for multilayer boards
	Conformal coating techniques and capacities to prevent dendritic growth
	Glass manufacturing technology for liquid crystal displays
Information systems	Systems architecture that permits secure use of commercial-off-the-shelf computers, software, and networks
	Defense logistics systems that are interoperable with the diverse systems used by suppliers
	Network management and control protocols to ensure data security in distributed design and manufacturing operations
	Product models with multiple levels of resolution for simulation-based design

(*continued*)

Table 20.1   (*continued*)

Technology Area	Manufacturing Capability
	Databases containing weapons system life-cycle costs for integration into design systems
	Production process capabilities and cost databases for integration into design systems
	Product data models and storage and retrieval architectures capable of handling data seamlessly
	Product structure directories that are open and meet commercial standards
	Intelligent agents for locating and retrieving information
	Automated reverse-engineering systems based on scanning of the actual part
	Parametric modeling to enable design trade-offs
Manufacturing processes and technologies	
Production rate transparency	Flexible production line
	Procurement of materials in bulk
	Methods for modeling production processes during design
	Adaptive process controls to enable 100 percent first-time yields
Composite repairs	Automated composite repairs
	On-system, on-site repair technologies and processes that are affordable and efficient
Dimensional control	Manufacturing processes and assembly sequences that determine dimensional tolerance stack-ups for modular construction
	Design methods that incorporate tolerance stack-ups at interfaces between modules or assembled parts
	Measurement systems that provide highly accurate electronic information on as-built parts
	Computer-aided visualization techniques Non-contact inspection during manufacturing operations
	Process data systems that integrate product analysis and design, manufacturing process analysis and design, tool analysis and design, and inspection/control system analysis and design
	Computer-aided design systems that integrate design, production processes, measurement processes, and compare ideal and as-built products

Table 20.1 (*continued*)

Technology Area	Manufacturing Capability
Titanium processes	Automated, highly accurate dimensional control systems using advanced photographic or laser technology
	Non-destructive inspection technology for titanium castings
	Method for coating structural titanium investment castings that produces limited reaction with molten titanium and where inclusions are detectable
	Process for producing titanium honeycomb from alloy 15–3
Overall process optimization above the plant floor	Non-recurring manufacturing process control with plant floor single view management, single numbering system, visual statusing system

Defense Manufacturing in 2010 and Beyond: Meeting the Changing Needs of National Defense;
Copyright © 2009 National Academy of Sciences. Reprinted with permission.
www.nap.edu/catalog/6373.html.

Table 20.2 Broad Categories of Required Defense Manufacturing Capabilities

Category	Manufacturing Capability
Composites processing and repair	Design methods and processes for low-cost structural composites
	Design methods for low-cost composite materials
	Composite materials for advanced propulsion systems
	Low-cost composite surfaces for tactical missiles
	Automated composite repairs
	On-system, on-site composite repair technologies that are affordable and efficient
Electronics processes	Intelligent health monitoring systems
	Electronic systems able to withstand high loads and severe vibrational environments
	High-density packaging for functional elements using monolithic microwave integrated circuits
	Electronics packaging with increased structural reliability
	Built-in test diagnostics
	Commercial programmable network protocols to replace existing buses and networks

(*continued*)

Table 20.2   (*continued*)

Category	Manufacturing Capability
	Software engineering tools to facilitate upgrades
	Lightweight chip-on-board technology for miniaturization
	High-precision, high-reliability connectors, back planes, and traces
	Interruption-free connector systems
	Optical interconnections for ultra-high data rates
	Designs to prevent dendritic growth in high-density electronics
	Manufacturing technology for liquid crystal displays
Information technology systems	Commercial software systems to replace proprietary systems
	Systems architecture that permits secure use of commercial off-the-shelf computers, software, and networks
	Defense logistics systems that are interoperable with the diverse systems used by suppliers
	Network management and control protocols to ensure data security in distributed design and manufacturing operations
	Databases containing weapons systems life-cycle costs for integration into design systems
	Production process capabilities and cost databases for integration into design systems
	Product data models and storage and retrieval architectures capable of handling data seamlessly
	Product structure directories that are open and meet commercial standards
	Intelligent agents for locating and retrieving information
	Automated reverse-engineering systems based on scanning of the actual part
	Non-recurring manufacturing process control with single view management, single numbering system, and visual statusing system
Sustainment	Repair techniques for aging systems
	Non-intrusive, real-time monitoring techniques for flight loads and damage
	Maintenance and upgrade technologies for aging systems
	Automated validation tools to replace flight testing
	Avionics packaging with increased structural reliability and reduced connector problems for aging systems
	Built-in test diagnostics for aging systems

Table 20.2 (*continued*)

Category	Manufacturing Capability
Design, modeling, and simulation	Modular components to facilitate maintenance of aging systems Software engineering tools to facilitate upgrades
	Product models that enable accurate life-cycle performance versus cost trade-offs
	Integrated product and process development
	Virtual prototyping
	System designs based on common subsystems
	Process simulations based on finite-element analysis of materials characteristics during forming
	Product models that enable stealth versus other performance characteristics trade-offs
	Designs for affordable, high-performance radomes and infrared windows
	Designs for affordable, easy-to-install electro-optical systems with minimum drag and signature
	Product models with multiple levels of resolution to enable simulation-based designs
	Parametric modeling to enable design trade-offs
	Integrated product, tool, and manufacturing process designs
	Design methods that incorporate tolerance stack-ups
	Computer-aided design systems that integrate design, production processes, measurement processes
Production processes	Affordable processing methods for launch equipment with reduced drag and signature
	High-yield, robust fuse production process
	Methods for precise filling of explosives in munitions
	Automated filling of explosives in munitions to increase safety, improve process yield, and ensure performance
	Methods to reduce cycle time and non-recurring costs in production processes
	Precise, automated methods for applying low observability coatings
	Affordable manufacturing techniques, processes, and tools that can form complex shapes
	Conformal mold line technology
	Manufacturing processes for multilayer boards
	Conformal coating techniques to prevent dendritic growth

(*continued*)

Table 20.2 (*continued*)

Category	Manufacturing Capability
	Glass manufacturing technology for liquid crystal displays
	Flexible production lines
	Adaptive process controls to enable 100 percent first-time yields
	Manufacturing processes and assembly sequences that determine tolerance stack-ups for modular construction
	Measurement systems that provide highly accurate electronic information on as-built parts
	Computer-aided visualization techniques
	Non-contact inspection during manufacturing operations
	Automated system for accurate location of assembly tools and components
	Non-destructive inspection for inclusions in titanium castings
	Process for producing titanium 15–3 honeycomb

Defense Manufacturing in 2010 and Beyond: Meeting the Changing Needs of National Defense; Category Manufacturing Capability. Copyright © National Academy of Sciences. Reprinted by permission. www.nap.edu/catalog/6373.html.

Table 20.3 Leveraging Advances in Commercial Manufacturing
Defense Manufacturing Challenges Supported by Commercial Advances

Challenge	Supporting Commercial Advances	Elements
Low-cost rapid product realization	Industry collaboration	Activity-based accounting
	High-performance organizations	Cost-as-an-independent-variable accounting
	Adaptive enterprises	Integrated product and process design
	Advanced manufacturing processing technology	Three-dimensional digital product models
		Simulation and modelling
		Tool-less assembly
		Teaming among organizations
		Virtual enterprises
		Long-term supplier relationships

Table 20.3 (*continued*)

Challenge	Supporting Commercial Advances	Elements
		Lean, adaptive, and agile enterprises
		Knowledge-based and learning enterprises
		Simulation and modelling
Expanded design capabilities	Life-cycle perspectives Advanced manufacturing processing technology	Simulation and modelling Three-dimensional digital product models Life-cycle design Cost-as-an-independent-variable accounting
Environmentally compatible manufacturing	Shared information environments Life-cycle perspectives Environmentally compatible manufacturing	Seamless data environment Life-cycle design Coating systems Cleaning systems Material selection, storage and disposal
Adaptation of information technology	Shared information environments Adaptive enterprises Advanced manufacturing processing technology	Simulation and modeling Data interchange standards Seamless data environments Knowledge-based enterprises Simulation and modeling
Security of product and process data	Advanced manufacturing processing technology	Data exchange standards Seamless data environment Three-dimensional product models
Challenge	Supporting Commercial Advances	Elements
Access to production sources	Industry collaboration Shared information environments Adaptive enterprises Advanced manufacturing processing technology	Rapid prototyping Three-dimensional product models High-speed machining Simulation and modeling

(*continued*)

Table 20.3   *(continued)*

Challenge	Supporting Commercial Advances	Elements
		Adaptive machine controls
		Tool-less assembly
		Agile enterprises
		Teaming among organizations
Use of commercial manufacturing capacity	Shared information environments Life-cycle perspectives Adaptive enterprises Advanced manufacturing processing technology	Rapid prototyping Simulation and modeling Tool-less assembly Data interchange standards Seamless data environment Life-cycle design Cost-as-an-independent-variable accounting Agile enterprises
Sustainment of weapons systems	Life-cycle perspectives Advanced manufacturing processing technology	High-speed machining Embedded sensors Cleaning systems Coating systems
	Shared information environments Environmentally compatible manufacturing	Life-cycle design Cost-as-an-independent-variable accounting Seamless data environments Data interchange standards

Defense Manufacturing in 2010 and Beyond: Meeting the Changing Needs of National Defense;
Challenge: Commercial Advances Elements; Copyright © National Academy of Sciences.
Reprinted by permission.

Action Steps

Principled Business Leaders Must:

1. Overcome past losses with new innovation and technology offerings to close existing gaps and to create new technological advantages.
2. Avert the future loss of expensive technologies to international interests notwithstanding lax enforcement of existing statutes and regulations.

3. Manage technology with every innovation at their disposal and oversee licensing and patents assiduously, especially publicly owned technologies.

4. Constantly pursue innovation to protect and extend their product, service, and market share lead in every industry.

5. Determine which, if any, defense needs can be met with technologies that they may have developed or are in the process of developing.

Key Measures of Success

Technology Need	Sector	Best Opportunities	Development Action	Date to Complete
1. Weapons platforms				
2. Weapons systems				
3. Production processes				
4. Information systems				

Suggested Reading

Gertz, Bill. *Enemies: How America's Foes Steal Our Vital Secrets—And How We Let It Happen*. New York: Crown, 2006, 304 pp.

Johnson, Rob, PhD. *Analytic Culture of the U.S. Intelligence Community*. Washington, DC: Center for the Study of Intelligence, 2005, 100 pp.

Schwartz, Peter. *Inevitable Surprises: Thinking Ahead in a Time of Turbulence*. New York: Gotham Books, 2003, 256 pp.

Limiting the Impact
of Terror

The world is a dangerous place to live not because of the people who are evil,
but because of the people who don't do anything about it.

—Albert Einstein

The Copenhagen Shock

Ross Gregory often thinks about the one stunning event that marked his otherwise wonderful trip with former classmate Ed Sipos to Denmark. It was the day that there was a terror threat in the center city near the castle. The stark reality of the moment still lives in his mind as though it were yesterday.

Ross and Ed were asleep in their hotel room. The fire alarm sounded, followed by a public address announcement in Danish. Since they didn't know the language, Ross and his friend immediately threw on clothes and hurried into the lobby. The night clerk explained that there was an attempted bombing in the center city and that all hotels were asked to keep their guests in their respective rooms until noon as a precaution. The exhausted travelers were eager to comply.

As they discussed the event later, Ross and Ed were both so impressed to see that the hotel had a complete plan for guest care in the event of an attack. Their security was splendid, as were the thorough preparations that both the hotel and the city had made for terror emergencies.

It was reassuring to know that they could safely travel to this area again.

The Issue. Has your enterprise prepared for terror incidents as well as Ross's hotel did? Does your city have an evacuation plan—along with written instructions—that has been fully shared with every resident? Is the United States the world's best example of effective terror prevention and responsive action? Can we afford the steps that we are taking? Are we using our investments wisely? If so, your children will be grateful.

The History of Terror

For nearly 1,000 years, terrorism has been a strategy employed by small groups to attempt to overcome their perceived disadvantages or grievances against established institutions or states. The objective is for an outnumbered minority to acquire an advantage. It is without a civilized or moral basis; nonetheless, it is a reality. The economic system and welfare of business is at risk. As such, business must lead the charge in counterterrorism.

This practice has continued, as small groups of dedicated extremists work to change the international balance of power in the Middle East, North America, Africa, and Asia. A scant few persons have accomplished its astonishing impact on western civilization.

Purposes of Terror

Terror is the means by which a smaller group seeks to control a larger group of people. Using surprise as a vehicle, the smaller group can gain a temporary advantage over the larger one.[1] Because of terror's origins in oil-rich Middle Eastern states, the United States finds itself in the unique position of combating and simultaneously funding terror as its petrodollars find their way back to oil-producing nations and often into the hands of terrorists.[2]

Roots of Terror

Former Harvard professor Samuel P. Huntington offers four cultural factors that enable terror—a reality largely outside of the civilized West—to become a divider of the "seven or eight civilizations in the modern world (Western, Latin American, African, Islamic, Sinic, Hindu, Orthodox, Buddhist, and Japanese)."[3] These cross-civilization factors are:

1. The forces of integration are real and are precisely what are generating counter forces of cultural assertion and civilizational consciousness.

2. The world is in some sense two, but the central distinction is between the West as the hitherto dominant civilization and all the others, which, however, have little if anything in common among them. The world, in short, is divided between a Western one and a non-Western many.

3. Nation states are and will remain the most important actors in world affairs, but their interests, associations, and conflicts are increasingly shaped by cultural and civilizational factors.

4. The world is indeed anarchical, rife with tribal and nationality conflicts, but the conflicts that pose the greatest dangers for stability are those between states or groups from different civilizations.[4]

Although the West, one of the parties in Huntington's "clash of civilizations,"[5] is not a perpetrator of terror, it *does* have a significant economic stake in successfully confronting and defeating terror. One analyst puts it more bluntly in describing terror's most visible proponent: Osama Bin Laden's main goal is the destruction of the U.S. economy—and . . . so far, he appears to be succeeding.[6] He went on to conclude that "the main goal of the radical Islamic Jihad movement is to 'bring the U.S. economy to its knees.'"

Suggesting that Bin Laden and Al-Qaeda started to plan its moves against the United States after it attributed Moscow's exit from Afghanistan to Soviet economic difficulties resulting from the war, Dr. Gal Luft, director of the Institute for the Analysis of Global Security states, "Now Bin Laden thinks he can do the same thing to the United States, but more so." Dr. Luft explains that Bin Laden is deliberately focusing on U.S. economic targets. Al-Qaeda's attack on the World Trade Center on September 11, 2001, was planned to strike at the epicenter of the U.S. economy.

That attack, which cost the U.S. taxpayer $1 trillion in damages, and the subsequent war in Afghanistan and Iraq are "bleeding" the U.S. economy of its wealth. Bin Laden is also attempting to disrupt the U.S. economy by causing the price of oil to rise, concludes Dr. Luft. He claims that the sabotage of oil pipelines in Iraq and attacks on foreign oil workers in Saudi Arabia succeeded in raising the price of oil by $10 to $15 per barrel.

What the United States has to do, asserts Dr. Luft, is drastically revamp the inefficient transportation sector. He proposes that the United States lead a massive international project to improve transport fuel efficiency. He points out that the technology already exists. "There's no need for new research and development" to have cars running on 60 to 70 miles per gallon, he explains.

Dr. Luft claims that improving fuel economy in the transportation sector is the most important thing the United States can do to strengthen its economy "and win the war on terror."

So far, however, without U.S. leadership on this issue, it appears that Bin Laden is gaining the upper hand. "Bin Laden says he wants oil to go [back] up to $140 per barrel."[7]

A Canadian writer quotes a former CIA director who warns, "there is every reason to expect more terror attacks in the coming months, because al-Qaida [*sic*] has not been destroyed."[8] He goes on to quote "a 1997 report on the scourge of terrorism," in which "the Pentagon's Defense Science Board observed: 'Historical data show a strong correlation between U.S. involvement in international situations and an increase in terrorist attacks against the United States.'"[9]

As a part of its status as the world's only *superpower*, the United States is the only country in the world that actively attempts to police regions outside its own, so it should come as no surprise that one-third of all terrorist attacks worldwide are perpetrated against U.S. targets. Far from providing security, U.S. policy is stirring up security threats, even as the government uses the aftermath of successful attacks as the rationale to expand government power.[10]

Another analyst puts it more forcefully by claiming, "In the interest of peace, security, and the freedom of global commercial relations, all Americans and non-Americans the world over must forcefully oppose the hyper-interventionism of the United States government, which by its own admission endangers the lives and property of Americans. Interventionism and jingoism are not the solutions to terrorism, but rather its motive force."[11] Regardless of the origins of terror, business leaders must have a comprehensive plan to address and mitigate its risks.

Lesson for Principled Business Leaders. Business leaders must have a long-term view of terror and its risks. They must systematically assess these risks, develop structured approaches to mitigating them, and emphasize variable- and not fixed-cost solutions to counter them.

Lesson for Principled Business Leaders. Terror must be one issue evaluated in new product offerings, entry to new markets, and outsourcing manufacturing. It is an element of variable cost planning.

Lesson for Principled Business Leaders. Counterterror planning and activities must be strategic (addressing long-term threats and business interests) and tactical (covering immediate operations, response, and security).

Lesson for Principled Business Leaders. Business leaders must incorporate counterterror planning into every local business activity—manufacturing plants, retail locations, distribution points, transportation and delivery, and supply chain management. This planning should include systematic outreach to relevant local, state, and federal officials and maintenance of up-to-date contact information and counterterror plans.

Lesson for Principled Business Leaders. Counterterror planning for business must include public information and awareness training, preparedness and preventive actions, comprehensive/layered security for all locations, reliable communications systems, response planning and rehearsal, and continuous systematic risk assessment. Planning addresses all functions—operations, production, transportation, storage and distribution, finance, and administration.

Stretch Goal for My Enterprise. Is our business able to reduce terror risks, make mitigation investments, and develop high-success response actions to an acceptable level at all of its locations?

Stretch Goal for My Enterprise. Is our terror protection plan sufficient, in that we are assured of continuity of operations and minimum disruption of the supply chain in the event of the temporary loss of a facility? A transportation route? A transportation terminal?

Stretch Goal for My Enterprise. Is there a role that our organization can play in local counterterror protection and improved security for our critical community infrastructure?

Questions to Ponder. Are our enterprise managers aware of any forthcoming credible, specific, and/or corroborated terror threats against commercial facilities on a real-time basis? Do they know what actions to take? Is our critical business infrastructure protected? Are there other likely terror targets in the communities in which we are located that might cause ancillary damage to our business operations in the event of a terror incident or attack?

Action Steps

Principled Business Leaders Must:

1. Develop a realistic, systematic assessment of terror risks, required mitigation actions, and responses to plausible terror scenarios for their facilities, critical infrastructure, and operations.

2. Make employees, families, and vendors aware of any plausible terror threats or intelligence that comes to their attention.

3. Direct the mitigation and response to any terror threats or incidents.

4. Manage employee participation in averting terrorism and promoting safe practices and security.

5. Use technology to best advantage in monitoring unusual behavior, managing enterprise installations, and carefully assessing all internal and external risks.

6. Complement the limited public safety security services available in many vulnerable areas.

7. Maintain a real-time planning and counterterror coordination program in their enterprises.

8. Set the example for other businesses by using best practices on all counterterror issues.

Key Measures of Success

Terror Management	Persons Responsible	Mitigation Priorities	Resources Required	Date to Complete
1. Risk assessments				
2. Terror plan				
3. Public coordination				
4. Critical infrastructure				
5. Employee education				

Suggested Reading

Ahmed, Akbar. *Journey into Islam*. Washington, D.C.: Brookings Institution Press, 2007, 323 pp.

Armstrong, Karen. *Holy War*. New York: Anchor Books, 2001.

Barnett, Thomas P.M. *The Pentagon's New Map: War and Peace in the Twenty-First Century*. New York: G.P. Putnam's Sons, 2004, 628 pp.

Enderlin, Charles. *The Lost Years: Radical Islam, Intifada, and Wars in the Middle East, 2001–2006*. New York: Other Press, 2006, 356 pp.

Friedman, Thomas L. *From Beirut to Jerusalem*. New York: Anchor Books, 1995, 571 pp.

Huntington, Samuel P., PhD. *The Clash of Civilizations and the Remaking of World Order*. New York: Simon & Schuster Paperbacks, 1996, 448 pp.

Lewis, Bernard. *The Middle East*. New York: Scribner, 1995, 448 pp.

Business Solutions for the Developing World

Globalization could be the answer to many of the world's seemingly intractable problems. But this requires strong democratic foundations based on a political will to ensure equity and justice.

—Sharan Burrow

The Visit

Some years out of college, Ross and his friend Lee Warren, an employee of a non-profit microlending organization, decide to take a trip to Zimbabwe, where his classmate Ellis did such great work among the villagers a few years earlier. After an exhausting 24-hour flight, the two friends are met by the village chief, who shows them to his 1960 Opel to make the three-hour trip over the mountains to the village. When they arrive in the early morning, they immediately fall asleep in their small hut, totally wiped out.

The new day brings a warm welcome from the villagers. Ellis's well is still working, and the schoolhouse is still standing. The people are moderately happy, but they have a nagging problem—no jobs.

Lee has seen this situation before. His organization has a remarkable record of success in nearby Kenya in stimulating rural employment in areas that had suffered chronic job losses and economic hardships for years. There were some real miracle stories. Lee begins to talk to villagers about their lives and work. Lee is spellbound as the grade school interpreter lights up with the stories from men and women in the village. This goes on for five days.

Then there is a meeting in the school building, for which virtually every one of the 100 adults in the village is present. Lee begins to talk about his company's microlending program—small loans to individuals to launch their own craft, service, animal, or food enterprises. Often less than $100, these loans are paid back over the course of a year with the earnings of the little businesses that they enable. The funds are then loaned to others to start or expand their businesses—all under the careful supervision of a government representative, who acts as banker.

The villagers are ecstatic to hear Lee tell of the small village nearby where his company saw 50 jobs created for new cottage industries in less than a year at a cost of less than $1,000, all of which was repaid. As he sees the villagers become more excited about this potential plan, Ross is glad to have made the trip.

The Challenge

One-fifth of the world's population lives in underdeveloped, third-world nations. These people drink unclean water; have massive problems with disease and inadequate health and nutrition; and suffer from devastated and underdeveloped economics that do not provide them with sufficient employment. Just staying alive is an ordeal of immense proportions.

The United States has attempted to ameliorate failed economic conditions in many countries with money. But the grants and loans have not made alleviating human suffering a priority. As a result, money often finds its way into the hands of corrupt politicians and bad governments, where it has benefited only bureaucrats and government officials. Additionally, many corporations that extract resources from developing countries ignore the desperate conditions in which local citizens live in impoverished economies like Nigeria, Liberia, and countless others. As a result, human poverty and suffering has persisted, despite the investment of hundreds of billions of U.S. dollars in foreign aid since World War II.

More recently, China and other Asian nations have been surpassing the United States in these third-world economies. The Asians not only buy commodities, but they also invest in urgently needed projects to benefit local citizens in a demonstrable and highly visible way. They have learned to build friendships and to add value, instead of just extracting value.

America must take a hard look at friendship-building and economic development. Business can provide innovation and support for a new ethic in international relationships, where the business case exists for their involvement. Perhaps the cornerstone of this process should be to provide the greatest of all human needs—fresh, clean water to drink and sanitary living conditions.

An international relations strategy for developing and underdeveloped nations built around clean water is a revolutionary concept—an unassailable good. Water development and resource management in the third world could replace international lending organizations' special-interest-driven projects and the mountains of debt piled on these struggling economies. Most important, the water policy would meet the most urgent of human needs and be far cheaper. How can business aid this process?

Perhaps there is a second pillar to international assistance that should be considered—small-scale job creation through microlending.

Putting Competence to Work

Business can lead the way to new technology and to a responsible strategy for systematic third-world development. Leaders can not only participate in the debate, but can also demonstrate the principles of microlending in developing markets where it operates by:

1. Bringing capacity building to microenterprises;
2. Creating new jobs where they are most needed;
3. Building trust with local people;
4. Helping needy businesses in difficulty; and
5. Being a catalyst for socio-economic development.[1]

These principles can apply at many levels. On an individual level, microloans can be provided to budding entrepreneurs individually, and the lender can supervise the use and repayment of the money. On a regional level, a microlending bank can be established to run hundreds of microloans in many urban and rural locations. The principles are the same in both scenarios: teaching business fundamentals—purchasing raw materials, product development, production, sales, and, most importantly, cash and financial management—when the loan is repaid. Jobs are created, people develop, and market needs are met.

The same concept can be implemented at the national level by one primary bank that is responsible for administering a series of regional banks, all of whom engage in local level microlending as well. The National Bank for Agriculture and Rural Development (NABARD) in Bangladesh finances a total of 500 small banks who lend funds to self-help groups (SHGs), small groups of local entrepreneurs and employers. The SHGs meet regularly for training on a business function. They then contribute small sums of money to a group fund from which members can borrow for business projects the group supports. If larger sums are needed, the SHG can borrow from the regional bank, the NABARD, or other groups. There are 1.4 million SHGs with some 20 million female members in the India "SHG-Bank Linkage Model," the largest in the world.[2]

Farmers, for example, are able to purchase seed and fertilizer for seasonal crops. Home businesses are formed. Improved business practices are taught on the individual scale. Responsible financial practices are demonstrated with the strong oversight of the borrowers' peers in the small group. These case histories are being repeated in Africa and Southeast Asia with the assistance and support of numerous international organizations like Opportunity International, Catholic Relief Services, CARE, AMPAS, and Oxfam.[3] Interest is charged on the loans ranging between annual rates of 12 to 24 percent, since many loans are paid back in months and not years.[4]

Business leaders can engage in microlending from a distance, as well. India's Rang De and dhanaX enable international entrepreneurs to connect with a local farmer in Tamil Nadu.[5] Kiva.org does microloans from the United States in which interested business persons can contribute to microloans for entrepreneurs, whose photos and stories are available on the site.

Aptly named "one-click high leverage giving" by blogger Kevin Kelly, Kiva.org provided the photo of Jocelyn, a furniture maker in the Philippines. She needed a loan of $175 in 2009. U.S. contributors/lenders provided the funds, and Jocelyn began a repayment schedule of amounts ranging from $21.00 to $36.50 over a six-month period beginning in May 2009. Reports were posted on each month's repayment within 15 days of the due date. And the contributors' loan to Jocelyn was monitored by a *field partner*, Alalay as Kaunlaran, Inc. (ASKI), who rated the loan for risk and monitored the repayment for the donor. ASKI, interestingly, serves 491 Kiva.org entrepreneurs with total loans of $80,900. The delinquency rate on the portfolio is 0.52 percent, and the default rate is 0.00 percent—a remarkable record by most lending norms.[6]

Batasayan Suhbaatar is a livestock herder in Mongolia. A resident of Arhangay Province, Batasayan has a wife and two children. His wife does tailoring to earn money and cares for their children. Batasayan has 120 livestock in his herd, many of which he was forced to sell at low prices after the cold Mongolian winter in April 2009. He applied for a $350 loan to purchase livestock. A repayment schedule of 14 months was established, and lenders were offered shares in his loan beginning at $25 each. Kiva.org's field partner in Mongolia is XacBank, which had 108 Kiva entrepreneurs and $89,600 in loans outstanding in only two months.[7]

These stories have brought miracles to each of the families who were fortunate enough to participate in a microlending program. A generation was given a helping hand. Many family members were helped. In other instances, several generations can be similarly affected, or several businesses can be launched. The story of Frew Wube in Ethiopia is one such multi-business miracle.

A Small Shop

When his parents could no longer afford to support him and his six younger siblings, Frew Wube decided to leave his native village of God-jam in northern Ethiopia in search of a better life in the capital city Addis Ababa. That was more than ten years ago, and like many other young children in his country, Frew—then only 14 years old—learned quickly to survive on the streets on his own. He landed his first job cleaning tables in a restaurant, working hard to make just enough money to eat one meal a day and pay for the bed he rented for ten cents a night in the slum area of town. Whenever possible, he would also try to send money to help support his family in Godjam.

"One day I was talking with a co-worker at the restaurant, who mentioned that the kebele [the local government administration] was giving business loans to people in the area," Frew says. However, when he inquired about the program, he was told that he was too poor to qualify for loans. Instead, he was directed to a Trickle Up partner agency, and was selected to receive a Trickle Up seed capital grant to start his first business. Frew used the capital to purchase a small stock of clothes to resell for a profit and saw his income increase progressively.

"There are tricks you learn," Frew explains, "such as when are the best days to sell and the first days of the months when people generally receive their paychecks."

As his economic situation improved, Frew was able to leave the bed he rented for ten cents a night and pay for a small room for $15 a month. He continued to send money home to support his family. Two years ago, he sent for his two younger sisters, Haimanot and Melkan, to join him in the city.

"I thought they would have more opportunities here. They could work and maybe go to school," he says.

Haimanot and Melkan quickly learned the ropes of the job and started working with their brother in the business. Soon, the two girls managed the clothing business on their own, and Frew began to think about other income-generating opportunities.

"I also save every month," says Frew, who has over $40 stored in a cooperative savings fund. The capital he has saved with other people in his group is used to provide loans to group members at a low interest rate. Frew, now able to access credit thanks to his Trickle Up clothing business, has taken progressively larger loans from the group, including his latest loan of $300 to start a candle business.

"Church is an important part of people's lives here in Addis," Frew explains. "Some people go to Church two or three times a week and purchase candles to burn for their prayer. I thought making candles could be a good business since people consume them in such large quantity and regularly."

Frew used his loan and the profits he earned from his Trickle Up business to purchase a charcoal stove, utensils, wax, and thread to launch a candle business. At first, he and his siblings sold a small quantity of candles directly to individuals. Frew soon learned that they could sell larger quantities to wholesalers, which would require less time spent on the market and larger sales.

"There are days when we get large orders and produce several hundred candles," he says.

The family now earns an income of about $30 per week, which in their local context allows them to pay rent for the room they share, eat sufficient meals, and continue to send money to their family in Godjam.

"We used to eat one meal a day that we had to buy outside our home.... Now we can afford to buy our own cooking materials, like grain, and make our own injera [bread] here at home for our meals," they say. The siblings were even able to buy a radio-cassette player and a mattress—two luxuries they couldn't enjoy before.

Frew's ambition grows. "Eventually, I'd like to open a small shop in the market where I can sell my products," he says determinedly. "When you're not selling on the streets, that means you have succeeded."[8]

Lesson for Principled Business Leaders. Regardless of the size of your enterprise, there is a role that you can fill in bringing opportunity to others around the world. The challenge is to match the opportunity with your organization's interests and the applicable business case in that market.

Lesson for Principled Business Leaders. Businesses can make microloans to U.S. entrepreneurs in depressed domestic markets and low-income areas, just as they can be made in overseas markets. (See Grameen Foundation.)

Lesson for Principled Business Leaders. Businesses can consider micro-enterprises in overseas markets as the first step in accessing new sources of raw materials or products where quality standards can be enforced.

Stretch Goal for My Enterprise. Is there a business case for our enterprise to engage in international markets for mutual benefit? Are our horizons larger than my immediate business enterprise?

Stretch Goal for My Enterprise. What opportunities exist for our organization to join a public-private partnership (PPP) as a first step in developing international markets, sales opportunities, or business relationships? Can we meet the criteria for a successful PPP?

Questions to Ponder. Has my enterprise looked systematically at the short-term and long-term impacts of globalism on our product lines, services, and markets? Are overseas suppliers and service providers committing unfair or inappropriate labor practices that would not be permitted in a similar domestic operation? Am I prepared to demonstrate best practices in overseas operations in human resources, finance, safety, worker compensation, worker benefits, and management even if there is a cost to meeting these standards, when the business case can sustain such changes?

Action Steps

Principled Business Leaders Must:

1. Accept, adapt to, and adopt globalism—systematically searching for business opportunities for their enterprise.

2. Consider developing nations as a potential market for innovation and new products.

3. Consider developing nations as a potential market for microloans and small business investments and as a means to explore new markets and new opportunities.

4. Consider investments and donations to developing nations as a means to contribute to the welfare of others and to demonstrate the validity of micro-enterprise.

5. Give back as strongly as they take resources in extraction and mining industries in overseas markets by setting the best possible example of meeting employee and local needs, as part of the business planning and execution process.

6. Set the best possible example for other nations in applying U.S. best practices and standards in international operations.

7. Be transparent in the manner in which they operate enterprises in developing nations.

Key Measures of Success

International Markets	Person Responsible	Urgent Business Needs in Priority Order	Alternate Sourcing Options	Date to Complete
1. Selling opportunities				
2. Materials sourcing				
3. Finished product sources				
4. Options for manufacturing				
5. Microloan strategy				

Suggested Reading

Counts, Alex. *Small Loans, Big Dreams: How Nobel Prize Winner Muhammad Yunas and Microfinance Are Changing the World*. Hoboken, NJ: John Wiley & Sons, 2008, 410 pp.

Yunus, Muhammad. *Banker to the Poor: Micro-Lending and the Battle Against World Poverty*. Blackstone Audio Books, 2008.

Yunus, Muhammad. *Creating a World Without Poverty: How Social Business Can Transform Our Lives*. New York: Perseus Books Group, 2007, 296 pp.

CHAPTER 23

Business and International Environmental Resources

Earth provides enough to satisfy every man's need ... but not every man's greed.

—Mahatma Gandhi

International Environmental Risks

R oss Gregory is on assignment in California. As a long-time surfing enthusiast, Ross finds himself in San Diego for the weekend, a few miles north of Imperial Beach. He can't wait until business is finished for the week on Friday so that he and his friend Fritz Elliott—a biologist at the San Diego Water Management Laboratory—can take off for the beach. Imperial Beach is good surfing when the evening tides come in, and the two are on their way by four o'clock in the afternoon. Caroline and Emma Kelley are to join them at Imperial Beach for a day of surfing.

Unfortunately, when Ross and Fritz arrive at Imperial, posted signs indicate that the beach is closed for most of the day. They learn from the lifeguard that the closure is due to higher-than-normal discharge of untreated and partially treated sewage from the Tijuana River that has washed landward from the ocean outlet and polluted the beach, making it highly unsafe for bathing and surfing. The problem is further complicated by the north-ward flow of untreated sewage from the city of Tijuana that is discharged over the beach in nearby northern Mexico. Caroline and Emma can only hold their noses. They leave in minutes.

Fritz informs Ross that sewage from the Mexican side of the Tijuana River watershed flows north at a rate of nearly 60 million gallons per day into the United States. It receives primary treatment at a U.S.-operated plant in San Ysidro before it is piped straight into the Pacific Ocean three miles offshore from San Diego. Ross is astonished to learn that this water is lost forever.

To his surprise, Ross also learns from Fritz that this problem has been in existence since the closing days of World War II, when the small joint commission established by the United States and Mexico to regulate joint waterways was formed. After 60 years, money has been appropriated to build a second treatment station to provide secondary treatment to the water before it goes to the Pacific. This is a help, Ross thinks, but can't we avoid losing the water?

Fritz lets Ross in on a shocking reality: More than one billion peo-ple worldwide do not have access to clean water, even for drinking. The resulting scourges of diarrhea, dysentery, typhoid, and malaria are killing thousands each day. Ross learns that nearly half of the world's population, including many parts of Asia, do not have adequate water access to main-tain minimum health and nutrition levels. Unfortunately, certain farming and animal industries are massive users of water to the exclusion of the population in other downstream areas on many of the world's waterways. The problem is all the worse, he finds, because so many waterways touch as many as five countries. International water problems have gone unresolved for decades. Ross is stunned.

Issue Summary. The United States has an opportunity—and even a responsibility—to assume leadership in restoring the environment world-wide and playing a strategic role in water management because it has viable clean water technologies and because the problem has been unresolved for so long. Moreover, the health of one-fifth of the earth's population is at risk. Business leaders can also assert environmental leadership as they consider new markets, overseas materials procurement, and urgent human needs in these markets, when there is a viable business case.

If this can be done, there is no better place for the nation or its business leaders to start than in advocating for clean water and sanitary living condi-tions in the markets in which they work. Unfortunately, this goal is far from the present reality. The international water business is the adopted stepchild of countless international aid organizations, worldwide water enterprises, and regional special interests, many of whom serve every interest but those of the local citizens. As a result, millions of people have suffered, while the near-violent war for control of water resources is played out in one country after another. International water businesses installed by Western aid organizations have often been at the core of dramatically worsening local and regional dislocations. Disease and starvation have been rampant in the wake of massive inequities in the collection, treatment, and distribution of water. Suffering has often occurred at the hands of these unscrupulous interests. Northern Mexico is only one sad water story; other such stories abound throughout the world. Can business stop the advance of this growing disaster?

Can Business Lead the Debate on Worldwide Environmental Issues?

In light of the urgency of global environmental needs, business may finally be forced to take a lead role in making the case for new ecological priorities when there is a business case to do so. The pervasive absence of clean water, massive amounts of untreated wastewater flowing in community streets, outdated infrastructure, absence of clean air, wasteful farming practices, lack of conservation, growing population pressures, countless destroyed rivers and streams, numerous dissipated underground water aquifers, unwise farming and manufacturing policies, frequent illegal disposal of toxic wastes, seething transboundary water disputes, and improper use of chemical fertilizers that destroy both the soil and the water supply all argue for a new worldwide ethic of environmental pragmatism.

A transformational environmental ethic will come only at an enormous tangible expense and political courage. But continuing to ignore these needs will cause only a greater future expense, crisis, or outright collapse. Pragmatic, principled business leaders have the knowledge, sense of urgency, capacity, and capability to focus the debate, to launch the educational process, to move aside political obstacles, and to step carefully but purposefully into this virtual environmental minefield. But where should they start?

Water and Wars   Water should be the first priority. Water is the unseen hand behind some of the world's most bitter disputes.[1] One can hope that serious water-related conflicts can be resolved through formal negotiations. Unfortunately, the tensions over international water issues remain white hot, and few if any disputes have been resolved in the past decade. Moreover, there is a strong connection between water and energy, which few leaders understand because the implications are so daunting.

As one analyst observed, "if the world fought for oil in the 20th Century, the war will be about water in the 21st Century."[2] Prudent use of this resource over the long term will be an essential element of the health and welfare of the 7 billion people on the planet and, surely, for the 300 million Americans and their descendents during this pivotal century.

Former USSR President Mikhail Gorbachev reminded attendees at the 2003 Third World Water Conference in Kyoto, Japan, that water had been the cause of 21 recent armed disputes. Moreover, 18 of them had involved Israel. Yehezkel Lein, a water expert for B'tselem—an Israeli human rights group—went even further in saying, "There is a clear linkage between the gap in water availability and the occupation."[3]

Clearly, the Middle East is water-war prone, but it is only one such area: "water scarcities and allocation will pose significant challenges to governments in the Middle East, Sub-Saharan Africa, South Asia, and northern China. Regional tensions over water will be heightened by 2015." By 2015, nearly half the world's population—more than 3 billion people—will live in countries that are "water-stressed."[4]

One such case is the Middle East and the Israeli Six-Day War. The little known element of Israel's 1967 War (and other Israeli conflicts in this region) was the importance of water in the territorial seizures and still-contested border areas. Israel has since become a model of agricultural modernization, while the region still lags in food production. "For Israel, the water question was the key to the land question."[5]

Water silently drives many political actions in other regions. Because of its misuse, it is also driving massive natural resource and wealth transfers.

Use and Misuse of Water   There are numerous instances of man-made destruction of major watersheds, urbanization, dumping of wastewater into oceans, production of toxic wastes from desalinization, and misuse of water for petroleum production. One of the more tragic examples is the virtual loss of the Aral Sea Basin in Asia, described in the following passage from Maude Barlow's compelling work, *Blue Gold: The Fight to Stop the Corporate Theft of the World's Water*.

> The Aral Sea basin shared by Afghanistan, Iran and five countries of the former Soviet Union was once the world's fourth largest lake. Excessive river diversions (part of a massive Soviet irrigation project) have caused it to lose half its area and three-fourths of its volume, while its surrounding wetlands have shrunk by 85%.[6]

Other Clean Water Technologies

Unfortunately, and contrary to the convictions of many officials in Asia and the Middle East, desalination is not a solution to the world's water shortages. It's expensive, it's an energy consumption monster, and it produces large amounts of a concentrated, harmful saline brine. It is a dangerous ocean polluter in and of itself. However, despite these detrimental effects, Saudi Arabia and other oil-rich states plan continued widespread use of desalination plants.[7]

Urbanization and the accompanying paving-over of large areas further complicate the world water problems. Water runoff from paved areas to storm sewers, once treated, is released to nearby oceans rather than being reintroduced to aquifers or recycled for manufacturing. Fossil-fuel production and automobile manufacturing are also big users of water:

Petroleum refining is one of the most water-intensive of all industrial activities. Tar Sands oil represents 66 percent of the world's supply of petroleum,[8] and it requires huge amounts of fresh water for refining. High-pressure steam (heated by natural gas) is required to wash heavy oil from sand (tar sands production).[9] The water-energy equation is clearly out of balance in fossil-fuel production, as it is in many types of manufacturing.

Producing one automobile, for example, uses nearly 119,000 gallons of fresh water. If the world's consumers seek to buy 700 million alternative energy cars to replace the existing fleet, the water cost reaches more than 83 quadrillion (83,213,900,000,000) gallons of fresh water. The post-manufacturing polluted water is often lost to further use.[10] Other massive losses are caused by man's leadership failures.

These staggering losses and illustrations of water misuse are tragic. Consider agriculture—the primary user of water. International water expert Peter Gleick describes these water uses and water losses in practical terms, beginning with the definition of consumptive water use.

> Consumptive water use refers to water that is not returned to streams after use. For the most part, this is water that enters the atmospheric pool of water via evaporation (from reservoirs in arid areas) and from plant transpiration (especially from "thirsty" crops such as cotton and alfalfa). Irrigated agriculture is responsible for most consumptive water use and decreases [in] surface run-off. "An extreme example is the Colorado River, which has most of its water diverted to irrigated agriculture, so that in a normal year, no water at all reaches the river's mouth."[11]

Agriculture is responsible for 87 percent of the total water used globally. In Asia it accounts for 86 percent of total annual water withdrawal, compared with 49 percent in North and Central America and 38 percent in Europe. Rice growing, in particular, is a heavy consumer of water: It takes some 5,000 liters of water to produce 1 kg of rice. Compared with other crops, rice production is less efficient in the way it uses water. Wheat, for example, consumes 4,000 m^3/ha, while rice consumes 7,650 m^3/ha.[12]

Since agriculture is consumptive, correcting its inefficiencies should be a high priority in any transformational environmental policy. Business could bring innovation to this much-needed transformation worldwide. Gleick provides further justification for the needed non-consumptive water transformation from the vital perspective of world health challenges.

> A great deal of water use is non-consumptive, which means that the water is returned to surface runoff. Usually that water is contaminated however, whether used for agriculture, domestic consumption, or industry. The WHO (World Health Organization) estimates that more than 5 million people die each year from diseases caused by unsafe drinking water, and lack of sanitation and water for hygiene. This has economic effects as well: an outbreak of cholera in Latin America killed hundreds of people, and cost hundreds of millions of dollars.[13]

The Bottom Line   Gleick further points to Asia as the newest frontier in the water crisis, as he acknowledges Africa's long (and failed) battle against dire water shortages and for clean water. Enormous human health and survival outcomes are at stake in both Africa and Asia.

> Some believe that fresh water will be a critical limiting resource for many regions in the near future. About one-third of the world's population lives in countries that are experiencing water stress. In Asia, where water has always been regarded as an abundant resource, per capita availability declined by 40–60% between 1955 and 1990. Projections suggest that most Asian countries will have severe water problems by the year 2025. Most of Africa historically has been water-poor.[14]

He goes on to explain that agriculture, unfortunately, loses a large share of the water devoted to it due to inefficient irrigation. Asia's water losses are all the more severe, because that continent begins with only 36 percent of the world's water supply (available only on a highly seasonal basis), despite the fact that it has 60 percent of the world's population.[15] Asia suffers from a much greater pollution problem as well, because of unregulated water disposal from industry, and much higher bacteria levels due to the absence of wastewater treatment.[16] The tragic price of leadership failures in water management in Asia—500,000 deaths per year—is "from dirty water and poor sanitation."[17] The international water problem cries out for pragmatic solutions—solutions that are not coming from the large global water companies. International environmental challenges don't end with water, however.

Destruction of Rain Forests　　Loss of rain forests is also a major blight, and a key contributor to the buildup of greenhouse gases. While some limited progress has been made in slowing rain forest destruction—particularly in Brazil—the ongoing devastation continues at alarming rates. This is a particular problem in poorer countries, where forest destruction has already destroyed some civilizations, and it threatens others.[18]

Protecting Endangered Plant and Wildlife　　The loss of endangered plant and animal species is also a global environmental concern, particularly in tropical climates. Fish stocks are another victim, given the fact that a majority of all of the world's marine fisheries are already over-fished, "over-exploited, depleted, or slowly recovering from collapse."[19] Whole communities and industry groups are at risk. *Time* magazine concluded a recent series on the modern losses of endangered species, suggesting that the sixth and current decimation of endangered animal species and wildlife would be due not to the forces of nature as in the past five waves of extinction but rather to the misguided and self-serving actions of Earth's humans.[20]

International Persistent Organic Pollutants Contamination Proposals
Health risks posed by polluted waterways filled with persistent organic pollutants (POPs) contamination is epidemic in some underdeveloped areas. Ignoring existing conventions, many manufacturers leave a wake of POPs pollution, often containing low-level remnants of allowable DDT and PCBs. DDT, needed in some areas for malaria control, has not yet been replaced as a preventive for malaria despite significant international debate promoting development of alternatives.[21]

World Deforestation　　It is a strange irony that the current outcry to combat global warming largely ignores one of the solutions and underlying causes of excess greenhouse gases into the atmosphere—the systematic and continuing loss of rain forests and trees. The United States has only a small fraction of its original forestland, as was pointed out earlier. And worldwide losses continue to mount. A recent survey reported that "Worldwide there are 3.9 billion hectares of forests which cover 29.6% of the worlds 13.1 billion hectares of land. Regrettably, the loss of forest land during the decade beginning in 1990 was 9.3 million hectares or .2% of the total forest coverage."[22] Many current misguided land and animal management practices are unlikely to reverse these net losses. So the greenhouse gases continue to belch into the atmosphere. Can prudent business leaders influence these errant practices? Are there not best practices to share?

Genetically Modified Foods　　Altering the genetic makeup of a basic agricultural commodity by introducing genes from other species yields genetically modified foods.[23] "Some environmentalists argue that the dangers posed by GM (genetically modified) foods involve the possibility that the food will produce a protein that is toxic or allergenic to some or all human beings, the nature and potency of that protein's toxicity or allergenicity, and the magnitude of dietary exposure to that protein. They note that 81 scientific studies financed by the European Commission have all shown no evidence of risk to human and animal health or to the environment from genetically modified crops. The European Union has been a highly vocal opponent of GM foods."[24] Is there an environmental relevance to genetically modified foods that would argue for their broader use?

Finding and Implementing Solutions

There are three major first-step solutions—irrigation improvements, conservation and efficiency of use, and allowing water to be priced at real cost while charging for it at the source. But there are also big potential rewards, as Gleick details in the following excerpts:

> Improvements in the efficiency of water use (e.g., irrigation systems often perform poorly, wasting as much as 60 percent of the total water pumped before it reaches the intended crop).[25]

> Efficient management and modern technology can stretch even scarce water supplies much further. Israel, for example, supports its population, its growing industrial base, and intensive irrigation with less than 500 cubic meters per person per year.[26]

> Water is often wasted because it is underpriced. Direct and indirect subsidies (especially for agricultural use) are still common in both developed and developing countries. Removing such subsidies and letting water prices rise can provide incentives for conservation and for the investments needed to spread more efficient technologies.[27]

Water solutions will require that respected, principled leaders come forward. Will these leaders come from business?

Similarly, solutions to the world's challenges in reversing the destruction of rain forests; protecting endangered species of plant, sea, and animal life; ridding the earth of persistent organic pollutants; changing world deforestation to world forestation; or promoting safe advances in genetically modified foods and plant species all require a new breed of leaders and a new ethic of leadership. Will this ethic come from business? Will new environmental solutions come from business? Will principled leaders on environmental issues come from business? What environmental realities will the children of the world inherit?

Lesson for Principled Business Leaders. Environmental issues are taking center stage for all business leaders because of the proven past impacts of environmental failures on the survival of cultures, the long-standing and wasteful environmental damage of past practices in many international markets, and the criticality of and search for certain natural resources in an advancing global economy.

Lesson for Principled Business Leaders. Environmental best practices should be a high priority in any international sourcing decisions by business.

Lesson for Principled Business Leaders. ISO 9000 manufacturing should be broadened in international locations to include environmental practices.

Lesson for Principled Business Leaders. There is a role for principled business leaders in reversing international environmental degradation. This approach should be adapted for underdeveloped country markets, as well, and perhaps as a higher priority.

Stretch Goal for My Enterprise. Is there a public-private partnership alliance that my organization can form or join to assist in meeting a global need and opening up new markets? Are there worldwide markets in which our enterprise is already engaged, where we can assist in meeting human needs and creating a business opportunity?

Questions to Ponder. Are international environmental deficits too important to be left to bureaucrats, bloated institutions, and politicians any longer? Should mission-minded business leaders step into this massive set of gaping problems? Is there any more important cornerstone of international policy and relationships than water? Should clean water be the U.S. standard for the developing world in the twenty-first century? What role can or should principled business leaders play in launching this debate? How should clean water for the world be implemented?

Action Steps

Principled Business Leaders Must:

1. Look systematically at international environmental realities in any potential future international market.

2. Make international manufacturing decisions only after carefully assessing the environmental implications of both production and growth.

3. Consider the enormous international environmental needs as potential new markets for products and innovation.
4. Make needed environmental remediation a component of capital investment decisions.
5. Use best practices for all aspects of international environmental good citizenship.
6. Conserve water in every process and location as a high priority.
7. Reward good environmental performance by international managers and employees.
8. Recognize good environmental practices by international vendors and producers.
9. Publicize their environmental victories as an example to other enterprises.

Key Measures of Success

Environmental Issue Review	Person Responsible	Areas of Greatest Need	Corrective Action Steps	Date to Complete
1. Water use/conservation				
2. Wastewater reuse/processes				
3. Greenhouse gas review				
4. POP contamination				
5. Critical resources				

Case History

ABBOT LABORATORIES: WASTEWATER RECYCLING, FRESHWATER SAVINGS— AND NOW REUSING WATER FOR COOLING AND STEAMBOAT LABORATORIES

Abbott's bulk pharmaceutical manufacturing facility in Puerto Rico is a U.S. plant that continues to benefit from water management practices long in place and that still finds ways to conserve and reuse resources.

(continued)

(continued)

An Abbott bulk pharmaceutical manufacturing facility located in Puerto Rico has experienced some marked success over the past decade in implementing water-recycling projects. These projects strive to maximize the reuse of treated wastewater from the facility's on-site wastewater treatment plant, which processes approximately 2.5 million gallons per day (MGD). The reclaimed water now is used within various plant systems that require large amounts of water. Collectively, these projects avoid in excess of 1.3 MGD of groundwater extraction and reduce wastewater discharges to the local publicly owned treatment works by an equivalent amount.

Specifically, in the mid-1990s, a project was completed to recycle treated wastewater from the secondary stage of the facility's biological wastewater treatment plant. The recovered water now provides 100 percent of the makeup supply to a process wet scrubber air emission control system at the facility. This wastewater-recycling project yielded a water savings of over 900,000 gallons per day.

Source: Global Environmental Management Initiative.

Suggested Reading

Barlow, Maude. *Blue Covenant.* New York: New Press, 2007, 208 pp.

_____. *Blue Gold: The Fight to Stop the Corporate Theft of the World's Water.* New York: New Press, 2002, 288 pp.

Diamond, Jared. *Collapse: Why Societies Choose to Fail or Succeed.* New York: Penguin Books, 2005, 575 pp.

Gleick, Peter. *The World's Water.* Washington, DC: Island Press, 1988, 304 pp.

Klare, Michael T. *Resource Wars.* New York: Henry Holt, 2002, 304 pp.

Business: Leading or Following—The Choice Is Ours

CHAPTER

24

The Role of Principled Leadership in America's Turnaround

My reading of history convinces me that most bad government results from too much government.

—Thomas Jefferson

New Resolve

R oss and his friends have developed a new name for their monthly meetings—*The Future Team*. The new name and a logo created by Karen Alexander, one of the members, helped to put a light touch on a number of serious issues. They have been gathering once a month for the past six years. It is now Christmas 2017, and they all agree that it is time to celebrate the holidays and to set aside the serious discussions.

Bill Woolfolk offers a toast to the New Year and thanks each of his classmates for their friendship and their honest appraisal of the challenges before them. He expresses his gratitude for their good ideas and the proposals for helping their organizations set a new course for the future. Every member of the team agrees with Bill that the old ways of gauging success and failure are over, and the music resumes.

Issue Summary. The United States typically judges its economic success against regular measures of the gross domestic product (GDP). Not only does this single measure distort the present realities, but it also foregoes the deeper accountability imposed by standard financial reporting of assets, liabilities, revenues, and expenses. Unfortunately, the nation has steadfastly refused to account for its resources at the national level using the standard measures of stewardship and accountability. The reasons are probably quite varied, and the penalty is that our children and their children will pay an enormous financial price not of their own making. Is it already too late to reverse this course? Is there a leader that has the courage and ability to make the needed—and massive—course corrections?

The United States' inability to operate under a single value system that matches the vision of the Founding Fathers will hinder the ability of any leader or leaders to confront the challenges of the years ahead. If there is no universal moral value system, it will be difficult to have sound economic values. Is it time for business leaders to advance a value system that will enable the nation to survive and prosper? Is it time for a course change? Or is it time for a turnaround?

Which Leaders Will We Choose?

If it is indeed time for us to set a correct course, then there is only one criterion for every action, namely to ask, "Does this work for the long-term benefit of our children and their children?" If business leaders are to advance the case for turnaround, every business action must be taken within a balanced national moral and economic model that achieves solvency, security, infrastructure modernization, improved domestic and international relations, and debt retirement in a 20-year period. The choice is ours. Will principled business leaders allow the nation to continue down the wrong path? Should success continue to be measured in GDP, or instead, in more telling terms?

Measuring Success As was previously mentioned, numerous authors and economists have, to this point, primarily used one particular measure of success: the nation's GDP. This serves as the primary indicator of success, as well as determining the acceptable level of national debt. This is the total of all transactions of the goods and services of the United States, and it is the primary indicator of the country's economic welfare. But is it a valid measure of how well (or poorly) we're doing?

In looking at the economic health of the United States, economists suggest that the continuous rises in the GDP from one quarter to the next indicate that we are in the best of shape. But a second look may also show that "While the GDP of other nations has struggled at times to remain positive, America's GDP appears to increase in good times and bad."[1] The post-Katrina period was a case in point:

"Referring to growth after Hurricanes Katrina and Rita, The *Wall Street Journal* said of the GDP expansion of July–September 2005, 'Increased consumer and federal government spending contributed heavily to the increase.' "[2] Growth was deceptive. Goods and services consisted of government hurricane relief. Oops!

Perhaps there is a better example. Consider the heavy importance of trade as a measure of our economic activity over the past decade, as described by one of the nation's favorite scorekeepers, the *Wall Street Journal*:

> First we need to realize that a product, let's say a microwave oven, could be made in China, shipped from California to Maine by a Mexican trucking company and sold in a Dutch-owned store, with each step in this process adding to America's GDP.[3]

> What has added most to GDP growth is the volume of foreign goods sold in America. As late as 1975 the country had a trade surplus of $9 billion. By 1980 that turned into a trade deficit of $24 billion. In 1995, the deficit soared to $150 billion; in 2000, to $436 billion; in 2003, to $532 billion; and in 2004, to $600 billion.[4] And they continued to grow through 2007 . . . until the meltdown of 2007–2009.

> The unique part is how America could make GDP grow so much without a corresponding increase in national productivity. In other words, how can the United States spend so much more money without Americans making more money? Good question. In 2004 when the trade deficit was $600 billion, the U.S. government also overspent its budget by $400 billion. You could say the nation "lost" $1 trillion. . . . And yet it seems to be going forward.[5]

We're just spending borrowed money. Is that growth? There's another problem. We've spent our Social Security Trust Funds, as well, contributing to that same GDP *growth*. "[D]uring the Reagan administration, America's Social Security money was moved from a 'locked box' to U.S. treasury bonds so the money could draw interest. This money is in the same pool as the treasury bills purchased by other nations as well as U.S. investors."[6] And much of it has been spent. Where else has all of this added GDP "growth" come from? Yes, it came from the housing boom of the late 1990s and 2000 to 2010.

> The second big gusher of money comes from the private sector. The world's pension funds, mutual funds and insurance money have $46

trillion at their disposal globally. In order to tap into this huge pool of money, the Federal Reserve dropped its lending rates from 6 percent to 1 percent in a single year. This caused an avalanche of new home buyers and builders, as well as corporate building.[7]

The equation becomes clear; more debt = more GDP. Therefore, borrowing is good, until you're *broke*.

In general, the United States has become the *Great Consumer* while many other nations have become the *Great Lenders*. It is an illusion that spending borrowed money is good for the economy, because, of course, it has to be paid back at some point. The United States is recklessly spending money it is borrowing from foreigners.[8] This has long been foretold; the resounding warning in the following passage from the Bible is unmistakable.

> The alien who is among you shall rise higher and higher above you, and you shall come down lower and lower. He shall lend to you, but you shall not lend to him; he shall be the head, and you shall be the tail. Moreover all these curses shall come upon you and pursue and overtake you, until you are destroyed, because you did not obey the voice of the Lord your God, to keep His commandments and His statutes which he commanded you.[9]

This was Moses' clear instruction to the Israelites in approximately 1406 or 1407 BC, as they entered the Promised Land after 40 years in the wilderness following their departure from Egypt. He is simply telling his people, "mistakes should not be repeated; commitments made should be fulfilled; and the memory of special events can encourage us to move into action."[10]

Lesson for Principled Business Leaders. Don't be fooled by economists' measures of growth and by the growing tendency to seek progress on the back of debt and foreign savers. Measure your success one dollar at a time. Cash is king.

Lesson for Principled Business Leaders. Is your business investment not worth saving the currency upon which it has been built? Are your business assets headed for devaluation because your money is going in that direction? Take a careful look at your pensions, business assets, and lifetime of service to an enterprise. It can all be lost in a matter of hours if you don't act to help bring your nation and its finances back into balance.

Lesson for Principled Business Leaders. Don't be misled by the deception, delusion, and denial that have taken over your country. The facts don't support the nonsense you are hearing in the media, reading in many newspapers, and hearing from politicians. They're only saving a job, and it's not yours.

Questions to Ponder. Is either your enterprise's market share or its markets safe, if the dollar collapses? Is your business secure if America is *broke*? Is America secure if the nation is *broke*? Is the United States' current situation and economic state good for the future of any business?

Action Steps

Principled Business Leaders Must:
Take responsibility. Consider the following call to action:

> There was a most important job that needed to be done,
>
> And no reason not to do it, there was absolutely none.
>
> But in vital matters such as this, the thing you have to ask
>
> Is who exactly will it be who'll carry out the task?
>
> Anybody could have told you that everybody knew
>
> That this was something somebody would surely have to do.
>
> Nobody was unwilling; anybody had the ability.
>
> But nobody believed that it was their responsibility.
>
> It seemed to be a job that anybody could have done,
>
> If anybody thought he was supposed to be the one.
>
> But since everybody recognised [*sic*] that anybody could,
>
> Everybody took for granted that somebody would.
>
> But nobody told anybody that we are aware of,
>
> That he would be in charge of seeing it was taken care of.
>
> And nobody took it on himself to follow through,
>
> And do what everybody thought that somebody would do.
>
> When what everybody needed so did not get done at all,
>
> Everybody was complaining that somebody dropped the ball.
>
> Anybody then could see it was an awful crying shame,
>
> And everybody looked around for somebody to blame.
>
> Somebody should have done the job
>
> And Everybody should have,

But in the end Nobody did

What Anybody could have.

—Charles Osgood[11]

Key Measures of Success

Journalist Bill Moyers provided a sobering measures of our success in preparing the way for future generations in a recent address to a graduating class, when he said:

> Frankly, I'm not sure anyone from my generation should be saying anything to your generation except, "We're sorry. We're really sorry for the mess you're inheriting. We are sorry for the war in Iraq. For the huge debts you will have to pay for without getting a new social infrastructure in return. We're sorry for the polarized country. The corporate scandals. The corrupt politics. Our imperiled democracy. We're sorry for the sprawl and our addiction to oil and for all those toxins in the environment. Sorry about all this, class of 2006. Good luck cleaning it up."[12]

Is it time for principled business leaders to bring about a course change in the United States? If your answer is *yes*, start with your business to make sure that it is at least 80 percent in top shape using the measures laid out in Chapter 5. Once this is done, mobilize your Chamber of Commerce, your trade association, and your community to get the United States out of debt (Chapter 13) and cleaned up (Chapters 14 and 17). Then, look at opportunities to make a contribution to the wider world using the approaches outlined in Chapters 18 through 23.

Or, you can let someone else do it. Chapter 25 will give you the outcomes—one if principled business leaders fail to act ("America Without a Turnaround") and one if principled business leaders act decisively ("America With a Turnaround and a Vision for the Future"). You make the call.

A Tale of Two Nations—Which Path Will We Choose?

If not us, who? If not now, when?

—Anonymous

America Without a Turnaround

Ross and his father are fishing at their Idaho home, which is now more beautiful than ever, and a welcome relief from the electric grid meltdown at home. That meltdown followed the break in a large regional gas pipeline and hundreds of local fires, one of which took out the high-voltage transmission lines serving the city. It was awful. Local waterlines also ruptured from overload when the fires hit the waterlines near gas lines.

When word of waterline ruptures got around, so did the reports of low water quality and the possibility of a disease outbreak. Ross and his father couldn't wait to get out of town, especially since his company had also closed down after the gas pipeline burst on the same street. That was the last straw. The mountains of Idaho are now home.

The last dinner in the old house was particularly sad, since Ross had grown up in that house and his father had stayed there in the years since his mother's death. They often had dinner together. One night, it became clear to both of them that it would be better to move to the small tract in Idaho that his parents had held onto. As they packed to go, they were haunted by the nagging realization that business leaders had failed so miserably in turning this national mess around.

First there was the economic meltdown. The market and investment losses at home reached nearly $18 trillion, and the government bailout and guarantees came to $20 trillion. Then, many of the failed subprime CDOs (approximately $1.5 trillion in purchase value, and $200 billion in market value) turned up overseas in central banks and private and sovereign wealth funds. Investors and foreign governments were understandably outraged. They had relied upon the nation's integrity to buy those instruments, but they had been defrauded by gutless white-collar crooks in the Wall Street financial houses. It would take two generations for the United States to restore its international reputation. The moral authority and worldwide financial leadership that had taken 170 years to establish was gone in less than three years.

Then there was the controversy over financial ratings, followed soon by the Treasury's default on redeeming its bonds on time—the first such incident in history. Consumer trust in both the federal government and in the private banking system both began to erode so badly that there were riots in Washington, Chicago, New York, and Los Angeles in 2014. San Francisco had filed for bankruptcy in 2017 after the City Hall was burned down following the public announcement that a number of city social programs would be discontinued. It was ugly.

Technology and business innovation also plummeted with the economic downturn. Consumer confidence and demand dropped like a rock. Many big names in retail were gone—Sears, Penny's, Macy's, and even Best Buy went bankrupt. Worldwide leadership in innovation and new product development moved to Asia.

The biggest loss, however, was the collapse of the dollar. The massive increases in federal debt taken on to overcome the economic meltdown of 2007 to 2009 became the Achilles heel of the dollar in 2014. Early rollovers of T-Bills were refinanced at several interest points higher. Soon, the 2 to 3 percent interest rate premium became an 8 percent rate premium just to sell out. Many Treasury auctions later closed without being sold out. So much capital had been sucked into the federal financing system that commercial offerings virtually stopped, and businesses that needed debt financing went *broke*.

Instantly, oil-rich countries like Russia, Venezuela, Iran, Iraq, and Bolivia all successfully pressed for oil to be valued and sold in gold and euros. The United States, now buried in debt at all levels, was powerless to stop them. Canada and Mexico had cut off oil shipments due to non-payment by the United States. It was the last blow for the dollar. Suffering around the world reached catastrophic levels.

The United States never did get control of its debt. Federal borrowing for the Middle East wars, bank bailouts, overspending on the stimulus, and auto bailouts continued unchecked from 2008 to 2012. The $56.7 trillion in all forms of debt in 2010 nearly doubled by 2013 to $98.7 trillion, as did unfunded liabilities, which shot up to $200 trillion. Thousands of companies, 12 states, 944 counties, and 2,420 cities and towns had all filed for bankruptcy protection by 2012. Many towns had regular riots, as public safety officials abandoned their jobs in the face of the local uprisings.

The two unexpected natural disasters of 2011—a hurricane on the Gulf Coast that narrowly missed New Orleans and the $500 billion in damages from the San Andreas Fault earthquake—just made it worse. Bankruptcy by the state of California in late 2016 closed out the decade of disaster since the 9/11 attacks in New York City in 2001. The state was powerless to respond. Some towns were taken over by gangs, as the police and firefighters abandoned their jobs.

Shortages of domestic manufactured goods, food, and capital all fed the inflation monster in many markets. The 1980 record of 21 percent inflation was broken in many urban centers as prices skyrocketed. Unemployment spiked at 50 percent in many areas. Price increases vastly outpaced middle-class wage growth, decimating personal savings and private investments. Soup lines returned to New York for the first time since 1934.

Most private sector pensions also collapsed, as did state and local pensions, while benefits inflated well beyond the ability of prior contributions to pay them. The federal government had never addressed its debt problems; so the rampant inflation emptied the Social Security Trust Fund by 2014. Sadly, the pension crisis never ended, as unfunded pension liabilities (private and public) became the norm.

Cities emptied out, as social and local domestic protests over health care, drugs, and crime reached epidemic levels. Unfunded liabilities for Medicare and Medicaid skyrocketed. Countless hospitals closed because of non-payment of patient bills, failed health insurance programs, and staff losses. The illegal immigration debate was shut down by total amnesty. The population of 44 million illegal immigrants in 2010 nearly doubled to nearly 80 million by 2012. County school systems, public health care programs, and many public services were all but immobilized less than halfway through the budget year for lack of added funding. Treatment programs for illegal drugs, alcohol, gambling, and prescription drugs were halted in many jurisdictions.

Public education was also a victim. The 2010 stimulus money for new schools benefited only the large urban jurisdictions. Local political self-dealing from the 2009 stimulus had already left thousands of unfinished construction projects standing. Student performance slipped further from the 2003 and 2006 OECD PISA scores—twenty-fifth in reading and science, and twenty-sixth in mathematics in 2012. U.S. education was near collapse. Postsecondary education (colleges) declined sharply, as nearly one-third of all colleges and universities closed before the end of the 2012 academic year.

Families were under the greatest stress. Fifty million middle-class families filed for bankruptcy in 2012. Nearly 40 million homes, 40 percent of the national housing stock, had also been foreclosed by 2012. Home values stabilized at the end of 2012 at one-half of their 2007 levels.

State and federal courts were the last to collapse. Groaning under staggering civil and criminal caseloads, the courts scrambled to find enough judges and staff to keep hearing dates below five years. Trial rates for felony offenders dropped to 1 percent of all arrests. Convictions remained high, however, so prison populations swelled to nearly 20 million—one-third of whom were undocumented or illegal immigrant inmates. Growing court politicization opened the way for gangs and drug dealers to operate in the open and without restraint in many jurisdictions.

Ross and his father brought all of their firearms from home to Idaho, just for personal protection. They never went out without a gun.

Water quality and availability declined to catastrophic levels, and water wars broke out in many farm counties. California lost 100,000 farm jobs as water flows were diverted before they reached the needy farms. Salinas and many small cities in California were overflowing with unemployed migrant workers. Food prices jumped by 30 percent every year after 2010, and victory gardens reminiscent of World War II times sprung up everywhere.

Energy remained in short supply as a result of the cut-off of Middle Eastern oil in 2012. Venezuela cut all of its sales to the United States by 50 percent, shipping all of its exports to China via the Panama Canal. China picked up all shipping costs and took delivery direct from the Caracas terminals starting in 2014, when the dollar collapsed. The renewable energy program never got off the ground. Whole communities had no power.

Brownfield environmental cleanup initiatives and Superfund projects were halted. The stimulus funding for wastewater plant modernization fell way short. Ross and his father had their own well, and they didn't waste a drop of water. All baths and washing were done with rainwater. Some years it was tight.

It was not a good picture. But the United States could blame only itself. The year 2015 was the worst—such a tragedy for a nation that had been so great a mere 15 years before. The United States of 2025 is a rural, third-world economy.

America With a Turnaround and a Vision for the Future

Ross and his father are fishing in Idaho, now more beautiful than ever. They often visited the small cabin and 100-acre tract on the Salmon River. They are particularly pleased to be there this year (2025), because Ross's father, now 67 years old, knows that it might be one of his last trips to the river. The weather is spectacular, the fishing is great, and they have a full week to be there together. They are almost giddy at the end of each day, as they hurry back from each day to engage in several hours of stimulating conversation. The turnaround of the United States is their favorite topic.

They speculate at length on how it all got started. Ross's father thought that it had been the amazing leadership of the Chamber of Commerce that jump-started the turnaround, while Ross credited a ballot initiative in Missouri on budget balancing that caught fire and was adopted by 21 states and the Congress. Most agreed that it had been the people in business who seized the initiative and led the nation's transformation. But the biggest surprise was how *few* years it took to succeed.

Principled business leaders awakened in 2011 to the reality that they had squandered their moral authority for four decades. They realized that national prosperity couldn't be built on debt. Surprisingly, they put the blame for U.S. failures squarely on themselves—starting with the Fortune 500 CEOs. States, cities, counties, and localities had done the same thing—seeking special preferences at the expense of taxpayers for years on end. It had been tragic.

The ugly truth was that it had all gone too far. The United States found itself technically bankrupt in 2011. The dollar was near collapse. The national debt was out of control. The federal government couldn't publish an audited financial report. Many states, counties, and municipalities went bankrupt. These and hundreds of other failures galvanized the nation's 100 top CEOs into action.

And as if this weren't enough, was a massive worldwide loss of prestige of the U.S. financial system that started with the subprime mortgage meltdown in 2007 to 2009. Investors who had trusted the U.S. rating systems for investment grade instruments were badly misled only to find themselves holding billions of dollars' worth of deeply discounted financial instruments. Sadly, these international firms and individuals were often small cities, senior citizens, and innocent banks.

The year 2011 saw worldwide school closings, a second spike in national bankruptcies, huge jumps in oil prices from OPEC nations trying to offset their losses, and a host of other sad stories of U.S. financial engineering gone wrong. It was a pretty dreadful state of affairs.

Business leaders realized that they were in danger of losing their economic platform and forfeiting their economic future if these harmful practices weren't stopped. The CEO group that started the nation's long march back to solvency operated out of the glare of publicity for nearly five years. They had a clear, simple strategy to restore the nation's finances. It took only two years for business to regain its moral authority after this highly private enterprise became public knowledge. Financial reporting improved, and transparency became a reality.

Innovation and new product research nearly tripled in three years, and new offerings often had marketing and promotion experts panting to catch up. Public-private partnerships sprang into action on scores of domestic and international issues. Words gave way to action.

There was a second axis of citizen activity that no one would have expected. It began in downtown Washington, DC, in the most surprising of all places—the middle and high schools and the local universities. Two African-American pastors had been preaching for years about the wide disparity between what they saw in the nation's values and what they knew from their study of the Bible. They learned that many of their members had been hurt badly by the 2007 to 2009 meltdown. They were deeply disappointed at their nation's lack of integrity, from the lowest to the highest levels. Pastor Brewster Clarkson and Pastor Terrance Wendell Miller, along with several gifted women leaders who worked with them, became widely known. Both were highly gifted preachers, and both had vital experience in business. They mobilized their church youth to partner with the students of Washington's middle and high schools and universities in a series of rallies in the spring of 2013 and again in 2014. The rallies provided information on all of the major issues to the students and sent them away quietly outraged that (1) the Social Security Trust Fund was empty; (2) Washington, DC, was on the verge of bankruptcy; (3) Maryland had two insolvent employee pension plans; (4) many counties in Virginia were already bankrupt despite record property tax levels; and (5) 30-plus million manufacturing jobs had moved offshore since 1993 because of high corporate tax rates. The students were angry.

The amazing part about this second, but very civilized, student uprising was that the students began to march on the Congress; a few at a time at first, but soon by the hundreds, as congressional and committee staff aides airily dismissed their questions. Each time, the students returned days later to these meetings with hundreds of their peers. Soon they demanded political donor lists. They insisted upon legislative voting lists. Many of them knew more about key issues than did the congressional staffers. As they recruited Congressional cosponsors for the turnaround legislation, their confidence and determination grew after each visit. Congress began to pay attention, and to act accordingly!

Transparency began to emerge slowly. Short-term administration objectives were folded into long-term goals and strategies and the needed turnaround legislation to repay all public debt and to modernize the nation's infrastructure on a short timetable. The big step of debt payoff was accomplished with a national transaction fee of 2 percent on every dollar spent. The pressure on Congress to pass this transaction fee for debt repayment became an international spectacle, and television viewers around the world howled with laughter week after week, as the evening broadcasts pictured students going from school to Congress. And the students didn't stop until Congress finally acted to pass the transaction tax—for debt retirement *only*! The President signed the Rebuild America Act on June 6—the anniversary of the landings at Normandy that turned World War II around. The students were ecstatic.

Congress also acted to lower business tax rates to 5 percent so that U.S. companies no longer paid the world's highest corporate taxes, but rather the lowest in the world. Unfortunately, the outsourcing of more than 30 million jobs as a result of the high tax rates of the 1980 to 2010 tax years had taken their toll. Ironically, some of the outsourced jobs had been refilled by undocumented workers during this period. When tax rates changed, however, domestic jobs were restored at a rate of four million per year starting in 2014. Illegal workers left the United States in droves, and the illegal population dropped from forty-four million to five million in less than five years.

Education also changed dramatically, as local public school parents were issued vouchers to cover the cost of education from pre-kindergarten through secondary school. The United States rose to fifth in reading, science, and math in the 2015 OECD PISA exams. Vocational education was expanded dramatically, using the same voucher payment system. English was made the national language for all residents.

With the vastly improved business self-regulation and the astonishing improvements in debt retirement by government at all levels, inflation became a non-issue by 2015. Excess liquidity and money creation also came under control. Ironically, the federal lending rate stayed steady at 1.5 percent for nearly a decade, from 2011 until 2020. The Fed also sold all of the Troubled Asset Relief Program assets and commercial paper that it had acquired in 2008 to 2009 over the next six years. Private investors purchased TARP bonds at 20 percent of face value and reaped big profits on their collections.

The most welcome improvement was the increase in value of the U.S. dollar and its retention as the world's reserve currency. Under the new tax policies, general revenues rose quickly, while debt curtailment lowered the balance of payments deficit and sharply reduced foreign governments' holdings of dollars. Pension investments soared after the economy recovered in

2014, and the levels of unfunded pension liabilities (private and public) went from –$4.9 trillion to +$100 billion by 2018.

The second joint demand of the business committees *and* the students—mandatory public service for young adults—turned out to have profound impacts. The cost of government dropped, as 18- to 24-year-olds worked at the minimum wage for 4,000 hours as interns in government positions. Education qualifications rose, since every single student had to have at least a GED when he or she left the program. It was an astonishing turn for the better. Illegal drug use dropped by 70 percent, and interns demanded an end to the debate on drug legalization.

Law enforcement also benefited from the education improvements in the national service corps and the GED requirement. Some youth had to work for six years before they earned the GED, kicked the drug habit, and gained a work skill. But it changed the nation's culture forever.

Natural resource management also improved. Fifteen million government interns worked to clean up waterways and brownfields across the nation. Water conservation programs were launched nationwide, as wastewater treatment projects were implemented in 2,000 counties. Environmental improvements skyrocketed as well. The national service corps planted nearly 100 billion trees to restore U.S. forests to 60 percent of the level that existed at the time of Washington, Jefferson, and Adams. Waterways were cleaned up, and citizen pride against polluters and unchecked manufacturing byproduct disposal in waterways reached deafening levels. Citizens refused to tolerate environmental abuses any longer.

Energy use and availability was the biggest single winner. The year 2013 ended the century-old game played between big oil and big autos. The year 2014 was the end of the many delays to modernize the electric grid. The smart grid was put on a 10-year development program that year. Capacity jumped by 80 percent, and the expanded coverage even included new access to wind energy production areas.

The year 2014 also launched a new era for nuclear power in the United States. Twenty new plants came online with the modernized power grid in 2019, just as millions of urban delivery vehicles were retrofitted for electric power. Electric cars also blossomed in cities, and over-the-road trucking converted to natural gas. Energy for transportation went from first to third place in overall demand, and energy imports dropped by two-thirds.

As states, counties, and localities saw their prior debt disappear, capital became available for school bond issues, highway bonds, and other infrastructure projects. Although the 2009 stimulus money fell far short of its advertised impact on infrastructure, the states, counties, and cities quickly filled the funding gap with local bonds. Transportation, schools, and water treatment became the top three infrastructure modernization targets.

The United States also took on a new and more conscientious global leadership role. Beginning in 2014, clean water became the cornerstone of its foreign policy. The improvements in health levels around the world were truly staggering. Africa was revolutionized, as national service corps intern teams installed shallow wells in 100,000 villages, while others built 200,000 new classrooms. Many acted as teaching aides in the new classrooms. Literacy levels skyrocketed worldwide.

The Middle East was a different challenge. Some 50,000 national service corps interns volunteered in Palestine alone to build roads, housing, and infrastructure. There was even a new nuclear power plant built in Israel dedicated to meeting the power needs of Palestine! The Israeli-Palestinian border was slowly opened so that agricultural and manufactured goods could move more freely.

A new leadership model emerged. Politicians became servant leaders. Control of the destiny of the United States again rested with its people. Leadership accountability shifted to objective performance benchmarks, and leaders were judged on their performance and ability to improve an organization's value to future generations. The nation's recovery was a classic business turnaround. The standard by which every action was measured was: "Does this work to the long-term benefit of our children and their children?"

Education achievement, youth crime, and youth unemployment showed remarkable improvement in five years. Domestic health levels began to improve as the risk-rated insurance came into force. Incidences of poor nutrition, lack of preventive care, and unhealthy lifestyles dropped as families benefited from a one-hour annual physical evaluation program modeled on fast-exam technology from Shanghai, China.

Citizens formed petition drives, while others led voter movements to make the nation *Debt-free in '23* (D23). These, and countless other steps, served to reestablish a broad set of values that reflected the original U.S. Constitution—financial prudence, sound leadership, accountability, social order and behavior, and a strong sense of patriotism. The changes were gradual, but they were highly effective, because the United States had come to its senses—just in time. The world became a better place, and U.S. business had led the way.

Ross and his father agree. *It's a great day to be alive!*

America's Economic/Business Leadership Failures: 1965 to the Present

Time Period	Economic Leadership Failure Event
A New Policy—Guns and Butter	It began in the 1960s, when America decided to fight a war in Vietnam and to launch a Great Society—all without raising the taxes needed to pay for either. So they borrowed from the future and made both "guns and butter" a twentieth century reality for the World War II baby boomer generation.
1965–1975	War is waged with the simultaneous launch of massive social programs—much of which was funded on debt—at a cost in excess of one trillion dollars.
1965–	Social Security is amended to add Medicare and to move funds from the Social Security Trust Fund to the U.S. General Fund to allow them to be used for current operations of the government.[1]
1973–1975	Arab oil embargo over Israel policy, energy price spikes, unemployment, and inflation.

(continued)

(*continued*)

Time Period	Economic Leadership Failure Event
1977–	President Carter triples Social Security withholding to compensate for drain of Johnson years benefit increases. "Now this legislation will guarantee that from 1980 to the year 2030, the Social Security Funds will be sound."[2]
1979–	Iranian oil crisis brings new unemployment and inflation to the United States and the West.
1973–1980	Inflation and high unemployment in the United States and Western Europe.
1980–1982	Rampant inflation and high interest rates in the United States with worldwide consequences.
1981–1983	Third-world government debt defaults causes crisis and further impoverishment.
1983–	Social Security eligibility is scaled back to accommodate Trust Fund shortfall. Other changes include taxing benefits and taking the Trust Fund "off-budget."[3]
1983–	Congress invests Social Security Trust Fund cash in non-negotiable U.S. Treasury securities and cash is spent by Treasury.[4]
1986–1995	Savings and Loan Crisis—1,043 bank failures—$152.9 billion in losses.[5]
1986 (Dec. 31)	FSLIC is insolvent and unable to insure unprecedented losses in S&L industry.[6]
1987 (Aug. 10)	FICO created to fund FSLIC[7]
1987–	Black Monday—October 19, 1987—market investments lose 23 percent.
1989 (Aug. 9)	Creation of FIRREA to replace FSLIC; FRP created to take FSLIC assets and liabilities; SAIF created to handle thrift failures after August 9, 1992; RTC created to resolve thrifts placed into conservatorship or receiverships between January 1, 1989, and August 8, 1992; REFCORP created to fund RTC.[8]
1990–1991	U.S. real estate industry crisis resulting from the S&L collapse.
1994–	Peso crisis in Mexico—saved by $50 billion loan from U.S. taxpayers.
1997–	Asian economic crisis—IMF crisis—high interest rates brought capital collapse.
1998–	Long-term capital management—hedge fund—derivatives—public bailout.

Time Period	Economic Leadership Failure Event
2000–	Dot.com/"dot.bomb" collapse of tech bubble—billions in investor losses.
2001–	Enron collapse—fraudulent accounting—billions in investor losses.
2004–	WorldCom collapse—fraudulent accounting—billions in investor losses.
2007 (Feb. 27)	Federal Home Loan Mortgage Corporation (Freddie Mac) announces that it will no longer buy the most risky subprime mortgages and mortgage-related securities.[9]
2007 (April 2)	New Century Financial Corporation files for Chapter 11.[10]
2007 (June 1)	Rating agencies downgrade 100 bonds backed by subprime mortgages.[11]
2007 (June 7)	Bear Stearns suspends redemptions from its High Grade Structured Credit Strategies Enhanced Leverage Fund.[12]
2007 (July 11)	S&P places 612 securities backed by subprime residential mortgages on a credit watch.[13]
2007 (July 24)	Countrywide Mortgage warns of "difficult conditions."[14]
2007 (July 31)	Bear Stearns liquidates two hedge funds that invested in various mortgage backed securities.[15]
2007 (Aug. 7)	American Home Mortgage Investment Corporation files for Chapter 11.
2007 (Aug. 16)	Fitch downgrades Countrywide to BBB+ (third lowest rating) and Countrywide borrows $11.5 billion from bank credit lines.[16]
2007 (Oct. 9)	Dow Jones Average reaches high of 14,164.3.[17]
2007 (Oct. 10)	Treasury and HUD establish HOPE NOW to help mortgagees in default.[18]
2007 (Fall)	Financial meltdown continues despite lower Federal Reserve lending rates.[19]
2007–	Subprime mortgage crisis in full bloom—exposure is estimated at five trillion dollars in mortgages in danger of default.
2008 (Jan. 11)	Countrywide Mortgage collapses—company purchased by Bank of America for four billion dollars.[20]
2008 (Jan. 18)	Ambac Financial Group (monoline bond insurance entity) downgraded by Fitch and S&P.[21]
2008 (Feb. 13)	President Bush signs Economic Stimulus Act of 2008.[22]
2008 (March 24)	Bear Sterns collapse—purchased by JP Morgan Chase—$27 billion in losses.

(continued)

(continued)

Time Period	Economic Leadership Failure Event
2008–	Fannie Mae and Freddie Mac fully nationalized—fraudulent accounting found.
2008 (July 11)	IndyMac Bank seized by FDIC—second largest U.S. bank failure in history.[23]
2008 (July 13)	Federal Reserve Board authorizes New York Fed to lend to Fannie Mae and Freddie Mac (GSEs); U.S. Department of the Treasury authorizes credit line increases to both on same day.[24]
2008 (July 15)	SEC suspends naked short selling in Fannie Mae, Freddie Mac, and primary dealers.[25]
2008 (July 30)	President Bush signs Economic Recovery Act of 2008, authorizing Treasury to purchase GSE obligations.[26]
2008 (Sept. 7)	Federal Housing Finance Agency places Fannie and Freddie in conservatorship.[27]
2008 (Sept. 15)	Bank of America announces purchase of Merrill Lynch & Co. for $50.0 billion.[28]
2008 (Sept. 15)	Lehman Brothers bankruptcy—$613 billion in debts—CEO earns $400+ million.
2008 (Sept. 17)	SEC suspends short selling on financial companies.[29]
2008 (Sept. 20)	Secretary of Treasury submits plan to Congress for purchase of troubled assets.[30]
2008 (Sept. 25)	Office of Thrift Supervision (OTS) closes Washington Mutual Bank (largest bank collapse in U.S. history). JP Morgan purchases assets.[31]
2008 (Sept. 29)	FDIC announces that Citigroup will purchase assets of Wachovia Corporation.[32]
2008 (Oct. 3)	Wells Fargo announces intent to purchase assets of Wachovia without FDIC assistance.[33]
2008 (Oct. 3)	President Bush signs Emergency Economic Stabilization Act of 2008 with $700 billion for purchase of troubled assets.[34]
2008 (Oct. 8)	First installment for AIG Loan Bailout of $38.7 billion in form of Fed of New York borrowing of investment grade securities.[35] Ultimate cost of AIG assistance is $121 billion in taxpayer loans—caused by derivatives.
2008 (Oct. 13)	Federal Reserve approves Wells Fargo purchase of Wachovia Corporation assets.[36]

Time Period	Economic Leadership Failure Event
2008 (Oct. 14)	U.S. Treasury announces troubled asset purchase program (TARP); $125 billion is subscribed by nine U.S. banks.[37]
2008 (Oct. 24)	PNC Bank purchases National City Corporation to create fifth largest U.S. bank.[38]
2008 (Oct. 29)	IMF creates short-term liquidity credit facility for market-access countries.[39]
2008 (Nov. 10)	AIG bailout is expanded to include TARP funds, loans, and new LLC to buy CDOs.[40]
2008 (Nov. 11)	U.S. Treasury joins with HUD and HOPE NOW to establish streamlined loan modification program.[41]
2008 (Nov. 12)	Secretary of Treasury announces that it will not purchase troubled assets.[42]
2008 (Nov. 17)	Three large life insurance companies seek TARP funds by becoming savings banks.[43]
2008 (Nov. 18)	Three automakers (GM, Chrysler, and Ford) request access to TARP funds.[44]
2008 (Nov. 20)	Fannie Mae and Freddie Mac suspend mortgage foreclosures until January 2009.[45]
2008 (Nov. 21)	U.S. Treasury purchases $3.0 billion in preferred stock from 23 U.S. banks under Capital Purchase Program.[46]
2008 (Dec. 5)	U.S. Treasury purchases $4.0 billion in preferred stock from 35 U.S. banks under Capital Purchase Program.[47]
2008 (Dec. 12)	U.S. Treasury purchases $6.25 billion in preferred stock from 28 U.S. banks under Capital Purchase Program.[48]
2008 (Dec. 13)	U.S. Treasury Department authorizes $13.4 billion loan for GM and $4.0 billion for Chrysler under TARP.[49]
2008 (Dec. 23)	U.S. Treasury purchases $15.1 billion in preferred stock from 43 U.S. banks under Capital Purchase Program.[50]
2008 (Dec. 24)	Federal Reserve Board approves GM subsidiary GMAC and IB Financial to become bank holding companies so as to receive TARP funds.[51]
2008 (Dec. 29)	Federal Reserve announces that it will purchase $5.0 billion in equity from GMAC and that it will lend another $1.0 to GM under the "bank" program.[52]
2008 (Dec. 30)	Federal Reserve announces purchases of mortgage-backed securities from Fannie Mae, Freddie Mac, and Ginnie Mae in 2009.[53]

(continued)

(*continued*)

Time Period	Economic Leadership Failure Event
2008 (Dec. 31)	U.S. Treasury purchases $1.91 billion in preferred stock from seven U.S. banks under Capital Purchase Program.[54]
2008–	Stock markets experience serious declines as funds dump stocks through much of the fall.
2008–	Federal CDO purchases—$700 billion with $106 billion added in earmarks.
2008 (Dec. 31)	Pending bank failure estimates range from 140 to 1,437.
2009 (Jan. 8)	Moody's Investor Services reports that Federal Home Loan Banks face write-downs of $76.2 billion on MBS portfolios; only four in twelve banks have adequate capital ratios.[55]
2009 (Jan. 9)	U.S. Treasury Department purchases $4.8 billion in preferred stock from 43 banks.[56]
2009 (Jan. 16)	U.S. Treasury Department purchases $1.4 billion in preferred stock from 39 banks.[57]
2009 (Jan. 23)	U.S. Treasury Department purchases $326 million in preferred stock from 23 banks.[58]
2009 (Jan. 30)	U.S. Treasury Department purchases $1.15 billion in preferred stock from 42 banks.[59]
2009 (Feb. 6)	U.S. Treasury Department purchases $238.5 million in preferred stock from 28 banks.[60]
2009 (Feb. 13)	U.S. Treasury Department purchases $429 million in preferred stock from 29 banks.[61]
2009 (Feb. 17)	President Obama signs $789 billion American Recovery and Reinvestment Act of 2009.[62]
2009 (Feb. 18)	President Obama signs $75 billion The Homeowner Affordability and Stability Plan.[63]
2009 (Feb. 24)	U.S. Treasury Department purchases $365.4 million in preferred stock from 23 banks.[64]
2009 (Feb. 26)	FDIC problem bank list grows from 171 institutions with $116 billion in assets to 252 institutions with $159 billion in assets.[65]
2009 (Feb. 26)	Fannie Mae reports a loss of $25.2 billion for 2008; Federal Housing Finance Agency requests $15.2 billion from Treasury to eliminate Fannie Mae's net worth deficit.[66]

Time Period	Economic Leadership Failure Event
2009 (Feb. 27)	FDIC charges 0.20 percent emergency bank assessment in insured deposits for collection on September 30, 2009.[67]
2009 (Feb. 27)	U.S. Treasury Department purchases $394.9 million in preferred stock from 28 banks.[68]
2009 (March 2)	AIG reports loss of $99.2 billion for 2008 and receives $30 billion in additional capital.[69]
2009 (March 3)	Dow Jones average drops to 12-year low at 6,763.29.[70]
2009 (March 3)	U.S. Treasury Department announces Troubled Asset Loan Facility (TALF) and provides $200 billion in credit to AAA asset-backed securities.[71]
2009 (March 6)	U.S. Treasury Department purchases $284.7 million in preferred stock from 22 banks.[72]
2009 (March 13)	U.S. Treasury Department purchases $1.45 billion in preferred stock from 19 banks.[73]
2009 (March 19)	FDIC completes sale of IndyMac to OneWest Bank. IndyMac reports 2008 losses of $2.6 billion. FDIC losses on IndyMac reach $10.7 billion.[74]
2009 (March 23)	U.S. Treasury Department announces Public-Private Investment Program for Legacy Assets to purchase distressed (toxic) assets.[75]

APPENDIX

B

Repaying America's Debt: Staffing the National Service Corps—2010 to 2030

Borrowing Levels—2008	Borrowing Annual Levels IV Qtr.—2008 ($ Billions)	Debt Level IV Qtr. 2009 ($ Billions)	Interest Amount ($ Billions)	Interest Percentage	Unfunded Liabilities ($ Billions)	Notes	Total Current Funded/ Unfunded Unfunded ($ Billions)	Percent
1. Consumer credit	−83	2,596.2	168.8	6.5		1	2,765.0	1.6
2. Consumer home mortgages	−163	10,453.7	679.5	6.5		1	11,133.2	6.5
3. Business—non-corporate	28.5	3,992.1	339.3	8.5		1	4,331.4	2.6
4. Business—corporate	156.8	7,103.7	426.2	6.0		1	7,529.9	4.5
5. State/local government	26.7	2,239.6	134.4	6.0	2,250.0	1,2,5,6	4,624.0	2.7
6. Federal government	2,155.2	12,100.0	514.3	4.3	5,000.0	3	17,614.3	10.4
7. Social Security[1]					15,800.0	2	15,800.0	9.4
8. Medicare et al.[1]					85,900.0	2	85,900.0	50.9
9. Domestic financial sectors	1,221.6	1,7216.5		4.5		1	17,216.5	10.2
10. Foreign borrowers	−456.1	1,858.3		4.5		1	1,858.3	1.1
TOTAL ($ Billions)	2,886.7	57,560.1	2,262.4		108,950.0	4	168,772.5	100.0
TOTAL PUBLIC DEBT ($ Billions)	14,339.6				108,950.0	4	123,936.2	73.4

#	Retiring Outstanding Public Debt—2008	Principal—20-Year Payoff ($ Billion)	Average Annual Interest[3] Percent	Average Annual Interest[3]	Pay-Off Years	Annual Payment Unfunded Liability ($ Billions)	Years	Public Debt Annual Payments Total ($ Billions)	Federal Only ($ Billions)
1	Consumer credit		6.5		20	0.0	20		
2	Consumer home mortgages		6.5		20		20		
3	Business—non-corporate		8.5		20		20		
4	Business—corporate		6.0		20		20		
5	State/local government	112.0	6.0	67.2	20	112.5	20	291.7	
6	Federal government	605.0	4.3	257.1	20		20	862.1	862.1
	Federal unfunded amount		6.5	0.0	20	250.0	20	250.0	250.0
7	Social Security[1]		6.5	0.0	20	790.0	20	790.0	790.0
8	Medicare et al.[1]		6.5	0.0	20	4,295.0	20	4,295.0	4,295.0
9	Domestic financial sectors		4.5		20				
10	Foreign borrowers		4.5		20				
		717.0		324.3		5,447.5		6488.8	6,197.1

Staffing the National Service Corps

	2000	2004	2008	2012	2016
Under 5 years	19,175,798				
5 to 9 years	20,549,505	19,175,798			
10 to 14 years	20,528,072	20,549,505	19,175,798		
15 to 19 years	20,219,890	20,528,072	20,549,505	19,175,798	
20 to 24 years	18,964,001	20,219,890	20,528,072	20,549,505	19,175,798
25 to 29 years	19,381,336	18,964,001	20,219,890	20,528,072	20,549,505
30 to 34 years	20,510,388	19,381,336	18,964,001	20,219,890	20,528,072
35 to 39 years	22,706,664	20,510,388	19,381,336	18,964,001	20,219,890
40 to 44 years	22,441,863	22,706,664	20,510,388	19,381,336	18,964,001
45 to 49 years	20,092,404	22,441,863	22,706,664	20,510,388	19,381,336
50 to 54 years	17,585,548	20,092,404	22,441,863	22,706,664	20,510,388
55 to 59 years	13,469,237	17,585,548	20,092,404	22,441,863	22,706,664
60 to 64 years	10,805,447	13,469,237	17,585,548	20,092,404	22,441,863
65 to 69 years		10,805,447	13,469,237	17,585,548	20,092,404
70 to 74 years			10,805,447	13,469,237	17,585,548

Source: U.S. Bureau of the Census

Retiring the U.S. Public Debt: Late Retirement (74 Years) vs. Existing Retirement (64 Years)

	2000	2004	2008	2012	2016
Optimistic—retire at 74					
Total eligible taxpayers			206,704,850	216,448,908	222,155,469
Total taxpayers (at 67 percent)			137,872,135	144,371,422	148,177,698
Total investors (at 67 percent)			137,872,135	144,371,422	148,177,698
Tax filers with positive AGI (55 percent)			75,829,674	79,404,282	81,497,734
Public debt principal and Interest ($ Billions)	6,488.8	6,488.8	6,488.8	6,488.8	6,488.8
Annual cost per nominal taxpayer ($)			**47,064**	**44,946**	**43,791**
Annual cost per actual taxpayer ($)			**85,571**	**81,716**	**78,619**

(continued)

285

(continued)

Standard—retire at 64

	2000	2004	2008	2012	2016
Total taxpayers (at 67 percent)	110,693,244	116,972,678	121,680,921	123,657,880	123,046,504
Total investors (at 67 percent)	110,693,244	116,972,678	121,680,921	123,657,880	123,046,504
Public debt principal and Interest ($ billions)	6,488.8	6,488.8	6,488.8	6,488.8	6,488.8
Annual cost per taxpayer ($)			53,326	52,474	52,734
Federal/other debt interest ($ billions)	324.3	324.3	324.3	324.3	324.3
Annual cost per taxpayer ($)			2,665	2,623	2,638
State/local pension debt burden ($ billions)	291.7	291.7	291.7	291.7	291.7
Annual cost per taxpayer ($)			2,397	2,359	2,370

	2000	2004	2008	2012	2016
OBLIGATION SUMMARY					
Federal debt payoff per year ($)			53,326	52,474	52,734
Interest payment per year ($)			2,665	2,623	2,636
State debt payoff per year ($)			2,397	2,359	2,370
Consumer debt payoff per year					
Payoff per taxpayer per year					
Consumer mortgage payoff per year					
Payoff per taxpayer per year					
Non-corporate business per year					
Payoff per investor					
Total annual payment per taxpayer ($)			58,389	57,455	57,741

APPENDIX
C

Meeting America's Growing Power Demands

	Total All Plants	Total Key Plants	2007 Supply (Billion Kwh)	% Power Share	Supply per Plant	% 2030 Mid	New 2030 Demand Mid-Level	Total Plants Mid	New Plants Mid	% 2030 High	New 2030 Demand High Level	Total Plants High	New Plants High	Cost per Plant 2015 ($ Billions)	Mid-Range New Plants 2015 ($ Billions)	High Cost Plants 2015 ($ Billions)
Total electricity demand			3,913,700,000,000			20.0	4,696,800,000,000			36.0	5,323,000,000,000					
Energy plants—nuclear plants	104	104	900,000,000,000	21.4	8,653,846,154		1,000,000,000,000	116	12		1,000,000,000,000	116	12	15.0	180.0	180.0
Energy plants—coal plants	1,470	1,470	2,100,000,000,000	50.0	1,428,571,429		2,400,000,000,000	1,680	210		2,600,000,000,000	1,820	350	1.0	210.0	350.0
Geothermal plants	224															
Hydroelectric conventional	3,992															
Energy plants—natural gas plants	5,439	5,439	900,000,000,000	21.4	165,471,594		1,000,000,000,000	6,043	604		1,000,000,000,000	6,043	604	0.9	543.6	543.6
Other gas	105															
Other biomass plants	1,229															
Petroleum	3,743															
Pumped storage	151															

Renewable energy plants—total	815		300,000,000,000	7.1	368,098,159.51	700,000,000,000	1,902	1,087	800,000,000,000	2,173	1,358	0.3	326.1	407.4
Solar thermal per photovoltaic	38													
Wind power	389													
Wood derived	346													
Other	42													
Conventional plants	17,168													
Total plant scope per investment	17,272	7,828	4,200,000,000,000	100.0		5,100,000,000,000	9,741	1,913	5,400,000,000,000	10,152	2,324		1,259.7	1,481.0

Source: U.S. Department of Energy; Energy Information Administration/Annual Energy Outlook, 2009, p. 71 (demand growth data only).

Notes

Preface

1. Dr. Vernon L. Grose, Chairman, Omega Systems Group, Inc.; Author of *Managing Risk—Systematic Loss Prevention for Executives and Science but not Scientists* (Story of the California text book controversy of the 1970s); Englewood, NJ: Prentice-Hall, 1999, 404. Originally published as *Science But Not Scientists* (Bloomington, IN: Author House, 2006), 707.
2. Ibid.
3. Bob Slosser, *Reagan Inside Out* (W. Pub Group:1984), 140–153.
4. Slosser, Ibid., 140.
5. Dr. P. T. Bauer, Professor, London School of Economics, "Why Conservatives Govern in Name Only," *Wall Street Journal*, Editorial Section, 3/29/83.
6. Slosser, Ibid., 141.

Chapter 1

1. The quote on the Athenian Republic appeared in three web sites in the spring of 2006 as follows: www.actionhistorique.blogspot.com; www.rantburg.com/poparticle, posted by Besoeker May 22, 2006, 09:00 AM; www.huntingnet.com.
2. The cycle is also referred to by Internet blogger John Eberhard in www.commonsensegovernment.com, in a posting dated September 15, 2003, discussing a 2002 education seminar presented by Dr. Shannon Brooks at the George Wythe College in Salt Lake City. The lecture was titled "The Liber," a reference to one who is "educated for freedom." The word comes from the same root as the words *library* and *liberty*.

    Eberhard pursued his research with Dr. Brooks, who was able to help with the proper spelling of Tytler's name, but little more than he had provided in the lecture. See www.commonsensegovernment.com; www.snopes.com/politics/ballot/athenian.asp; www.famousquotessite.com
3. "... attitude, beliefs, character, code, conduct, conscience, ethics, ideals, integrity, morals, mores, scruples, sense of duty, sense of honor, standards,"

as outlined in Roget's Thesaurus in Dictionary Form (Barnes & Noble, Inc., 1999), 854.

4. Bob Slosser, *Reagan Inside Out* (W. Pub Group, 1984), 140.
5. C-SPAN Broadcast of Congressional Testimony, April 19, 2006.
6. C.S. Lewis Institute Seminar, November 2005, Falls Church, Virginia.
7. Thomas L. Friedman, *From Beirut to Jerusalem* (Random House, Inc., 1995), 230.
8. Jared Diamond, interview on National Public Radio, March 2009.
9. "Potted histories," Karavans.Com, Copyright 2006.
10. Cadet Prayer, United States Military Academy at West Point, as reprinted in *Forging the Warrior's Character*, McGraw-Hill—Learning Solutions, Inside cover.
11. Edward N. Flynn, January 2006.

Chapter 2

1. National Center for Education Statistics, U.S. Department of Education, Highlights from PISA 2006.

Chapter 3

1. John B. Mumford, paper written for the president and founder (Campus Crusade for Christ International, 1985).
2. Dr. Vernon L. Grose, meeting, December 4, 2006.
3. Ibid.
4. Dr. George Labovitz, and Victor Rosansky, *The Power of Alignment* (Hoboken, NJ: Wiley, 1997), 156.
5. Ibid.
6. David McCullough, *1776* (Simon & Schuster, 2005), 41, 48, 118, 148.

Chapter 4

1. Warren Buffett interview, CNBC, March 9, 2009, 7:00–10:00 A.M.

Chapter 5

1. Timothy Curry and Lynn Shibut, "The Cost of the Savings and Loan Crisis: Truth and Consequences," *FDIC Banking Review* 12, no. 2 (1999).
Added Note: FICO was created by the Competitive Equality Banking Act of 1987 (CEBA) as the vehicle for recapitalizing the insolvent FSLIC. The law authorized FICO to raise funds for the FSLIC by selling bonds to the public; as noted, FICO had $8.2 billion of outstanding debt as of the passage of FIRREA in August 1989. Initially the thrift industry was to be responsible for payment of interest and principal on the outstanding debt. Later FIRREA permitted the FICO bonds to be paid for by annual assessments from the newly created SAIF insurance fund. Because of concern over the low reserves of the SAIF, the Deposit Insurance Funds Act of 1996 (PL 104-208) provided for the SAIF's

capitalization. As part of the capitalization effort, future interest payments on the FICO bonds were to be paid for by all FDIC-insured institutions.
2. Ibid.
3. Ibid.

Chapter 6

1. Congressman Ron Paul, U.S. House of Representatives, February 15, 2006.
2. Hugo Chavez, OPEC Opening Meeting Address, June 1, 2006.
3. Martin D. Weiss, et al., *Money and Markets*, www.moneyandmarkets.com. *Money and Markets* is a free daily investment newsletter from Martin D. Weiss and Weiss research analysts offering the latest investment news and financial insights for the stock market, including tips and advice on investing in gold, energy, and oil.
4. Lothar Kemp, "Executive Intelligence Review," weekly newsletter published by EIR News Services, Inc, August 10, 2001.
5. Brian Hunt, *DailyWealth*, www.dailywealth.com, online newsletter published by Stansberry and Associates Investment Research, May 9, 2006.
6. David M. Walker, U.S. Comptroller General, Excerpts of a November 9, 2005, speech, as published in MoneyNews.com on November 11, 2005.
7. Clyde Prestowitz, president of the Economic Strategy Institute and author of the book *Three Billion New Capitalists*, as reported on MoneyNews.com, September 6, 2005.
8. Paul Volcker, *Liberty Dollar*, April 15, 2005, www.LibertyDollar.org.
9. *Liberty Dollar*, article was written by Bernard von Nothavs, Volume 7, no. 7, July 20, 2005, www.LibertyDollar.org.

Chapter 7

1. Federal Reserve Board, G.19 Release, Consumer Debt, March 6, 2009, pp. 1–2. See also Appendix B with a full data set on the existing debt loads by sector, population changes through 2016, and notes on all sources of information.

Chapter 8

1. Sir Julian Hodge, memo, dated November 1990, to senior executives of the Cardiff-based Julian Hodge Bank, quoted in the *Western Mail*, February 28, 1995.
   "Unlike Warren Buffet, Sir Julian Hodge, the Welsh banker, issued his apocalyptic warning three years before the first rash of derivatives disasters involving Metallgesellschaft, Orange County, Sears Roebuck, Proctor & Gamble, happened in 1994. More was to come in 1995 in the form of the Daiwa and Barings scandals. None of those on their own, however, threatened to bring the world financial system to its knees. The crisis that came closest to doing so, so far, involved LTCM in September 1998, but could a mega-catastrophe lie around the corner. . . .?"[1]
2. Bank of International Settlements, Page A 190, March 26, 2009.

3. "Gambling on Derivatives—Hedging Risk or Courting Disaster?" www.exeter .ac.uk. (accessed: June 13, 2006).

4. This is the claim made by the Futures Industry Association in their 1984 publication *An Introduction to the Futures Markets 2*. It is cited by Jerry Markham in two instances. Jerry W. Markham, 1994. " 'Confederate bonds,' 'General Custer,' and the 'Regulation of Derivative Financial Instruments.' " *Seton Hall Law Review* (1994); and Jerry W. Markham. *The History of Commodity Futures Trading and Its Regulation* (New York: Praeger Press, 1987).

5. It is not entirely clear from the available translation whether these derivatives were options or forward contracts.

6. Edward J. Swan. *Building the Global Market: A 4000 Year History of Derivatives.* (London, United Kingdom: Kluwer Law International, 2000) Article previously published in *The Development of the Law of Financial Services.* (London, United Kingdom: Kluwer Law International, 1993).

7. Edward J. Swan. *The Development of the Law of Financial Services.* Op. cit, 1993.

8. Randall Dodd, Derivatives Study Center, Financial Policy Forum, November 15, 2001.

9. Ibid., Randall Dodd.

10. Derivatives Markets: Sources of Vulnerability for U.S. and World Financial Markets: Randall Dodd, director of the Washington, DC-based Financial Policy Center (which includes the Derivatives Study Center), summarized the way in which derivatives markets pose several types of public interest concerns by exposing the U.S. economy to new and greater sources of vulnerability in a paper dated November 15, 2001. Mr. Dodd is now a senior staff member at the International Monetary Fund.

Chapter 9

1. History Channel, *The San Francisco Earthquake*, April 18, 2006.

2. Joint FEMA/NOAA Press Conference, National Press Club, August 12, 2006.

3. Federal Emergency Management Agency web site (access date: March 15, 2009).

4. Federal Emergency Management Agency, Emergency Management Guide for Business and Industry, October 1993.

Chapter 10

1. Eddie Willers, "The Non-Neutrality of Government Intervention," ewillers@ LaissezFaireRepublic.com, August 23, 2004.

2. Professor Michael Hudson is an independent Wall Street financial economist. After working as a balance-of-payments economist for the Chase Manhattan Bank and Arthur Anderson in the 1960s, he taught international finance at The New School in New York City. Presently, he is Distinguished Professor of Economics at the University of Missouri (Kansas City). He has published widely on the topic of U.S. financial dominance. He has also been an economic adviser to the Canadian, Mexican, Russian, and U.S. governments. His books include *Trade, Development*, and *Foreign Debt* (Pluto Press, 1992, 2 vols.). He is the author of *Super Imperialism* (Pluto Press, 1993).

Standard Schaefer is an independent economic journalist, a cultural histo-
rian, literary critic, national award-winning poet, and short fiction writer. He
is the fiction and the non-fiction editor of *The New Review of Literature*. He can
be reached at ssschaefer@earthlink.net.

3. Xie, Danyang, *China Daily*, March 28, 2006, 4.

Chapter 11

1. Michael Chossudovsky, Professor of Economics, University of Ottawa,
   addressed the growing problems of poor financial practices on the world stage
   because of its influence on large-scale money creation, central bank plundering,
   and the potential for a failed dollar in the future.

   Professor of Economics, University of Ottawa, author of *The Globalisa-
   tion of Poverty, Impacts of IMF and World Bank Reforms* (London: Zed Books,
   1997; Panang, Malaysia: Third World Network, 1997). He is also the author of
   "Dismantling Yugoslavia, Colonizing Bosnia," *Covert Action Quarterly* (CAQ)
   56, Spring (1996); and "The Business of Crimes and the Crimes of Business: Globalization and the Criminalization of Economic Activity," *Covert
   Action Quarterly* (CAQ) 58, Fall (1996). The author can be contacted at:
   Michel.Chossudovsky@uOttawa.ca. Address he can be reached at is : Department of Economics, University of Ottawa, 55 Laurier Avenue East, Desmarais
   Building, Room 10111, Ottawa, Ontario, Canada, telephone number : (613)
   562–5800, ext. 5753.

2. United Nations Development Program, Human Development Report, New
   York, 1997, 2.

3. Robert O'Harrow Jr., "Dow Dives 513 Points, or 6.4," *Washington Post*,
   page A, September 1, 1998.

4. Bob Djurdjevic, Return looted Russian Assets, Truth in Media's Global Watch,
   Phoenix, August 30, 1998.

5. *See* "Society under Threat-Soros," *The Guardian*, London, October 31, 1997.

6. Statement at the Meeting of the Group of 15, Malacca, Malaysia, November
   3, 1997, quoted in the *South China Morning Post*, Hong Kong, November 3,
   1997.

7. *See* Michael Hudson and Bill Totten, "Vulture speculators," *Our World* 197,
   Kawasaki (August 12, 1998).

8. Nicola Bullard, Walden Bello and Kamal Malhotra, "Taming the Tigers: The
   IMF and the Asian Crisis," Special Issue on the IMF, Focus on Trade No.
   23, Focus on the Global South, Bangkok, March 1998. Article located at
   www.focusweb.org.

9. Korean Federation of Trade Unions, "Unbridled Freedom to Sack Workers Is
   No Solution at All," Seoul, January 13, 1998.

10. Jung-tae Song, "Insolvency of Construction Firms Rises in 1998," *Korea Her-
    ald*, December 24, 1997. Legislation (following IMF directives) was approved,
    which dismantles the extensive powers of the Ministry of Finance while also
    stripping the Ministry of its financial regulatory and supervisory functions. The
    financial sector had been opened up, a Financial Supervisory Council under the
    advice of Western merchant banks arbitrarily decides the fate of Korean banks.
    Selected banks (the lucky ones) are to be "made more attractive" by earmarking

a significant chunk of the bailout money to finance (subsidize) their acquisition at depressed prices by foreign buyers—i.e., the shopping spree by Western financiers is funded by the government on borrowed money from Western financiers.

11. Michael Hudson, *Our World*, Kawasaki (December 23, 1997).

12. Michael Hudson, "Big Bang Is Culprit behind Yen's Fall," *Our World* 187, Kawasaki (July 28,1998). *See also* Secretary of State Madeleine K. Albright and Japanese Foreign Minister Keizo Obuchi, Joint Press Conference, Ikura House, Tokyo, July 4, 1998 contained in Official Press Release, U.S. Department of State, Washington, July 7, l998.

13. *See* Nicola Bullard, Walden Bello, and Kamal Malhotra, op. cit.

14. On July 15, 1998, the Republican dominated House of Representatives slashed the Clinton Administration request of $18 billion in additional U.S. funding to the IMF to $3.5 billion. Part of the U.S. contribution to the bailouts would be financed under the Foreign Exchange Stabilization Fund of the Treasury. The U.S. Congress has estimated the increase in the U.S. public debt and the burden on taxpayers of the U.S. contributions to the Asian bailouts.

15. *Financial Times* (London), December 3, 1997, 27–28.

16. Institute of International Finance, Report of the Multilateral Agencies Group, IIF Annual Report, Washington, 1997.

17. Letter addressed by the managing director of the Institute of International Finance Mr. Charles Dallarato. Mr. Philip Maystadt, Chairman of the IMF Interim Committee, April 1997 (quoted in Institute of International Finance 1997 Annual Report, Washington, DC).

18. Steven Forbes, "Why Reward Bad Behavior?" *Forbes Magazine*, editorial, May 4, 1998.

19. "Hot money" is speculative capital; "dirty money" is the proceeds of organized crime, which is routinely laundered in the international financial system.

20. International Monetary Fund, Communiqué of the Interim Committee of the Board of Governors of the International Monetary Fund, press release no. 98/14, Washington, DC, April 16, 1998. The controversial proposal to amend its articles on "capital account liberalisation" [*sic*] had initially been put forth in April 1997.

21. *See* Communiqué of the IMF Interim Committee, Hong Kong, September 21, 1997.

22. Ibid.

23. Christian Mulder, Senior Economist in the IMF's Policy Development and Review Department. "Spotting Vulnerability to Financial Risks Is Key to Preventing Crises," *IMF Finance and Development* (Quarterly Magazine of the IMF) 39, no. 4 (December 2002).

24. Jefferson, Thomas, during the debate on the Recharter of The Bank Bill, 1809, as reported in www.barefootsworld.net/prophesy.html (accessed: July 18, 2009).

Chapter 12

1. Charles Morris, The Century Foundation, February 10, 2006.
   Charlie Morris is the author of the Century Foundation report "Apart at the Seams: The Collapse of Private Pension and Health Care Protections." This

excerpt is taken from Chapter 3, "A System Under Stress." (Copyright 2006, The Century Foundation.)

NY Office: 41 East 70th Street—New York, New York—10021—Phone: 212-535-4441—Fax: 212-879-9197

DC Office: 1333 H Street, NW—10th Floor—Washington, DC— 2005—Phone: 202-387-0400—Fax: 202-483-9430

The Century Foundation was founded in 1919 by businessman Edward A. Filene. A non-profit public policy research institution, the Foundation focuses on the major challenges facing the United States within a context of advancing effective government, open democracy, and free markets. The current challenge priorities include:

- The problem of persistent economic inequality and the shift of financial risks from government to taxpayers;
- The aging of the population;
- Balancing effective terror mitigation with preserving civil liberties; and
- Restoring the United States' international credibility in an atmosphere of security and economic dangers.

Within this theme set Century produces materials Social Security and pensions, health care, education, tax and budget policy, homeland security, immigration, and others.

2. Ibid.
3. Ibid.
4. Ibid.
5. Ibid.
6. IBM's union web site, The Endicott Alliance, www.endicottalliance.org, shows "Where IBM is hiring in 2009." The Fiscal Survey of States is published twice annually by the National Association of State Budget Officers (NASBO) and The National Governors Association.
   Asia/Pacific: 13,376
   CEEMEA: 3,988 (Central/Eastern Europe and Middle East)
   Europe: 2,923
   India: 18,873
   Japan: 868
   Latin America: 7,112
   USA: 3,514
   Canada: 820
   The Company will hire 47,960 new employees overseas to replace the some 9,000 U.S. senior professionals laid off through the first half of 2009.
7. Rick Matoon, *The Economist*, Federal Reserve Bank of Chicago.

   Suggested reading on OPEB:

- The GASB 43 and 45 reporting guidelines For other post-employment benefits: A civic federation issue brief.
- "Clearly Unhealthy," *The Economist*, Vol. 376, Issue 8433 (July 2, 2005): 65-66 pp.

Standard & Poor's, "Funding OPEB Liabilities: Assessing the Options", December, 14, 2005.
*   Fitch Ratings, "The Not So Golden Years: Credit Implications of GASB Statement No. 45."

8. GASB no. 35 and no. 45.
9. E. McNichol, State Fiscal Crisis Lingers, Cuts Still Loom, Center on Budget and Policy Priorities, February 15, 2005.
10. Rick Matoon, *The Economist*, Federal Reserve Bank of Chicago.
11. National Governors Association and National Association of State Budget Officers, The Fiscal Survey of States: July 2005, June 2005, p. ix.

Chapter 14

1. Mongabay.com
2. Ibid.
3. Ibid.
4. V. Bolynev, Institute of Geography, USSR National Academy of Sciences, (Moscow, 1997).
5. President's Budget for FY 2009, Department of the Interior Summary, DH44.
6. President's Budget for FY 2009, Department of the Interior Summary, 80.
7. George W. Handy, Center for Strategic and International Studies, International Action Commissions, 1992–1996, Final Report, Washington DC, June 2006.

Chapter 15

1. Thomas Dyson, *Daily Wealth*, May 9, 2006.
2. U.S. Department of Energy, *2008 International Energy Outlook*.

Chapter 16

1. Newsbatch.org (access date: February 2006).
2. Ibid.
3. Ibid.
4. Pre-2000 Election Statement by George W. Bush.
5. Newsbatch.org, op cit.
6. Newsbatch.org, Ibid.
7. Newsbatch.org, Ibid.
8. Newsbatch.org, Ibid.
9. Newsbatch.org, Ibid.
10. Newsbatch.org, Ibid.
11. Newsbatch.org, Ibid.
12. Newsbatch.org, Ibid.
13. Newsbatch.org, Ibid.
14. Newsbatch.org, Ibid.
15. Newsbatch.org, Ibid.
16. Newsbatch.org, Ibid.
17. Newsbatch.org, Ibid.

18. Congressional Budget Office, Domestic Issue 14 (1996).
19. Newsblast.org.
20. Newsblast.org.
21. USEPA, Mid-Year Performance Report—FY 2005, 2.
22. Ibid., 5 pp.
23. Ibid., 7 pp.
24. Ibid., 9 pp.
25. Ibid., 13 pp
26. Ibid., 15 pp.
27. Ibid., 17 pp.
28. Ibid., 19 pp.
29. Ibid., 21 pp
30. Ibid., 23 pp.
31. Ibid.
32. Newsblast.org.
33. Newsblast.org.
34. Newsblast.org.

Chapter 17

1. Dr. Vernon L. Grose, Presentation to County Supervisor, Springfield District, Fairfax County, VA (10/1/08).

Table 17.1

2. FDIC Future of Banking Study, "The future of Banking," 2003; branch replacement value is estimated at an average of $2.0 million each. Modernization for security and communications enhancement is estimated at $500,000 per branch.
3. Greenpeace feature on Nuclear Terrorism, www.Greenpeace.org. (Note: 2.4 million people killed or injured by one attack on one plant National Infrastructure Protection Center.) Replacement cost is estimated at $0.3 billion each. Modernization for hardening, security, and updating technology is estimated at $0.1 billion per plant.
4. Commercial facilities are those with more than one employee working alone. There are 17 million such facilities. Replacement cost is estimated at $ 1.0 million per site. (115,074,924 employees here per Department of Commerce, 2004.) Modernization for hardening, security, and updating technology is estimated at $0.5 million per facility.
5. Nuclear plants are per U.S. Department of Energy; Energy Information Administration; www.eia.doe.gov/cneaf/nuclear/page/nuc_reactors/reactsum.html. Replacement cost is estimated at $5.0 billion per reactor. Modernization is estimated at $1.0 billion per reactor. Modernization for further site hardening, added security, and plant overhaul is estimated at $1.5 billion per reactor.
6. Dams—75,000 dams in the United States, blocking 600,000 miles (960,000 km) of river or about 17 percent of rivers in the nation per Wikipedia[1]
   The American Society of Civil Engineers reports that there are 4,000 dams in urgent need of rehabilitation to save downstream development.

The American Society of Civil Engineers reports that the expenditures needed per year through 2019 for critical repairs is $10.1 billion. Testimony before the House Ways and Means Committee by David G. Mongan, P.E. President, ASCE, October 25, 2008.

Levees—The American Society of Civil Engineers reports that there are 100,000 miles of levees, 85 percent of which are privately owned.

Source: USACE Report. 114 levees have been classified as so neglected that they cannot be repaired, and 177 are in urgent need of repair. None are expected to perform their functions in the event of a flood.

Replacement cost per dam is estimated at $30 million; maintenance cost per mile of levee is estimated at $1.0 million.

Modernization for dam and levee rehabilitation, added security, and equipment overhaul is estimated at $15 million per dam and $0.2 million per mile of levee.

Source: The Architect's Newspaper, March 17, 2009. Repair and modernization of public and privately owned levees is estimated at $100 billion by the American Society of Civil Engineers.

Source: The Architects Newspaper, March 17, 2009. The American Society of Civil Engineers reports that the average cost of replacement of river locks is $600 million.

There are 257 inland waterway locks, 30 of which were built in the nineteenth century. Total cost to replace is $125 billion.

7. The Defense Industrial Base is estimated at 1,200 installations—federal and private, with an estimated replacement value of $200 million each. Modernization for facility rehabilitation, added security, and equipment overhaul is estimated at $150 million per installation.

8. The EPA is responsible for water system safety and security. It reports that there are 53,000 community water systems in the nation and 21,400 non-profit (hospital et al.) water systems. The investment needed to modernize the system is $276.8 billion from 2003 through 2023 per the Report of the National Academy of Sciences, "Drinking Water: Understanding the Science and Policy behind a Critical Infrastructure" (undated). Wastewater treatment systems in the United States number 16,000 according to the Suburban Emergency Management Project (April 15, 2009).

The replacement value of both public and private non-profit water treatment systems is estimated at $20.0 million per facility (per ASCE web site, www.asce.org).

The American Society of Civil Engineers estimates the annual outlays for rehabilitation and modernization of the existing water treatment capacity at $11 billion per year.

9. Emergency services (fire, ambulance, and police services) are estimated at 60,000 facilities with a replacement cost of $1.5 million each and a modernization and security cost of $0.5 million each.

10. Energy facilities are estimated at 90,000 installations with an average value of $5 million. Modernization will require an additional $1.5 million per installation. Valuation and modernization of plants is shown in USD ($ millions) by each plant type below:

Coal plants	$ 5.0	$ 2.5
Geothermal plants	$ 6.0	$ 0.5
Hydroelectric conventional	$ 12.0	$ 4.0
Natural gas plants	$ 10.0	$ 3.0
Other gas	$ 6.0	$ 2.0
Other biomass plants	$ 6.0	$ 1.0
Petroleum	$ 25.0	$ 12.0
Pumped storage	$ 30.0	$ 6.0
Solar thermal/photovoltaic	$ 18.0	$ 6.0
Wind power	$ 15.0	$ 4.0
Wood derived	$ 5.0	$ 1.0
Other	$ 3.0	$ 1.0
Total conventional plants		

11. The power grid is estimated at a value of $500.0 billion with modernization requiring an additional $500.0 billion.

    The U.S. power grid consists of 300,000 kilometers of lines operated by 500 companies.

    Source: Wikipedia (access date: March 19, 2009). The total miles of the U.S. power grid are 186,420 miles..

    Source: Steve Hargreaves, CNN Money (January 8, 2009).

12. Estimates of the number of U.S. farm establishments are based upon the total census by USDA in 2007 of the number of potential establishments. 3.0 million forms were mailed, and 85 percent were returned (2.55 million). The value estimate per farm is $500,000, and the modernization estimate is $200,000 per farm.

13. There are 84,000 units of government in the United States. It is assumed that each unit has at least one installation and that there are a total of 10,000 additional installations. It is assumed that the replacement value of the buildings is $1.5 million and the modernization expense is $0.5 million.

14. It is assumed that critical information technology installations are valued at $15.0 million; modernization would cost $5 million.

    Source of number of installations: U.S. Department of Commerce; Census of Business Establishments, 2006; Adjusted for 2007.

15. Wikipedia Note: There are 100 national monuments managed or co-managed by one or more of four federal agencies. There are an estimated 1,400 national icons with a nominal value of $20 million each and a modernization and security budget of $10 million each.

    Source: 2002 Economic census, www.census.gov/econ/census02/data/us/US000-62.HTM#N621. Clinics numbering 25,750 in The United States employ 590,144 people.

16. Postal facilities are both public and privately owned. The total of U.S. postal service facilities is 32,741 according to the U.S. Government Accountability office's December 2007 report. An estimated 15,000 privately owned and commercial postal facilities is estimated for a total of 47,741 for the United States as a whole. The value of each facility is estimated at $1.0 million and modernization is budgeted at $0.25 million.

17. *Source*: U.S. Department of Commerce, Census of Business Establishments, 2006 (Adjusted for 2007). Estimated replacement value is $0.75 million per facility with modernization budgeted at $0.25 million.

18. *Source*: Bruce Clark "Means of Survival," *Waste Age*, March 19, 2009. The number 20,000 is an EPA estimate. The average value is estimated at $40.0 million and modernization is budgeted at $1.0 million.

19. The U.S. Department of Commerce; Census of Business Establishments lists 141,495 establishments in the information technology function. This has been divided into two segments for purposes of the information technology establishments and 100,000 for telecommunications establishments. Telecommunications establishments have been valued at $10 million for replacement and $5 million for modernization and security.

20. Airports are valued at $50.0 million. Modernization is budgeted at $20 million per installation.

    Bridges are valued at $4.0 million each; modernization is budgeted at $1.5 million per bridge.

    Canals are estimated at 2,000 total miles with ownership divided two-thirds public and one-third private. Value is set at $100,000 per mile with $50,000 per mile for modernization, dredging, and security.

    Source: Wikipedia (access date: March 19, 2009) for total ports. Value of ports is estimated at $100.0 million and modernization is estimated at $50.0 million each.

    Source: www.nemw.org/roadshighways.htm. There are four million miles of public roads in the United States.

    Roads are valued for replacement at $100,000 per mile. Modernization is budgeted at $50,000 per mile.

    Source: www.aar.com. Class I railroad miles are shown; total railroads are 140,000 miles per American Association of Railroads.

    Offshore oil platforms are valued at $200 million. Modernization is budgeted at $50 million per platform.

    Source: Report, U.S. Department of Homeland Security, National Monuments and Icons, 2007.

    Source: Wikipedia (access date: March 19, 2009). Pipelines are shown at 276,000 kilometers or 171,506 miles. Natural gas pipelines are shown at 331,000 kilometers or 205,683 miles. Total miles of pipelines are 377,189 miles.

    Source: Report, U.S. Department of Homeland Security, National Monuments and Icons, 2007.

    Petroleum pipelines are valued at $200,000 per mile and the modernization is budgeted at $75,000 per mile.

    Source: Wikipedia (access date: March 19, 2009). Port valuation is set at $100.0 million and modernization and security are estimated at $50.0 million per port.

Source: Enchanted Learning, March 19, 2009. There are 250,000 rivers in the United States. The total mileage is 3,500,000.

Source: Wikipedia (access date: March 19, 2009). Navigable rivers and canals—total navigable inland waterways is 41,009 kilometers or 25,843 miles.

There is no basis to put a value on rivers, but rehabilitation and restoration has been budgeted at $50,000 per mile.

21. *Source*: Data_Lists.com (access date: March 19, 2009). Schools are valued at $4.0 million each, and modernization has been budgeted at $1.0 million each.

Table 17.2

22. *Source*: www.hud.gov. Estimates of the number of brownfields vary between 425,000 (HUD) and 600,000 (EPA). The higher number has been used. Total acres in brownfields are estimated at five million. This is 60 percent of the total area of the United States' largest cities.
23. This is an average estimate of 1,250 acres of managed land in each of 3,181 counties.
24. This estimates an average of 31 parks in each of 3,181 counties.
25. This estimates an average of 945 miles of county-maintained roads in each county.
26. This estimates an average of 31 energy retrofit projects per county.
27. This estimates an average of 31 facilities in need of modernization in each county.
28. This estimates an average of 16 upgrade projects per county.
29. This estimates an average of 1,000 workdays per year per dam, with potential for public risk.
30. This estimates an average of 200 workdays per mile per levee, with potential for public risk.
31. This estimates an average of 500 days of lock maintenance work per year per lock.
32. This estimates that an average of 200 workdays per year is needed per mile of fire lane.
33. This estimates that 10 million acres are to be replanted per year with an average workload 100 days of work per acre per year.
34. This estimates that there are 150,000 local energy retrofit projects with an average workload of 100 days per year.
35. This estimates that there are 300,000 local maintenance projects requiring an average of 100 days of work each per year.
36. This estimates that 100,000 acres of local lands will require 100 days per year per acre to maintain.
37. This estimates that there are 50,000 city parks in the 30,000 largest cities needing 200 workdays of maintenance each per year.
38. This presumes that there are an average of 50 miles of local roads per city, requiring 100 workdays of maintenance each per year.
39. This estimates that the 1,500 national monuments and icons will require an added 1,000 workdays each per year.

40. This estimates that 50,000 national park projects will require 400 workdays each per year.
41. This estimates that the 91,957 primary and secondary schools will require 1,000 workdays each per year to upgrade.
42. This estimates that 50,000 state energy projects will require 200 workdays each per year to complete.
43. This estimates that 50,000 state park projects will require 200 workdays each per year to complete.
44. Airport projects are funded and staffed by federal and state airport authorities or privately.
45. Bridge projects are completed by established contractors under federal, state, county, or local supervision.
46. This estimates that 2,000 miles of canals will require 1,000 workdays of maintenance per year.
47. This estimates that all highway projects will require 400 days of maintenance and cleaning work per mile per year.
48. This estimates that 25,483 miles of rivers will require 1,000 workdays of maintenance and cleanup per mile per year.

Chapter 18

1. Tom Barry and others, "A Good Neighbor Ethic for International Relations," *Special Report*, International Relations Center, Silver City, NM, May 2005).
2. Ibid.
3. Ibid.
4. Ibid.
5. Ibid.
6. Ibid.
7. Ibid.
8. Ibid.
9. Consciouspolitics.org
10. Ibid.
11. David Ignatius, *The Washington Post*, May 21, 2006.
12. Ibid.
13. George W. Handy, Director, International Action Commissions, *Final Report (1992-2006)* (Center for Strategic and International Studies, Washington, DC, June 2006).
14. Ibid. Added Note: The International Action Commissions also made 177 substantial recommendations to benefit the partner organizations and nations.

Chapter 19

1. Legion XXIV, "A Short History of Rome", (LegionXXIV.org/history, revised December 22, 2002).
2. Ibid.
3. Ibid.
4. Ibid.

5. Ibid.
6. Ibid.
7. Ibid.
8. Ibid.
9. Averil Cameron, *The Mediterranean World in Late Antiquity, AD 395-600* (London, 1993).

   A.H.M. Jones, *The Decline of the Ancient World* (London, 1966).

   Hugh Elton, "The Collapse of the Roman Empire—Military Aspects," ORB Online Encyclopedia.

   Hugh Elton, *A Short Bibliography*. (Oxford Classical Monographs, year unknown).

   Hugh Elton, *Warfare in Roman Europe: AD 350-425* (Oxford, 1996).
10. Kirkpatrick Sale, "Imperial Entropy—Collapse of the American Empire," February 22, 2005. (web site: www.counterpunch.org/sale02222005.html).

    Kirkpatrick Sale is the author of 12 books, including *Human Scale*, *The Conquest of Paradise*, *Rebels Against the Future*, and *The Fire of His Genius: Robert Fulton and the American Dream*.
11. Ibid.

Chapter 21

1. "Failure of Intelligence," Discovery/*New York Times* Channel, June 25, 2006.
2. "Addicted to Oil," Discovery/*New York Times* Channel, June 25, 2006.
3. Dr. Samuel P. Huntington, *The Clash of Civilizations and the Remaking of the World Order* (New York: Simon and Schuster, 1996), 21–36.
4. Ibid., 6.
5. Ibid. The Clash of Civilizations and the Remaking of the World Order (New York: Simon and Schuster, 1996).
6. Dr. Gal Luft, "Bin Laden's Out to Destroy U.S. Economy," Interview, INN Television, Jerusalem, 18:09 April 11, 2005 (2 Nisan 5765), http://www.israelnationalnews.com/news.php3?id=79998.

   Dr. Gal Luft is the director of the Institute for the Analysis of Global Security.
7. Ibid.
8. Adam Young, Canadian freelance writer, analyzes the past two decades of unheeded warnings, the ensuing disasters, and the possible lessons to be learned.
9. Defense Science Board, *The Defense Science Board 1997 Summer Study Task Force on DoD Responses to Transnational Threats* (Final Report, Vol. 1, 15, Washington: U.S. Department of Defense, October 1997). Cited in "Does U.S. Intervention Overseas Breed Terrorism: The Historical Record" by Ivan Eland, *Foreign Policy Briefing, Cato Institute, December 17, 1998*. Much of the information in this article comes from Eland's excellent piece.
10. Ibid.
11. Adam Young, "A History of Terror," Ludwig von Mises Institute; 518 West Magnolia Avenue; Auburn, Alabama 36832-4528; Phone: 334-321-2100; Fax: 334-321-2119; AOL-IM: contact@mises.org; MainMises. (The Ludwig von Mises Institute is the research and educational center of classical liberalism and

the Austrian School of economics.) Posted on Wednesday, February 06, 2002. (Adam Young is studying computer science in Ontario, Canada. His articles have appeared in *Ideas on Liberty, Mises.org, LewRockwell.com,* and *The Free Market.*)

Chapter 22

1. Wikipedia, *Microcredit Principles,* 2 (access date: April 6, 2009).
   See also Small Loans, Big Business—*How Nobel Prize Winner Muhammad Yunus and Microfinance are Changing the World* (Hoboken, NJ: John Wiley & Sons, Inc., 2008).
2. Ibid.
3. Ibid.
4. Ibid.
5. Ibid.
6. Kiva.org.
7. Ibid., Jocelyn Manaligod, April 6, 2009.
8. Trickleup.org (access date: April 6, 2009).

Chapter 23

1. Subcommittee on Water Resources and Environment, U.S. House of Representatives, web site, and Ismail Serageldin, vice president of the World Bank, 1996. Serageldin web site: www.serageldin.com/SpeechDetail.aspx? SID access date: October 13, 2009). Statement on wars focused on water is also quoted on the following site: www.thehindu.com/fline/fl1609/16090890.htm (access date: October 13, 2009).
2. Ibid.
3. BBC News, "Water war leaves Palestinians thirsty," UK edition, June 16, 2003. http://news.bbc.co.uk/1/hi/world/middleeast/2982730.stm.
4. Global Trends 2015: A Dialogue About the Future With Nongovernment Experts, National Intelligence Council (NIC)—CIA web site, December 2000. http://www.cia.gov/cia/reports/globaltrends2015/index.html.
5. Michael Kane, "Beyond Peak Oil: Water Privatization, Water Wars, Water and Oil Don't Mix, Vapor Wars?, All Bottled Up," June 14, 2004, as printed in www.fromthewilderness.com. Kane was article writer, Stan Goff quoted.
6. Maude Barlow, Blue Gold, op. cit.; *also:* Spring 2001, www.canadians.org/documents/blue_gold-e.pdf.
7. Maude Barlow and Tony Clarke, "Who Owns Water?" *The Nation,* September 2, 2002, www.ratical.org/co-globalize/whoOwnsWater.html.
8. Tar Sands, www.fact-index.com/t/ta/tar_sands.html (access date: April 1, 2009).
9. Dale Allen Pfeiffer, "Oil Shortages Look Certain by 2007—LNG to the Rescue?" From the Wilderness Publications, February 19, 2004, http://www.fromthewilderness.com/free/ ww3/ 022304_lng_shortages.html.
10. Stuart Baird, "The Automobile and the Environment," *Energy Educators of Ontario,* 1993, http://www.iclei.org/EFACTS/AUTO.HTM (access date: Aprils 5, 2009).
11. Peter Gleick, The World's Water, Island Press, 1988.
12. Ibid.

13. Ibid.

14. Ibid.

15. Robin Clarke, *Water: The International Crisis*, Boston: MIT Press, 1993.

16. N.D. Kristof, 1997. "Across Asia, a Pollution Disaster Hovers," *New York Times*, A1, 11-28-97, citing WHO and World Bank.

17. Water-Wise Section, compiled by U.S. Agency for International Development, http://gsearch.info.usaid.gov (access date: October 13, 2009).

18. Newsblast.org (access date: April 10, 2009).

19. Ibid.

20. Brian Walsh, "The New Age of Extinction," *Time*, Planet on the Brink Section, April 1, 2009.

21. Newsblast.org (access date: April 10, 2009).

22. Ibid.

23. U.S. Department of Energy, Office of Science, Office of Biological and Environmental Research, Human Genome Program, www.ornl.gov/hgmis.

24. Newsblast.org (access date: April 10, 2009).

25. Peter Gleick, op. cit.

26. Ibid.

27. Ibid.

Chapter 24

1. "Economy Marks Solid Growth Despite Storms," *Wall Street Journal*, October 29, 2005.

2. Ibid.

3. Ibid.

4. Ibid.

5. Ibid.

6. "Huge Flood of Capital to Invest Spurs World-Wide Risk Taking," *Wall Street Journal*, November 3, 2005.

7. Ibid.

8. Ibid.

9. Deuteronomy 28:43–45, as explained on page 336 of the *Life Application Bible*. (Tyndale House Publishers, 1995).

10. Ibid., 336.

11. Attempts to determine whether CBS' Charles Osgood (Sunday Morning) is the author of this poem were not successful. It is provided with attribution.

12. Bill Moyers, *The Wise Guy*, June 11, 2006.

Appendix A

1. Wikipedia (access date: March 25, 2009).

2. Sylvester J. Scheiber and John B. Shoven. *The Real Deal: The History and Future of Social Security* (New Haven and London: Yale University Press, 1999), 182.

3. Roy Webb, "The Stealth Budget: Unfunded Liabilities of the Federal Government," Federal Reserve Bank of Richmond, Economic Review, 77, 2 May/June (1991).

4. Wikipedia (access date: 3/25/09).
5. Timothy Curry and Lynn Shibot, "The Cost of the Savings and Loan Crisis: Truth and Consequences," *FDIC Banking Review* 12, no. 2 (1999): 27, 31.
6. Ibid., 28.
7. Curry, Ibid.
8. Curry, Ibid., 28.
9. St. Louis Federal Reserve.
10–16, 18–69, and 71–75.   St. Louis Federal Reserve.
17. CNBC (access date: March 26, 2009, 8:23 A.M. EDT).
70. WSJ.com, (access date: March 26, 2009).

Appendix B

1. *Source:* Current debt statistics provided by The Federal Reserve Board, Statistical Supplement to the Federal Reserve Bulletin, Debt by borrowing sector, Section 1.59, lines 15–2, March 6, 2009.
2. Unfunded liabilities are for public debt issued by the federal government. Social Security and Medicare amounts are from the National Center for Policy Analysis; Brief Analysis #616, Social Security and Medicare Projections: 2008, dated April 30, 2008, 1.
3. *Source:* Federal Debt is as reported in the 2008 Financial Report of the United States; unfunded liabilities estimate; Total authorized U.S. debt has been projected at $12.1 trillion as of 12/31/09. Action by Congress to raise debt limit to this level is pending at time of printing. The Budget for Fiscal Year 2007, "The Nation's Fiscal Outlook," 21.
4. Total public and private secured, unsecured, and unfunded liabilities: $168,772.5 billion. The public portion is $123,938.2 billion or 73.4% of all public debt.
5. *Source:* Data on non-pension unfunded liabilities for state and local government: Reports by JP Morgan Chase, Cato Institute, and Pew Charitable Trust, as reported by The Heritage Foundation, February 11, 2008, in a summary by Gred D'Angelo. Amount: $1.5 trillion.
6. State and local government unfunded liabilities for retiree health plans have been estimated on the basis of approximately $2,500 in unfunded liabilities per capita for the state or $750 billion for all 50 states based upon a sample of 30 states, including several of the largest population centers, based upon a July 2008 report by the Center for State and Local Government Excellence, 6.

Bibliography

Ahmed, Akbar. *Journey Into Islam*. Washington, DC: Brookings Institution Press, 2007, 230 pp.

Allen, David F., MD. *In Search of the Heart*. Nassau, Bahamas: Eleuthra Publications, 1993, 237 pp.

Armstrong, Karen. *Holy War*. New York: Anchor Books, 2001.

Arnold, Daniel A. *The Great Bust Ahead*. Vorago-US, 2005.

Barlow, Maude. *Blue Covenant*. New York: The New Press, 2007, 196 pp.

_____. *Blue Gold: The Fight to Stop the Corporate Theft of the World's Water*. New York: The New Press, 2002.

Barnett, Thomas P.M. *The Pentagon's New Map: War and Peace in the Twenty-First Century*. New York: G.P. Putnam's Sons, 2004.

Bennis, Warren, and David A. Heenan. *Co-Leaders: The Power of Great Partnerships*. New York: John Wiley & Sons, 1999, 312 pp.

Black, Jim Nelson. *When Nations Die—America on the Brink: Ten Warning Signs of a Culture in Crisis*. Wheaton, IL: Tyndale House Publishers, 1994, 280 pp.

Bonner, William. *Empire of Debt: The Rise of an Epic Financial Crisis*. With Addison Wiggin. Hoboken, NJ: John Wiley & Sons, 2006.

_____. *Financial Reckoning Day: Surviving the Soft Depression of the 21st Century*. Hoboken, NJ: John Wiley & Sons, 2003.

Callahan, David. *The Moral Center: How We Can Reclaim Our Country from Die-Hard Extremists, Rogue Corporations, Hollywood Hacks, and Pretend Patriots*. Orlando, FL: Harcourt Books, 2006.

Colson, Charles. *God and Government*. Grand Rapids, MI: Zondervan Press, 2007, 447 pp.

Cooper, Jim. *Financial Report of the United States* Nashville: Nelson Current, a subsidiary of Thomas Nelson, Inc., 2006.

Counts, Alex. *Small Loans, Big Dreams: How Nobel Prize Winner Muhammad Yunus and Microfinance Are Changing the World.* Hoboken, NJ: John Wiley & Sons, 2008, 410 pp.

de Tocqueville, Alexis. *Democracy in America.* Boston: Tichnor and Fields, 1862, 805 pp.

Dent, Harry S., Jr. *The Great Depression Ahead: How to Prosper in the Crash Following the Greatest Boom in History.* New York: Free Press, Simon & Schuster, 2009.

Diamond, Jared. *Collapse: How Societies Choose to Fail or Succeed.* New York: Penguin Books, 2005.

_____. *Guns, Germs, and Steel: The Fates of Human Societies.* New York: W.W. Norton & Company, 1997.

Duncan, Richard. *The Dollar Crisis: Causes, Consequences, Cures.* Singapore: John Wiley & Sons (Asia) Pte Ltd., 2005.

Easterly, William. *The White Man's Burden: Why the West's Efforts to Aid the Rest Have Done So Much Ill and So Little Good.* New York: The Penguin Press, 2006.

Ellis, Joseph J. *Founding Brothers: The Revolutionary Generation.* New York: Vintage Books, 2000.

_____. *His Excellency: George Washington.* New York: Alfred A. Knopf, 2004, 312 pp.

Enderlin, Charles. *The Lost Years: Radical Islam, Intifada, and Wars in the Middle East 2001–2006.* New York: Other Press, 2006, 80 pp. (Partial Copy).

Freddoso, David. *The Case Against Barack Obama.* Washington, DC: Regnery Publishing, Inc., 2008, 290 pp.

Feiner, Michael. *The Feiner Points of Leadership.* New York: Warner Business Books, 2006, 265 pp.

Ferguson, Niall. *The Ascent of Money.* New York: The Penguin Press, 2008, 442 pp.

Fishman, Ted C. *China, Inc.: How the Rise of the Next Superpower Challenges America and the World.* New York: Scribner, 2005.

Fox, Stephen. *Transatlantic: Sameul Cunard, Isambard Brunel, and the Great Atlantic Steamships.* New York: HarperCollins, 2003, 468.

Friedman, Thomas L. *From Beirut to Jerusalem.* New York: Anchor Books, 1995.

_____. *The World Is Flat: A Brief History of the Twenty-First Century.* New York: Farrar, Strauss, & Giroux, 2005.

Gertz, Bill. *Enemies: How America's Foes Steal Our Vital Secrets—And How We Let It Happen.* New York: Crown Publishing Group, Random House, Inc., 2006.

Godwin, Peter. *When a Crocodile Eats the Sun: A Memoir of Africa.* New York: Little, Brown & Company, 2007, 341 pp.

Grose, Vernon L., DSci. *Managing Risk: Systematic Loss Prevention for Executives*. New York: Prentice Hall, 1982, 404 pp.

Guinness, Os. *The Case for Civility and Why Our Future Depends on It*. New York: HarperOne, HarperCollins Publishers, 2008, 214 pp.

Hacker, Jacob S. *The Great Risk Shift: The Assault on American Jobs, Families, Health Care, and Retirement and How You Can Fight Back*. New York: Oxford University Press, 2006.

Harris, Sam. *The End of Faith*. New York: W. W. Norton, 2005.

Heinberg, Richard. *Power Down*. British Columbia, Canada: New Society Publishers, Friesens Inc., 2005.

Heron, Patrick. *The Nephilim and the Pyramid of the Apocalypse*. New York: Kensington Publishing Corporation, 2004, 239 pp.

Higonnet, Patrice. *Attendant Cruelties: Nation and Nationalism in American History*. New York: Other Press, 2007, 350 pp.

Huntington, Samuel P., PhD. *The Clash of Civilizations and the Remaking of World Order*. New York: Simon & Schuster Paperbacks, 1996.

Iacocca, Lee. *Where Have All the Leaders Gone?* With Catherine Whitney. New York: Simon & Schuster, 2007, 274 pp.

Isaacson, Walter. *Benjamin Franklin: An American Life*. New York: Simon & Schuster, 2003, 590 pp.

Johnson, Bill. *Face to Face with God*. Lake Mary, FL: Charisma House, 2007, 227 pp.

_____. *When Heaven Invades Earth*. Shippensburg, PA: Treasure House, 2003, 190 pp.

_____. *The Supernatural Power of a Transformed Mind*. Shippensburg, PA: Destiny Image Publications, 2005, 175 pp.

Johnson, Rob, PhD. *Analytic Culture of the U.S. Intelligence Community*. Washington, DC: Center for the Study of Intelligence, 2005, 161 pp.

Juhasz, Antonia. *The Bush Agenda: Invading the World One Economy at a Time*. New York: Regan Books, HarperCollins Publishers, 2006.

Karmin, Craig. *Biography of the Dollar*. New York: Crown Publishing Group, Random House, Inc., 2008.

Kawasaki, Guy. *The Art of the Start: The Time-Tested, Battle Hardened Guide for Anyone Starting Anything*. New York: The Penguin Group, 226 pp.

Kemp, William H. *The Renewable Energy Handbook*. Ontario, Canada: Aztext Press, 2005, 560 pp.

Kirsch, Jonathan. *A History of the End of the World*. New York: HarperCollins Publishers, 2006.

Klare, Michael T. *Resource Wars*. New York: Henry Holt and Company, LLC, 2002.

Kosares, Michael J. *The ABCs of Gold Investing: How to Protect and Build Your Wealth With Gold*. Omaha, NE: Addicus Books, 2005, 175 pp.

Kunstler, James Howard. *The Long Emergency: Surviving the Converging Catastrophes of the Twenty-First Century*. New York: Atlantic Monthly Press, 2005.

Kupelian, David. *The Marketing of Evil*. Nashville: WND Books, 2005.

Labovitz, George, and Victor Rosansky. *The Power of Alignment*. New York: John Wiley & Sons, Inc., 1997.

Landorf, Joyce. *Joseph*. Old Tappan, NJ. Fleming H. Revell Company, 1979.

Lansing, Alfred. *Endurance: Shackleton's Incredible Voyage*. New York: Carroll & Graf Publishers, 1959.

Leeb, Stephen, PhD. *The Coming Economic Collapse*. New York: Warner Business Books, 2006.

Leeb, Stephen, with Donna Leeb. *The Oil Factor*. New York: Warner Business Books, 2004.

Lewis, Bernard. *The Middle East*. New York: Scribner, 1995.

Lewis, Nathan. *Gold: The Once and Future Money*. Hoboken, NJ: John Wiley & Sons, Inc., 2007, 447 pp.

Lieberthal et al. *Harvard Business Review on Doing Business in China*. Boston: Harvard Business School Press, 2004.

MacArthur, John F., Jr. *Nehemiah: Experiencing the Good Hand of God*. Nashville: W. Publishing Group, 2001.

Mann, Thomas E., and Norman J. Ornstein. *The Broken Branch: How Congress Is Failing America and How to Get It Back on Track*. New York: Oxford University Press, 2006, 270 pp.

Martin, James, *The Meaning of the 21st Century: A Vital Blueprint for Ensuring Our Future*. New York: Riverhead Books, 2006.

McCullough, David. *1776*. New York: Simon & Schuster, 2005.

McGann, Eileen, and Dick Morris. *Outrage*. New York: HarperCollins Publishers, 2007, 351 pp.

McGregor, James. *One Billion Customers: Lessons from the Front Lines of Doing Business in China*. New York: *Wall Street Journal*, published by Free Press, Simon & Schuster, 2005.

McKee, Jack. *Through Terror and Adversity*. Belfast, Northern Ireland: Alpha Publications, 2002, 183 pp.

McKillop, Andrew, and Sheila Newman, Eds. *The Final Energy Crisis*. London: Pluto Press, 2005.

Mearsheimer, John J., and Stephen M. Walt. *The Israel Lobby and U.S. Foreign Policy*. New York: Farrar, Straus and Giroux, 2007, 484.

Miller, Peter. *Author! Screenwriter!* Avon, MA: Adams Media, 2006, 299 pp.

Naughton, Barry. *The Chinese Economy*. Cambridge, MA, and London, England: The MIT Press, 2007, 528 pp.

Nierenberg, Gerald I., and Henry H. Calero. *How to Read a Person Like a Book*. New York: Barnes & Noble, Inc., 1990, 170 pp.

Pachter, Barbara, and Susan Magee. *The Power of Positive Confrontation*. New York: MJF Books, 2000, 271 pp.

Parker, Thornton. *What if Boomers Can't Retire? How to Build Real Security, Not Phantom Wealth*. San Francisco: Berrett-Koehler Publishers, Inc., 2002.

Peterson, Peter G. *Running on Empty*. New York: Farrar, Straus and Giroux, 2004.

Phillips, Melanie. *Londonistan*. New York: Encounter Books, 2006, 206 pp.

Rabin, Yitzhak. *The Rabin Memoirs by Yitzhak Rabin*. Boston: Little, Brown and Company, 1979, 337 pp.

Redlener, Irwin, MD. *Americans at Risk: Why We Are Not Prepared for Megadisasters and What We Can Do Now?* New York: Alfred A. Knopf, 2006.

Roberts, J.M. *The New Penguin History of the World* New York: Penguin Group (USA), Inc., 2002, 1, 184 pp.

Rubino, John, and James Turk. *The Collapse of the Dollar and How to Profit From It*. New York: A Currency Book Published by Doubleday, 2004, 252 pp.

Sanborn, Mark. *The Fred Factor*. Colorado Springs: WaterBrook Press, 2004, 110 pp.

Savage, Michael. *Liberalism Is a Mental Disorder*. Nashville: Nelson Current, Thomas Nelson, Inc., 2005, 221 pp.

Savinar, Matt, J.D. *The Oil Age Is Over: What to Expect as the World Runs out of Cheap Oil, 2005–2050*, Savinar Publishing—Printed in Kearney, NE: Morris Publishing, 2004.

Schiller, Robert J. *The New Financial Order*. Princeton: Princeton University Press, 2003.

Schwartz, Peter. *Inevitable Surprises: Thinking Ahead in a Time of Turbulence*. New York: Gotham Books, 2003.

Sears, Alan, and Craig Osten. *The ACLU vs. America: Exposing the Agenda to Redefine Moral Values*. Nashville: Broadman & Holman Publishers, 2005.

Sharansky, Natan, and Ronald Dermer. *The Case for Democracy: The Power of Freedom to Overcome Tyranny & Terror*. New York: Public Affairs, Perseus Books Group, 2004.

Shenkar, Oded. *The Chinese Century: The Rising Chinese Economy and Its Impact on the Global Economy, the Balance of Power, and Your Job*. Upper Saddle River, NJ: Wharton School Publishing, 2005.

Shlaes, Amity. *The Forgotten Man: A New History of the Great Depression*. New York: HarperCollins Publishers, 2008, 468 pp.

Siljander, Mark D. *A Deadly Misunderstanding: A Former Congressman's Quest to Bridge the Muslim-Christian Divide*. New York: HarperCollins Publishers, Inc., 2008, 260 pp.

Simmons, Matthew R. *Twilight in the Desert: The Coming Saudi Oil Shock and the World Economy*, Hoboken, NJ: John Wiley & Sons, Inc., 2005.

Skousen, W. Cleon. *The 5000 Year Leap: The 28 Great Ideas That Changed the World*. National Center for Constitution Studies, Fourteenth Printing, 2009, 337 pp.

Smith, Mark W. *The Official Handbook of the Vast Right-Wing Conspiracy*. Washington, DC: Regnery Publishing, Inc., 2008, 217 pp.

Suskind, Ron. *The One Percent Doctrine: Deep Inside America's Pursuit of Its Enemies Since 9/11*. New York: Simon & Schuster, 2006.

———. *The Price of Loyalty: George W. Bush, the White House, and the Education of Paul O'Neill*, New York: Simon & Schuster Paperbacks, 2004.

Talbot, John R. *The Coming Crash in the Housing Market: 10 Things You Can Do Now to Protect Your Most Valuable Investment*. New York: McGraw-Hill, Inc., 2003.

Vanden Heuval, Katrina, and the Editors of The Nation. *Meltdown: How Greed and Corruption Shattered Our Financial System and How We Can Recover*. New York: Nation Books, 2009, 310 pp.

Wattenberg, Ben J. *Fewer: How the New Demography of Depopulation Will Shape Our Future*. Chicago: Ivan R. Dee, 2004.

Wiggins, Addison. *The Demise of the Dollar and Why It's Great for Your Investments*. New York: John Wiley & Sons, Inc., 2005.

Woods, Thomas E., Jr. *Meltdown: A Free-Market Look at Why the Stock Market Collapsed, the Economy Tanked, and Government Bailouts Will Make Things Worse*. Washington, DC: Regnery Publishing, Inc., 2009, 194 pp.

York, Byron. *The Vast Left Wing Conspiracy*. New York: Three Rivers Press, 2006, 274 pp.

Yunus, Muhammad. *Banker to the Poor*. Blackstone Audio, Inc., Perseus Books Group.

Yunus, Muhammad. *Creating a World Without Poverty: Social Business and the Future of Capitalism*. With Karl Weber. Public Affairs, Perseus Books Group, 2007, 261 pp.

Index

About the Author

J ohn Mumford served in the administrations of three U.S. presidents and five secretaries of labor during his federal career. Selected as a White House Fellow during the middle years of the Nixon administration, he was appointed Deputy Assistant Secretary of Labor by President Ford and was retained in this position by President Carter.

In this assignment, he reported to the assistant secretary of labor for employment standards and directed three agencies in the execution and enforcement of over 100 federal statutes and executive orders. The agencies had a total of more than 3,000 full-time federal employees working in 346 offices throughout the United States and Puerto Rico. The annual budget was about $3 billion.

In 1982, he founded The Washington Group—Consultants, LLC, a consulting firm that has worked with Fortune 500 companies (AT&T, General Mills Restaurant Group, American Red Cross, and others) and more than a hundred private and non-profit clients. His consulting practice includes specialization in privately owned company turnarounds. Other firm work includes all phases of strategic and operations management. Earlier, he was project administrator for construction of Walt Disney World in Florida.

A graduate of the U.S. Military Academy in West Point, New York, he was later awarded the master of business administration from the Harvard Business School. While at Harvard, he was chairman of the student government. As an officer in the U.S. Army Corps of Engineers, he served two wartime tours of duty in Vietnam and three years in Europe. He received the Legion of Merit for exemplary service in Vietnam along with the Bronze Star and service medals.